T0304784

Climate Activism

What is activism? The answer is, typically, that it is a form of opposition, often expressed on the streets. Skoglund and Böhm argue differently. They identify forms of 'insider activism' within corporations, state agencies and villages, showing how people seek to transform society by working within the system, rather than outright opposing it. Using extensive empirical data, Skoglund and Böhm analyse the transformation of climate activism in a rapidly changing political landscape, arguing that it is time to think beyond the tensions between activism and enterprise. They trace the everyday renewable energy actions of a growing 'epistemic community' of climate activists who are dispersed across organisational boundaries and domains. This book is testament to a new way of understanding activism as an organisational force that brings about the transition towards sustainability across business and society and is of interest to social science scholars of business, renewable energy and sustainable development.

ANNIKA SKOGLUND is Associate Professor at Uppsala University, Sweden. Her research interests and teaching experience is closely linked to interdisciplinary approaches within climate social science and alternative entrepreneurship. She has published in journals such as *Renewable Energy, Sustainable Development, Human Relations* and *Organization Studies*.

STEFFEN BÖHM is Professor in Organisation & Sustainability at the University of Exeter Business School, UK, where he teaches a large Business and Climate Change module. His research focuses on the political economy and ecology of the sustainability transition. He has published widely in international journals such as *Organization Studies, Business Ethics Quarterly* and *Academy of Management Perspectives*. He is the Environment Section Editor at the *Journal of Business Ethics* and has co-edited the book *Negotiating Climate Change in Crisis* (Open Book Publishers, 2021).

Business, Value Creation, and Society

SERIES EDITORS:

R. Edward Freeman, *University of Virginia*
Jeremy Moon, *Copenhagen Business School*
Mette Morsing, *Copenhagen Business School*

The purpose of this innovative series is to examine, from an international standpoint, the interaction of business and capitalism with society. In the twenty-first century, it is more important than ever that business and capitalism come to be seen as social institutions that have a great impact on the welfare of human society around the world. Issues such as globalisation, environmentalism, information technology, the triumph of liberalism, corporate governance and business ethics all have the potential to have major effects on our current models of the corporation and the methods by which value is created, distributed and sustained among all stakeholder – customers, suppliers, employees, communities and financiers.

PUBLISHED TITLES:

Climate Activism

How Communities Take Renewable Energy Actions Across Business and Society

ANNIKA SKOGLUND
Uppsala University, Sweden

STEFFEN BÖHM
University of Exeter, United Kingdom

CAMBRIDGE
UNIVERSITY PRESS

CAMBRIDGE
UNIVERSITY PRESS

University Printing House, Cambridge CB2 8BS, United Kingdom

One Liberty Plaza, 20th Floor, New York, NY 10006, USA

477 Williamstown Road, Port Melbourne, VIC 3207, Australia

314–321, 3rd Floor, Plot 3, Splendor Forum, Jasola District Centre,
New Delhi – 110025, India

103 Penang Road, #05–06/07, Visioncrest Commercial, Singapore 238467

Cambridge University Press is part of the University of Cambridge.

It furthers the University's mission by disseminating knowledge in the pursuit of
education, learning, and research at the highest international levels of excellence.

www.cambridge.org
Information on this title: www.cambridge.org/9781108482646
DOI: 10.1017/9781108697194

First published 2022

A catalogue record for this publication is available from the British Library.

ISBN 978-1-108-48264-6 Hardback

Cambridge University Press has no responsibility for the persistence or accuracy of
URLs for external or third-party internet websites referred to in this publication
and does not guarantee that any content on such websites is, or will remain,
accurate or appropriate.

Contents

Figures

Foreword

This book delivers important insights on an often overlooked driver of transformation towards a more sustainable world by its focus on the changing political landscape for climate activism. Skoglund and Böhm critically analyse how 'activism' is emerging through forceful 'epistemic communities', shaped in collaborations between citizens, businesses and state actors, who share the ambition of decarbonisation. The empirical context is the renewable energy sector and the authors investigate how various forms of 'insider' and commercial activisms speed up a political agenda that has so far only moved slowly by the assistance of national and international organisations.

Skoglund and Böhm move the long-standing strands of environmental activism from an activity that is happening 'outside' political and business organisations – and oftentimes 'against' these organisations – to something that occurs 'inside' with 'support' of organisational constituents.

By advancing theory on the organisational force of knowledge movements, the book offers an important new and balanced perspective on a phenomenon that transcends prevailing studies of transformative change. At the same time, the authors acknowledge the substantial commercial interests that are at stake when 'non-partisan' citizens are stimulated to become activists in relation to renewable energy, and they critically point to how climate activism goes beyond old ideas of deliberative democracy when 'the will of the people' is increasingly detached from the democratically elected governors. While they do so, they also point our attention to how activism is animated 'from within' small towns, villages and among employees, and, importantly, take climate adaptation to a new level of climate action across organisational boundaries.

This book is a much welcomed contribution to the Business, Values Creation and Society. I hope it will serve to stimulate future debates on the different roles of activism to drive the social and environmental transformation of contemporary society.

Mette Morsing

Preface

It is spring. The leaves have just come out on the branches that hang gently over the narrow and muddy gravel road that leads to Decarbonised Living Project in Farmers Village (pseudonyms), deep in the countryside of south-west England. We pass custom-made signs with elaborate names of various sized estates behind closed entry gates. A mix of farmers, relatively rich landowners and people with summer houses live here. We get closer to the location where we are to meet a group of pensioners and a farmer who have got together with the ambition to decarbonise their village. After parking the car we walk slowly up the road to take some photos on the way. The first thing we encounter is a road sign in the shape of a snail, warning drivers to reduce their speed on account of the children who, during the week, attend a small, alternative school in a little round house, just in front of the old, renovated farm building where our meeting is to be held. The farm is used as a venue for parties, such as weddings and corporate team-building events. There are at least forty pairs of wellies, some hung on a wall and some spread on the floor, for guests to use in case there is an activity arranged in the muddy fields. We are guided around the property in the warm, soothing spring sun before being offered coffee and raw milk on the first floor of the damp and chilly stone barn. It is freezing indoors, and therefore hard to enjoy the conversation fully. Our hosts try their best to make us feel very welcome, and we are informed that the raw milk can only be given away as a gift, since the local farmer, who is part of the voluntary group, does not yet have a licence to sell it. They start to chat with us immediately about their life decisions and how they have come together to keep busy, make friends and belong, and as one of them enthusiastically summarizes:

Well, what happened, I mean, we were interested in renewable energy straight away and we'd have people talk to us about wind turbines. Community Energy Network certainly came and talked to us about, you know, wind turbines. And I remember going down to meetings at Community Energy Plus with Thomas and probably Peter, where they also talked to a wider audience, because they were keen on getting wind turbines started up here. And then, in late 2009, the government set up a challenge called the Decarbonised Living Challenge. And they were offering the people, or the communities that applied, half a million pounds, and there were, I think, twenty-four villages that, you know, got this.

So, I think, yeah, it was probably Thomas that said 'Well, yeah, we'll do this', so even though it seemed a bit ... yeah, you know, as a transition town movement that started in 2008 we hadn't been involved for that long. But we were able to say that, you know, we have been engaged in the whole exercise through some energy surveys, and we were able to put down enough things. But anyway, Community Energy Plus were keen, because you had to do it through an organisation, like Community Energy Network.

So we then had to put the bid in, so it was all a very rushed job of getting, you know, people who would be interested in having solar panels on their house and you know, other things. I think the idea was that it would be an example of all the different types of renewable energy installation available at the time. So, ground source, air source, hot water panels, PV, turbines. And one of the conditions was that all the work had to be done by the end of the financial year. So everything had to be done by March 31st. We had to get all the solar panels on the roofs, we had to get the wind turbine bought. We had to have bought all and have the wind turbine on site I think, even if it wasn't erected. And we had to get planning permission!

But we didn't manage to do all the installation we intended to do, because the people, we had people quote for this and well, I think they'd have to quote before we put the whole scheme in, so that we could say we could do it for half a million. And we had people rushing around here, you know, whole groups of contractors turned up mob-handed. I mean, one of the places to end up with a solar panel was my place, which is a converted barn. We had about five groups of people turning up there, because they're competing with each other to get the business anyway, you know.

We were going to take all the feed-in tariffs and renewable heat incentives, if they ever came, and use those to do further installations. So, that was the whole concept. The model that we adopted was to actually give these solar panels to the people, so that they took ownership and they wrote a contract with us, and our liability was to keep them maintained, in return for all the feed-in-tariffs coming back to us. Because we took the income, we could then roll it over into more insulation. So it is, I think, nearly unique in the community, and was pretty complex from a legal point of view. I think this is why we are unique, yeah, the fact that we've got a revenue stream, we are able to go well beyond what a lot of the transition groups have become, which is just talk shops. We're able to action initiatives on the ground; I think that's been key to probably the reason why you're here talking to us today.

Acknowledgements

Writing this book has been a long, empirical journey, with families supportive of academic research and its haphazard routes of curiosity. Our deepest thanks go to our respective, patient partners who have made the collaboration between Uppsala University, Sweden, and the University of Exeter, UK, practically feasible and more enjoyable.

Annika Skoglund would like to thank the Swedish Energy Agency for the grant that enabled her to research renewable energy and climate activism. Steffen Böhm would like to thank the Swedish Energy Agency for funding his guest professorship at Uppsala University. He is also grateful to the British Academy, which provided him with a mid-career fellowship, allowing this research to happen.

Various academic colleagues have greatly contributed to our thoughts about climate activism in this book. On 14 September 2018, we organised the workshop 'Prefiguring Activism: Free Spaces of Socio-Ecological Change' at the British Academy in London. We would like to thank all speakers and participants who helped to make this an enjoyable day full of creativity and debate. Mike Zundel, David Sköld, Johannes Stripple, Chris Land and Oscar Fitch-Roy very kindly commented on earlier versions of this book. Their comments and the comments from the anonymous reviewers, have been very helpful during the various revision stages. Our thanks also extend to the editors of the Cambridge book series Business, Society, and Value Creation, Mette Morsing, Jeremy Moon and Ed Freeman, who enthusiastically supported our project. The commissioning editor, Valerie Appleby, and her colleagues at Cambridge University Press have kept us on a straight line. Thank you.

We would also like to express our gratitude to all research participants, from representatives within village communities to managers within large corporations, and from public service workers to small business owners. Without your openness to our academic curiosity in your everyday work practices and activism, there would have been very little to say about epistemic communities in relation to climate

Figure 0.1 Wellies for collective walks in mud, Farmers Village. Photo: Annika Skoglund

activism. It has been a pleasure to learn from your rich experiences and devotion to various renewable energy technologies and, not least, the 'belonging' these have facilitated.

A final thanks goes to the Cornish artist Kurt Jackson who has allowed us to use one of his paintings as book cover image. It has been very inspiring to see how your art fathoms the changing aesthetics of renewables.

Introduction

Convinced that business-as-usual must be over, an increasing number of people have come together across national, disciplinary, cultural and other organisational boundaries to take climate actions and attain a more sustainable society. At the same time as organisations and state agencies have declared a 'climate emergency', people have taken decarbonisation into their own hands through direct and sometimes radical actions. Climate activists across generations and borders demonstrate in the streets, while people also take a stance via mundane professional actions at work and in their everyday lives. In this coming together, the pursuit of personal politics is merging with civic, state and corporate commitment to the point where, it might be argued, we are witnessing a rebirth of community relations and alternative ways of collective organising. As activism becomes increasingly dispersed and diffuse, communities are seemingly no longer tied to a specific geographical spot, organisation, group or even shared identity. This book is about this new configuration of the environmental movement and what it accomplishes – a bridging between business and society.

It is not only street protesters who proclaim climate change as a 'crisis', 'disaster' and 'emergency' (Höijer 2010, Hoggett 2011), but throughout history humans have experienced the climate as uncertain and have met it with fear, anxiety, mythologising and taming (Hulme 2008). To emphasise the seriousness of the situation, and to align the language of the people with scientific discourse, journalists have even proposed that we should no longer be told that there is human-induced 'global warming', but instead 'global heating' (Carrington 2019). In line with this increased emphasis on urgency, David Attenborough, a UK-based acclaimed natural world broadcaster, told UK Members of Parliament in July 2019 that 'we cannot be radical enough in dealing with [climate change]' (New Scientist 2019b). People across generations agree (Thunberg 2019), and popular culture is also littered with images of a dying planet, with pop artists who

1

directly engage their young fans in climate change and environmental issues (New Scientist 2019a, Reilly 2019, Abidin et al. 2020). This growing movement is reflected in opinion polls, showing that '93% of EU citizens see climate change as a serious problem' (European Commission 2019). Consequently, many people seem to have been influenced by a growing knowledge movement, furthered in different media, which has made it possible to express and understand personal experiences of storms, droughts, floods and heatwaves as being caused by human polluting behaviours (Painter 2013: Introduction). The expressed emergency has led to pockets of climate anxiousness (Weintrobe 2012) and fed practices of self-critique, generative of a broader eagerness to mobilise and transform the way humans are to live and thereby survive in 'togetherness' with other species on Earth.

Many politicians and business leaders mimic this climate change movement and have gathered their forces to publicly call for radical and economically beneficial climate change action. Business, it is proposed, can ramp up the speed of the transition and accelerate responses (Newell 2020). The United Nations (UN) Global Compact meeting in 2020 was tellingly entitled 'Making Global Goals Local Business' (United Nations 2020), and the World Bank report, 'Growing Green – The economic benefits of climate action', makes the strategic move beyond 'climate adaptation' clear. It is 'climate action' that is needed:

Adaptation will remain important as current heat-trapping emissions commit the work to further warming. But to prevent climate change that exceeds our adaptation capacity, climate action to significantly reduce emissions must become a greater priority to all countries. (Deichmann and Zhang 2013: Introduction xxi–xxii)

Climate Action through Renewable Energy

Renewable energy technology has become a focal point in the active response to knowledge about a potentially disastrous future of climate change, with its uncertainties and decision-making complexities (IPCC, Intergovernmental Panel on Climate Change 2011b, 2014, Howarth and Painter 2016). Most people can directly relate to 'renewables', as wind, wave and solar power technologies are often referred to. Involving both industrial actors and individual users, renewables have become one of the key paths to decarbonisation across business and society (Mitchell 2008, Vasi Bogdan 2011,

Dauvergne 2016). Although at heart quite technical and dry, renewable energy constitutes a cornerstone in policymaking, public and private investments, business as well as civil society activity, leading to a range of concrete organisational and corporate approaches, from large-scale wind and solar farms to grassroots, self-organised renewable energy communities to individual homeowners having solar panels installed on their roofs. Renewables complemented by energy saving insulation function as useful material objects and gadgets for the mobilisation of citizens (cf. Marres 2012), or even 'activists', governed as self-organised 'ethical consumers' (Dowling 2010:491), or 'prosumers', that is, people who produce, consume and at times sell by owning the means of production (Burke and Stephens 2017, Szulecki 2018).

Renewable energy technology is compelling for many reasons, politically and existentially. Renewables are said to decouple economic growth from greenhouse gas (GHG) emissions, thereby suggesting that it is possible to continuously progress economically (Jan, Farhat Durrani and Himayatullah 2021), albeit under the auspices of sustainable development (IPCC, Intergovernmental Panel on Climate Change 2011a:16). Given that both solar and wind are sources of infinite energy, they provide an optimistic image of the future, which stands in stark contrast to the dark, depressing thoughts about disaster and the finitude of humanity on Earth. This view of the infinity of renewables, and their seemingly indestructible non-exhaustive existence in nature, may be what creates such an alluring comfort for humans – a mentally and materially appealing focus for climate actions. This aesthetic dimension is perhaps best expressed in the art of Kurt Jackson, exemplified in the mixed media piece from 2020 *Late sunlight on the tumulus bracken, Warren's Barrow, Carland Cross*, reproduced on the cover of this book. In contrast to the criticism of progress raised in debates about the Anthropocene, driven by dismissal of modernist aspirations (e.g. see Haraway 2015, Latour et al. 2018), renewables seem to enable wanted technical fixes that succeed in repositioning ideals of progress and liveability. Renewables facilitate new structures, politically raised to be publicly enjoyed.

Located at the intersection of national, international and personal politics in the growing 'knowledge economy' (Powell and Snellman 2004), renewable energy has been heavily debated but also brought into citizen education programmes (Kandpal and Broman 2014). Renewable energy brings both obstacles and opportunities for citizens, engineers, investors and public officials, and has under these conditions thrived and resulted in a transformation of the environmental movement (Jamison 2001, Toke 2011a, Leach and Scoones 2015). The Alternative Technology Movement (Harper and Eriksson 1972), which grew out of environmental concerns in the 1970s, is partly responsible for this transformation and turn towards commercialisation via renewables (Eyerman and Jamison 1991, Smith 2005, Elliott 2016). Here, the technology itself is what holds hope and agency, conceived as it is to be an already existing utopia within an immature society (Eyerman and Jamison 1991:76). The domains of society and business have been bridged by such a hopeful conception of renewables, not only underpinned by climate regulations, subsidies and voluntary carbon markets, but by people who come together based on their shared belief in its promises (Walker et al. 2010). From village groups to businesses, and from 'green insider activism' in state agencies (Hysing and Olsson 2018) to employee activism in large polluting corporations (Skoglund and Böhm 2020) and 'green investor activism' (Belfiore 2021), we are witnessing the growth of a dispersed climate activism pursued by people who take renewable energy actions across organisations. In practice, these actions manage to merge the political idea of 'power to the people' with the equally popular notion of 'individual responsibility'. It is nevertheless unclear how this political entangling has succeeded in unfolding to such an extent, aided by renewables.

Despite existing climate scepticism and resistance to renewable energy, a shared worldview seems to have emerged among people who think positively about finding a solution to climate change. These people come together across national, disciplinary, cultural and other organisational boundaries to take action in the here and now. Instead of erecting structures for political change, new organisational forms arise with human efforts to accomplish change. To make sense of this broad and boundaryless movement, this book focusses on climate activism by investigating the community relations that animate it. With the growth of renewable energy solutions, we see a conglomeration of activist-business-state, massaged and glued together by a new outlook of both activism and community, which can no longer be easily distinguished as civic action (cf. Lichterman and Eliasoph, 2014), nor located in civil society. When environmental activism becomes boundaryless, communities become more fluid, linking the individual to the collective beyond local-ism and globalism (Reitan and Gibson 2012, Doherty and Doyle 2013). As the face of activism changes, so too does the way people are told to take action and choose to do so by gathering and pursuing their per-sonal politics collectively. The cult of the individual, charismatic, under-dog activist has in some cases been infused by, and in other instances replaced by, a communal inclusion of mundane everyday activism. We thus ask: how are community relations formed and how does climate activism bridge society and business via renewable energy technology? This is the main question this book seeks to answer.

Activism in Transition

In the 1960s and 1970s, environmental activism was, and still is, con-sidered part of broader civil rights movements and grassroots quests for increased democratic participation (Eckersley 1992). Yet, since at least the early 1990s, with the rise of neoliberal governance systems, green activism has engaged in ever closer dialogue with the private and public sectors (Hemmati 2002, Dauvergne 2016). Many transnational environmental activist groups, such as WWF, Greenpeace and Friends of the Earth, with millions of supporters worldwide, challenge and resist, but also work closely together with state institutions and corpo-rate organisations, to address environmental issues such as pollution and climate change (Wapner 1996). While studies of environmental-ism have focussed on how movements target private and public sector organisations, it has become evident that contemporary environmen-tal movements are active across the public and private divide (Ronit and Schneider 2013). At the same time as the environmental perfor-mance of corporations and public authorities can be challenged more or less aggressively from an external location (MacKay and Munro 2012), more subtle collaborative approaches are widespread and pop-ular (Kourula and Halme 2008, Pacheco, York and Hargrave 2014), especially in the advancement of 'corporate environmentalism' (Mirvis 1994, Hoffman 2001, Bowen 2014) and 'CEO activism' (Chatterji and Toffel 2018). This results in tight alliances between businesses and civil society that prosper based on multiplying notions of com-mercial activisms (see Table A.1 in Appendix).

Large parts of social theory nonetheless treat activism, and spe-cifically environmentalism, as something that happens externally, separate from state authorities and businesses, for example via 'challenger movements' (Bertels, Hoffman and DeJordy 2014) or even 'shareholder activists' (Goranova and Verstegen Ryan, 2014). This external position has furthermore been emphasised as being of theoretical importance. It secures the possibility of 'true critique' delivered from an outsider position with a clear political target or 'anti' (Dixon 2014:220). The question is nevertheless whether such a clean and clear-cut external position is still fruitful to uphold, empirically and theoretically, if we are curious about climate activism in the energy transition.

In the world of work, internal political acts have long been recognised as playing an important role. Whether through whistleblowing (e.g. Weiskopf and Tobias-Miersch 2016), union activism (Byford and Wong 2016) or humour (Taylor and Bain 2003, Fogarty and Elliot 2020), there are innovative ways in which people can enact their political imaginaries at work (Scott 1990). While the emphasis in such studies of resistance has been on organisational hierarchies, and how workers attempt to counter managers to improve exploitative work conditions (Bain and Taylor 2000, Ekman 2014), research on activism in workplaces underscores the existence of wider political movements and links to society at large (Meyerson and Scully 1995, Scully and Segal 2002, Skoglund and Böhm 2020). Here, activism is studied as a boundaryless political force, rather than as a co-construction of corporate responsibility (e.g. see Sonenshein, 2016, Girschik 2020), with the aim to understand how a political movement may take shape within organisations that on the surface look apolitical, or by contrast, are outspokenly political.

A clear case of the latter in the energy transition is Ecotricity, one of the UK's biggest renewable energy companies, founded by the activist and ecopreneur Dale Vince. Ecotricity not only lobbies for greener governmental policies and strict climate change targets, the company also takes an activist stance against fellow energy businesses, particularly the emerging fracking industry, producing campaign videos that have a lot in common with those produced by environmental activists. 'In fact, Ecotricity has teamed up with Friends of the Earth, one of the largest and most influential green NGOs, in its campaign to oppose fracking in the UK' (Böhm and Skoglund 2015). On the one hand, Ecotricity follows economic reasoning, clearly wishing to position itself as a green champion, gaining a competitive advantage in the energy market (Cronin et al. 2011). On the other hand, it also seems to follow, invent and sustain certain political imaginaries, fortifying the ideas and hopes many people have of a greener world to come, via very material means.

Descriptive insights on how the environmental movement, and specifically climate actions, are increasingly becoming enmeshed in a variety of organisational settings can be found in both popular culture and various academic fields. This book will engage with both to analyse a set of ethnographically collected empirical materials, mainly based in the UK, by finding common ground in social movement theory, political science and organisation and management studies. We need to establish a cross-disciplinary conceptual understanding between these three areas of thought, due to our research interest in a climate activism that is productive of a rich variety of organisational arrangements, and especially those that bridge business and society. This broad theoretical, and for some readers perhaps excessively panoramic, approach is also vital due to already established intellectual exchanges between these three areas, and a resonance with the empirical experiences we have had in the field. Instead of holding on to the academic canon, it thus seems more fruitful to let go and craft an experimental attitude towards existing studies.

While social movement theory mostly focusses its explanatory power on environmental non-governmental organisations (NGOs) and other civil society groups (Yaziji and Doh 2010, Vasi Bogdan 2011, Fisher and Nasrin 2021), political science authors have developed concepts of green deliberative democracy and citizen voicing (Smith 2009, Bäckstrand 2010, Dryzek 2013) that stretch to the remains of grassroots activism in political programmes of 'energy democracy' (Burke and Stephens 2017, Szulecki 2018). A blending of activism and formal politics is also advanced when ideas of 'ecological modernisation' (Hajer 1995) are brought into studies of renewable energy technology development (Toke 2011b). This focus on modernisation has been taken up by Corporate Social Responsibility scholars (e.g. see Curran 2015), especially those with an interest in 'ecological citizenship' (Crane, Matten and Moon 2008a:167, 2008b:151), including voluntary engagements driven by managers' personal values (Hemingway and Maclagan 2004). Conceptually, however, these studies keep the environmental activist in an external position, occasionally to be brought in to be managed or governed.

In contrast, scholars have slowly begun to investigate how 'internal activists' (Wickert and Schaefer 2015:107, also see Briscoe and Gupta 2016) and 'organisational activists' (Spicer, Alvesson and Kärreman 2009:552) enliven all sorts of political imaginaries in professional contexts. Among these approaches we find researchers who seek to understand how minorities and marginalised members change and recompose their world at work (Zald and Berger 1978, Scully and Segal 2002, Marens 2013). Early on, Meyerson and Scully (1995:589) developed the concept of 'tempered radicals' to describe organisational members who are 'outsiders within'. These are individuals who 'may be playing parts in movements bigger than themselves and their organisations' to accomplish change, starting with their organisation (Meyerson and Scully 1995:598). In contrast, 'internal activists' can also be conceived as less disruptive and more aligned with already established and accepted corporate responsibility and core values that need to be properly acted upon. Girschik (2020:35) states that 'internal activists believe in and identify with corporate responsibility and may mobilise others in an endeavour to promote different ways of thinking about and doing business'. The activist struggles undertaken are in this latter case often smoother since the internal activists seldom disrupt the core business. Yet how citizen-activists, businesses and state actors are entangled by activism pursued at work is still not well recognised and understood (cf. Briscoe and Gupta 2016:673).

These previous studies on business organisations show that activism is either seen to enter business, to work from the outside-in, or alternatively, that activism grows in a bottom-up manner, spurred by notions of corporate responsibility to work inside-out (Davis and White 2015). In the case of the energy transition and environmental employee activism, however, such empirical distinctions are hard to sustain (Skoglund and Böhm 2020). Focussing on the organisation as the level of analysis, with its inter-dynamics of 'inside-out' or 'outside-in', including diverse forms of 'boundary work' (Langley et al. 2019) is insufficient and unsatisfactory due to the boundaryless attribute of climate activism. Tellingly, the intensified calls for climate actions, with a spread of activism across domains, have thus also been studied by a growing number of scholars taking an interest in 'green inside activists' in state agencies (Hochstetler and Keck 2007, Olsson and Hysing 2012, Hysing and Olsson 2018, Abers 2019). While these studies still show how activists wish to transform how the green environment is treated within their own organisation (with policy implications), they also illustrate the existence of a much stronger will to connect actions taken 'from within' to others in efforts to accomplish a wider transformation. Hence, insider or employee activism can thus utilise a host organisation as a means for political ends.

Before the boundaryless attribute of activism was spotted in relation to employee activism and insider activism, it was well observed in digital activism (Hill and Hughes 1998, Maxey 1999, Postill 2018), and perhaps boundaryless activism is easier to accept when tracing activism digitally. Through digital tools, it has been suggested that political enactment travels in a less regulated manner, from keyboard to keyboard and screen to screen, across the Internet between interconnected countries via 'cybercitizens', 'transnational citizenship' and 'virtual communities' (Hill and Hughes 1998), for example in the case of the Arab Spring (Mason 2013) and the #MeToo movement. In contrast to a traditional leftist historicity of organised revolution, digital activism therefore resonates with theories of dispersed and disorganised activism, flowing flexibly across the political spectrum (Meyer and Tarrow 1998), shaped by digital networks and fluid communities that transcend local and global politics (Reitan 2010), disconnected from a specific activist citizen and target group (Mercea 2016).

The political dimension and effects of this expansive digital activism are nevertheless debatable (cf. Fileborn and Loney-Howes 2019, Dean 2019). The spontaneous and processual character of 'hashtag activisms', with their 'algorithmic politics' and affective potentialities, demand the recognition 'that there is no politically pure position from which to operate' (Pedwell 2019:134). There is no longer an 'outside' to neoliberalism and capitalism, or at least, no longer a safe one (Dean 2019:179). Digital activism performs from 'within' (Vlavo 2018), and the pressing question that both activists and academics ask themselves relates to this repositioning or even trans-valuation of politics: how can you work from within established structures, systems and hierarchies, with a wish to outmanoeuvre them, without yourself being defined by them (Scoones, Leach and Newell 2015)?

Inspired by this repositioning of activism, our main priority is not to better understand how activism permeates professional organisations and sometimes grows from the inside via so-called 'internal' activists. We are much more interested in thinking about climate activism as boundaryless and in relation to the 'complexity' that climate change repeatedly has been offering to political decision-makers (e.g. see,

Schneider and Kuntz-Duriseti 2002, Heazle 2010, IPCC, Intergovernmental Panel on Climate Change 2014:114, Incropera 2016). This has generated a wide range of 'uncertainties' that are not only making decision-making difficult but alongside which warnings of post-political conditions (Wilson and Swyngedouw 2014) and de-politicisation (Evans and Reid 2014) have grown. That is, hand in hand with the realisation that agreement on formal political decisions to mitigate climate change has been problematic, follows a general tendency to configure human behaviour based on adaptation and a capacity to cope (Chandler and Reid 2016). At the same time, as emphasised earlier in this Introduction, it is notable that calls for 'action' seek to complement 'adaptation', and that uncertainty is constructively met by the material-mental promises of renewable energy, its allure of infinity and hope.

There are very few question marks and precautions regarding renewable technologies, it seems. So, alongside all the political complexities and de-politicising uncertainties, climate activism spreads via renewables productively across organisations, but perhaps without any distinct cultivation of a political subject, namely an identifiable activist nurtured as a unified collective (Decreus, Lievens and Braeckman 2014). Hence, just as the energy system is in transition, it appears that so too is activism. The energy transition corrals and is infused by a boundaryless activism, indistinct political subjectivity and yet a forceful human relationality. To trace and understand this prolific environmental movement, we thus suggest there should be less focus on individuals identified as activists, and more analytical attention paid to the sort of human relationality and organisational force that underpins climate activism. To accomplish this shift in perspective, we turn to knowledge production about community formation, and specifically a theoretical expansion of the very limited concept of 'epistemic communities' (Haas 1992). This concept and slightly outdated framework were developed with other political complexities and uncertainties in mind: post-Cold War international affairs (Zito 2018).

Climate Activism and Community Formation

We only affiliate ourselves loosely with existing research on epistemic communities, previously mainly understood as a community of professionals and experts who share knowledge to steer changes in policy when there is high uncertainty and political complexity. In contrast to

Haas' (1992) analytical focus on hierarchies and causal relations that are assumed to follow instrumental and strategic flows of knowledge or discursive regularities, this book provides an analytical shift, more akin to a broader affirmation of epistemic movements (Knorr Cetina 1999). We are, however, not so interested in how scientists take the leading role in cultural machineries. Instead, we are fascinated by how everyone is assumed to become an expert, especially regarding an awareness of their own political capacities to be 'green', accessed and released as 'actions', via practical and reflexive knowledge mobilised by renewables.

The aim is to expand the conception of epistemic community as a vehicle to better understand the movement of knowledge that underpins climate activism and renewable energy actions, taken in the everyday, across different organisational domains (cf. Gough and Shackley 2001). This shared formation of knowledge or 'episteme' that spawns community formation can thus be more generatively conceived as a 'field of scientificity', moulded through discourses, institutions and laws, but grounded in philosophical and philanthropic historicities, including contemporary moral trends and practices (Foucault 1980:195–197). To make the most of a reconceptualisation of 'epistemic community', and give it the explanatory power it deserves, we will thus turn to a broad set of theories and definitions of community. This will make it possible to study climate activism and account for the boundaryless and dispersed mobilisations of knowledge that thrive on, and accomplish, the transition of the energy system.

A focus on knowledge movements and expertise is not necessarily novel, but there is still plenty of scope to further develop Haas' (1992) original conception (Zito 2001, Davis Cross 2013, Zito 2018), and especially so when taken out of a pure political science context. Just as we have seen a scholarly advancement of different types of activism, so too have definitions and studies of types of community prospered, from ecological communities (Böhm, Bharucha and Pretty 2015) to sustainable communities (Grim and Tucker 2014), policy communities (Stone 2008), occupational communities (Van Maanen 2010), brand and consumption communities (Antorini, Muñiz Jr and Askildsen 2012) and energy communities (Bauwens et al. 2022 in press). This shows that the dated field of community studies is going through a revival, giving rise to an increased awareness of the human will to gather and socialise, even professionally, building further on studies of close communities (Harrigan, Achananuparp and Lim 2012) or communities of practice (Wenger 1998, 2010).

Compared with how in the 1960s 'the community' was increasingly grafted onto a notion that could counter tensions and potential isolation of individuals in 'mass society' (Rose 1996:332), with climate change 'community' has grown in popularity and been extended to ethico-political programmes that seek to nurture resilient communities (Zebrowski and Sage 2017). Particularly in the German language, this present and historical moral function of community is still apparent. *'Aktiengesellschaft'* and *'Gesellschaft mit beschränkter Haftung (GmbH)'* are juridical terms for profit-oriented companies, while *Gemeinschaft* (community) implies that a group of people are assembled by ties other than, or beyond, just economic ties and instrumentality. In our study of climate activism, it will become evident that *Gemeinschaft* and *Gesellschaft* are intertwined (e.g. see Adler 2015, Bershady 2020), and fundamental for new political imaginaries of what 'a community' might become in the transition to a sustainable society.

A focus on how community relations unfold with the production and dissemination of knowledge about climate change will generate insights into the new outlook of activism, one that is mobilised by a personalisation that differs from the activist saying 'the personal is political' (Bennett and Segerberg 2011). There is a looser connection between the individual and the group, and a weaker construction of a 'we' against a 'them' (cf. Decreus, Lievens and Braeckman 2014). This makes the collective identity vague but therefore inclusive (Decreus, Lievens and Braeckman 2014), especially in 'pro' movements where the role of the adversary is either abstract or becoming distant. No longer can activism be understood as one coherent 'thing', located in one place and carried out by one set of people, with one shared identity, in one way only. Activism is rather conceived as, and constructed to be, multiple. By taking different empirical and theoretical positions, a greater variety has been identified, moulded through corporatism and deliberation to localism and 'prefiguration' (e.g. see Boggs 1977). Enabled by pluralist perspectives, it has become possible to talk about 'multiple green transformations' (Leach and Scoones 2015:119) and increased varieties of activism (Jamison 2001:147–175), for example pursued by 'the rich' (Dauvergne 2016). By empirically tracing renewable energy actions taken in the everyday, our study of epistemic communities will consequently enable us to better understand the organisational force of climate activism and how it revels in the asserted complexities of a changing political landscape, continuously redefined by the problem of climate change (e.g. see Wittneben et al. 2012).

Outline of the Book

Chapter 1, Boundaryless Activism, illustrates the changed outlook of activism. The boundaryless attribute of activism is clarified by examples of how activism has gone into business, and how business has gone into activism. The reader is introduced to the growing genre of commercial activism with a potpourri of activism notions: from activist entrepreneurship or enterprising activism to brand activism, CEO activism, employee activism and consumer activism (see Table A.1 in Appendix). By means of an overview of how these overlapping examples of commercial activism work based on environmentalism, the chapter points to how climate activism bridges the domains of business and society. The purpose is to acknowledge a more complicated picture of activism and move towards a conception of activism as disconnected from civil society, which is required to enable an empirical tracing of climate activism.

This commercial backdrop to climate activism will be useful for a better understanding of the four empirical chapters. By comparing different types of activist business strategy, the reader can additionally reflect on these aided by critical perspectives presented in both popular culture media and academic journals, and learn about their differences. A common difference between corporate engagement in formal politics (sometimes called corporate activism) and (business) enterprising activism is the creation of a coherent value chain in the latter – a strategic coherence that spans from the activist entrepreneur to the employee activist and consumer activist, offered to build a collective movement, sometimes in terms of a 'community' that bridges business and society. This insight prepares the reader for the empirics, and illustration of the dispersed way in which climate activism and its collective force is facilitated via renewable energy actions. We end by arguing that the various types of commercial activism presented in the chapter offer a significant change in speed, one that may become increasingly alluring when climate adaptations are extended to climate actions – actions to be taken sooner rather than later in the 'here and now' to respond adequately to the climate emergency. Conclusively, activism that thrives on business is, for some, considered as 'political', yet more effective, than any other form of activism.

Chapter 2, The Activist–Business–State Conglomeration, builds further on the boundaryless attribute of climate activism by illustrating how activism has gone into state authorities, and how state authorities have gone into activism. By tracing how the citizen is increasingly called on as a passionate and energetic force and potential activist, the chapter outlines how climate activism is becoming even more dispersed and diffuse when bolstered through formal political bodies. By means of a short contextualisation of the UK policy landscape on renewable energy, with an emphasis on how a deliberative democratic agenda has expanded and taken root, the chapter prepares the reader for contextual details in the four empirical chapters. The UK political agenda on climate adaptation, consensual deliberation and a top-down creation of market pull has been slowly revised by a call for climate actions and its collective force, resulting in community building and a bottom-up market push. To go beyond the view that policy drives activism, the latter part of the chapter is attentive to the formation of an activist–business–state conglomeration, important for the recognition of activism as boundaryless, increasingly commercially defined and without a confinement to civil society. The reader is introduced to examples of prosumer activism, investor activism and insider activism (see Table A.1 in Appendix).

The conclusion is that boundaryless climate activism predominantly speeds up the energy transition with an affirmation of affluent transformations and a fiscal energy 'revolution'. Climate activism can thus be governed in less counter-aggressive ways, with soft empowering approaches that seek consensus and behavioural change via knowledge co-production, including climate actions taken in good faith, especially via hopeful renewable energy community building. However, because of its characteristics of being less obvious and less aggressive, more about community relations than demonstrations in the street, climate activism can also find alternative ways to reproduce and prosper, before becoming governable anew. In light of this to-and-fro, the chapter problematises the analytical means for studying boundaryless activism. Somehow, there is a need to take into consideration the trendy talk about climate actions coupled with an overt embracement of its collective form and force – by policymakers, business organisations and citizens – as well as the pursuit of such actions and collectivity within specific empirical settings.

Chapter 3, Activism and Its Collective Force, first traces the basic theoretical assumptions in studies of activism, to then do the same for community. Especially in the energy transition, 'community' is a political imaginary that has been widely seen as a normative force to accomplish sustainable development through intimately connected people, embracing a biospheric vitality and relation to the Earth. 'Community' has historically been used more than 'activism', for a bridging across business and society. However, the question is how boundaryless activism can be thought of in relation to community formation when the notion of 'civil society' is slowly becoming redundant and affinities with nature are being emphasised. The aim is therefore to get closer to a new way of analysing activism and its collective force, or 'community', by first engaging in existing theories and three main basic assumptions in studies of activism: resistance, struggle and political subjectivity; a demarcation between words and actions; and the human capacity to relate in various ways to others and come together. This last aspect of coming together is thereafter discussed in relation to theories on community formation with a focus on community and togetherness, nihilism, locality, capitalism, business and neoliberalism.

We theoretically explore how the changing political landscape and trans-valuation of what can be considered 'political' is linked to a revival of community relations and political imaginaries of togetherness. At the same time as scholars have theorised 'the citizen' as less instrumental and more complicated – in effect a human with very diverse passions and will to take action beyond deliberation – community formation has been reintroduced as a potential host for the grouping of such complex human diversity. The chapter particularly notes the link between the autonomous individual, assumed to be found in expressions of activism, and how this individual has been differently balanced up by a collective formation of togetherness in expressions of community. This draws attention to the available conceptual resources and possibilities to study boundaryless climate activism in relation to its collective force, enabled by renewables and a knowledge movement, or 'epistemic community'.

Chapter 4, Epistemic Community, explores the different ways that communities of expertise have been studied previously, to then expand the reach of this analytical frame. This is of particular importance for a study of climate activism, which is infused by all sorts of pedagogic and educational trends, enacted by NGOs to pedagogues in nurseries, designed to be internalised and materially acted upon. As richly exemplified in the previous chapters, the applicability of this knowledge movement is also facilitated by technical and financial solutions, such as renewable energy technologies and European Union (EU)-sanctioned crowdfunding platforms. The epistemic movement, fortified by science on climate change, encompasses more than a scientific episteme – it vitalises a specific way of knowing, co-producing and applying knowledge. By reconceptualising epistemic community, the aim is to affirm this extensive knowledge movement to explain the workings of boundaryless climate activism in relation to its collective force.

We do so by turning to the historical notions of *Gemeinschaft* (community) and *Gesellschaft* (society/association), and Tönnies' (1957/2002) interest in the stimulation of public opinion via increased civic education. It is the interplay between *Gesellschaft*, which is based on knowledge, and *Gemeinschaft*, based on imaginings and relationality, that is still relevant in understanding more contemporary forms of activism. This conceptual pair can accomplish an analytical shift, from evident sources of expertise, to co-production of knowledge by the activist–business–state conglomeration. The chapter discusses how 'community', as an other-than-economic organisational force, combines with ideas about *Bildung*, renewed in the realisation that 'knowledge' itself is of utmost importance in the transition to a sustainable society. Contemporary *Bildung* processes, accordingly, secure human relationality based on unknowns and unknown outcomes within, what we call, an 'epistemic community'. This inclusion of *Bildung* within the epistemic community can thus help us to analytically grasp how renewable energy technology infuses 'action' by eliciting self-transformation and a reinvention of others. Acknowledging a more generative membership within the epistemic community furthermore facilitates an analysis of the dispersed actions and diffuse collective force that were experienced during the research in the field.

Chapter 5, Climate Activism at Vattenfall, mainly builds on our ethnographic study of people in Sweden and the UK who work with wind power development at Vattenfall, a multinational state-owned energy utility active across Europe (Skoglund and Böhm 2016). After contextualising the greening of Vattenfall and positioning this brand activism in relation to external activists, especially

Greenpeace, the chapter illustrates how Vattenfall early on adopted commercial activisms, such as CEO activism. The main empirics is nevertheless based on studies of the employees, both with regard to how they have been facilitated to form their own green activism and how they have taken initiatives beyond environmental management and efforts to harness their green personal politics via Green Human Resource Management. Despite all the green initiatives at Vattenfall, the company continued in parallel with a range of heavily polluting activities, creating dilemmas for how to manage a rich variety of personal politics and forceful passions acted out at work. So-called epistemic struggles emerged, enacted in meetings between employees within the various units at Vattenfall. Hence, these struggles refer to strongly differing opinions about the energy resources exploited, from nuclear to lignite, and from wind to hydropower. The struggles also meant that a collectivity was shaped by how renewables were spoken about on a daily basis, verbally constructed in clashes with other knowledge formations and concerns. An 'epistemic community' was consequently formed around a movement of employees who negotiated and co-produced knowledge about environmental degradation and climate change, including their hands-on actions in the office and beyond.

Chapter 6, Climate Activism via Small and Medium-Sized Enterprises, looks more closely at business organisations in the UK to grasp and illustrate how environmentally aware and concerned individuals, including individuals who self-identify as environmental activists, have started small and medium-sized businesses, collaborating closely with green NGOs and social movements, local government and other businesses. Here, climate activism is going into business, detailed in the case of Small R. Energy (pseudonym), a small, privately owned company based in south-west England, and in Localism for Renewables (pseudonym), also based in the south-west, which is a small community interest company. The chapter additionally introduces bigger companies, namely Ecotricity and Good Energy, known to be led by passionate environmentalists. Their activism has resulted in economically successful renewable energy start-ups, working UK-wide. Enterprising activism in this case refers to ambitions to utilise commercial means to reach environmental ends, seen in how activists schooled in business seek to accomplish environmental and social changes based on new business models, redistributive monetary flows and, commonly, a lot of passionate voluntary work. The chapter illustrates that it is often society and the planet as such that are considered to be at stake and that business is merely the vehicle to take action collectively to achieve faster social and environmental outcomes.

Chapter 7, Climate Activism in Governmental Authorities, is based on our interviews and observations of council workers and public servants in various authorities in south-west England. We specifically describe their work practices and environmental actions within county councils, analysing how they use their position to affect positive change and speed up the transition via business. They have deliberately chosen to work in local government councils to take actions to a collective level, and rely on a mix of educational backgrounds and previous experience of environmentalism, from environmental theatre, festivals and green documentary filmmaking to charity work and entrepreneurship in smaller businesses. Commonly with a left or centre left political agenda, they are based in the council offices where they become immersed in bureaucracy, learning how to utilise it for their enterprising environmental ambitions. This has resulted in what the chapter identifies to be horizontal organising, sometimes in parallel with, and at other times morphed into, top-down politics and deliberative democracy, knowledge co-production and renewable energy empowerment. This insider activism is fully focussed on working with and for local people, developing enterprising renewable energy solutions via the activist–business–state conglomeration. The chapter concludes that insider activism plays an intricate part in these public bureaucracies at the same time as it mobilises the epistemic community further to affect change at a local level.

Chapter 8, Climate Activism via Citizen Groups, describes climate actions taken by people who wish to be in control of their own production and consumption of renewable energy. Citizens are mobilised to facilitate public/private energy initiatives, whereby the 'citizen' and 'consumer' have become increasingly conflated and merged into the new category of 'prosumer'. Test sites and product advisory forums are initiated in a bottom-up manner, as the chapter illustrates in the case of the Decarbonised Living Project, launched in Farmers Village (pseudonyms), a small rural village in south-west England. By virtue of similar initiatives, information is gained about users interpellated as participative citizens, or even activists, at the same time as the implementation of technical solutions is facilitated via volunteer activities and free affective labour that constitute climate actions, as detailed in the case of Seaside Town Renewable Energy Network, a not-for-profit co-operative that is part of the transition town movement Love Seaside Town (pseudonyms). Love Seaside Town invests time and energy into enlightening their neighbours about green energy switching options and solar panel investments, seeking to make their fellow citizens more participative.

In this chapter we also get closer to the everyday struggles of climate activism, for instance illustrating how prosumers need consultancy aid to set up complex legal structures to be able to redistribute profits differently from normal businesses, to support life locally. The two cases thus clarify how environmentalism transforms with new knowledge, mobilised both by a 'grassroots innovation movement' that seeks control over the implementation phase (Smith and Ely 2015:107) and a consumption community that thrives on newness, progression and passion (West and Lakhani 2008). It becomes evident that renewable energy actions thrive on a positive and constructive perspective, turning hero stories about struggles with business into love stories about collaborations with business. Unavoidably with tensions between activism and business, the chapter highlights how a desire for sustainability and self-sufficiency leads to intensified local relations of exchange, either monetarily or as gift economies, concluding that people have experienced success in reaching their goals, at the same time as they have experienced exhaustion and a lack of longevity of activism.

Chapter 9, New Ways of Knowing, summarises how the various renewable energy actions presented in the four empirical chapters thrive on a knowledge movement, making individual actions into possible collective endeavours. The chapter discusses this formation of an epistemic community in relation to previously established movements, such as localism, collectivism, prefiguration and alternative forms of entrepreneurship, to further explore the boundaryless attribute of climate activism encountered in the empirical chapters. Through our conceptual expansion of epistemic communities, we also provide details on how activism bridges the domains of business and society differently. We summarise the main findings according to four themes on new ways of knowing, namely: experiment and Do-It-Yourself; share and Do-It-Together; wander and speed up; alter and materialise. This suggests that the epistemic community not only lays the foundations for the same topics – the climate emergency, renewable energy and swift action – but also opens up for a certain way of knowing through experimentation, sharing, wandering, altering and materialising.

Chapter 10, Horizontal Organising, summarises and critically reflects on the main findings and arguments to bring forth both theoretical and policy implications. The chapter concludes that a more inclusive and expanded concept of epistemic communities is useful for understanding how climate activism and renewable energy actions bridge business and society, speeding up the energy transition horizontally. The chapter elaborates on how renewable energy technology facilitates horizontality, to then discuss horizontal organising generated by an outsourcing of deliberation attempts, followed by horizontality that arises with the increasingly popular trend of prefigurative politics. Based on this emphasis on horizontality, the chapter ends by specifying four new elements of importance for a more generous conceptualisation of epistemic community: feral proximity, epistemic struggles, radical equality and human relationality. This broader understanding of epistemic community offers analytical possibilities to move beyond a study of activism and actions rooted in a specific source of activism, for example an activist conceived as a political subject, of importance for tracing boundaryless activisms, of which climate activism is a prime example.

1 | *Boundaryless Activism*

Efforts to decarbonise by means of a transition of the energy system have multiplied the ways in which the environment is merged with the economic and the social. Aided by renewables, sustainability has thus been mobilised and practically implemented across these domains. What otherwise could have been a difficult merger of contradictory rationalities and imaginaries hosted within the relaxed concept of sustainability seems to work unexpectedly well in the energy transition – at least on the surface. Corporations are engaging in different types of environmental politics, politicians are calling for a greening of business and citizen activities, and climate activists are desperately grasping for whatever they can to accomplish a real transformation. Citizens are envisioned as potential activists, by themselves and others, and, as explained briefly in the Introduction, hand in hand with this transition of the energy system, we can observe an activism in transition. This chapter will further investigate this mutual alteration by tracing the boundaryless attribute of activism, that is, how it is strategically mobilised and also flows freely in between various organisational domains. We will first address the tendency that businesses are going into activism, followed by how activism is going into business. Then we will narrow in on the boundaryless attribute of climate activism.

This boundaryless attribute of activism should not be mistaken for a simple movement, working back and forth, inside-out and outside-in, of organisations conceived as separate units in control. Instead, activism can be conceived as a widespread, dispersed and diffuse movement, a process that is hard to trace empirically and, by extension, difficult to represent in terms of theoretical assumptions about organisational boundaries and 'civil society'. With an accentuated will to take 'action' via renewables, across society and business, the boundaryless attribute of climate activism has become more dominant. The chapter closes in on this modification of activism by providing examples both from popular culture and academic literature. The purpose is to acknowledge a more complicated picture of activism, by interweaving the debates in social movement theory, political theory and management and organisation studies. It is our hope that this will prepare the reader for the rather messy, boundaryless character of activism presented in subsequent chapters in our empirical cases that span employee activism, CEO activism and brand activism at Vattenfall, a multinational energy corporation (Chapter 5); enterprising activism via small and medium-sized energy businesses (Chapter 6); insider activism in governmental authorities (Chapter 7); and prosumer activism undertaken by citizen groups in villages, homes, schools and sports clubs (Chapter 8).

1.1 Activism Goes into Business, and Business Goes into Activism

There is a long history of how business people have observed and engaged with formal political processes, including legitimate lobbying activities and networking, as well as illegitimate bribery and corruption. These traditional ways of steering political action and legislation from the world of business are nevertheless complemented by a broader spectrum of political engagements by contemporary businesses. With the growing conviction that corporate leaders and 'management' should be held responsible for hazardous emissions and their irreparable effects on a planetary scale (Rockström et al. 2009, Folke et al. 2010, Boyd and Folke 2012), businesses have been forced to bring environmental issues into the strategic centre of organisational decision-making. This has by extension led to an enrichment of stakeholder management and other inventive responses that stretch beyond an engagement with grassroots tactics applied by business to infuse formal political processes (Grefe and Linsky 1995), and has given birth to rejuvenated forms of commercial activism. We will now illustrate this span of corporate political engagement, from formal politics to activism, to better understand how and why activism has gone into business, and, conversely, how and why businesses have gone into activism.

1.1.1 Politics as Business Strategy

Corporations often choose to become political actors, directly involving themselves in political lobbying and sometimes campaigning. This

is referred to as corporate political activity (CPA).[1] Seen as a growing phenomenon around the world, CPA is defined as firms' attempts
to influence and sometimes shape governmental policies in ways that
are favourable to them (Baysinger, 1984: see reviews: Hillman, Keim
and Schuler 2004, Lawton, McGuire and Rajwani 2013). Within
the energy industry, for example, we have known for some time that
ExxonMobil has directly funded political campaigns to spread climate
change scepticism (MacKay and Munro 2012). Equally, we know
that the renewable energy sector in the United Kingdom (UK) and
elsewhere is actively trying to persuade governments to adopt more
climate friendly policies (Lockwood 2013, Sühlsen and Hisschemöller
2014). Businesses and their CEOs might be engaged in CPA out of
political, ethical and ideological convictions (Chin, Hambrick and
Treviño 2013) but they clearly also engage in CPA because they have
more than one eye on their bottom line (Lux, Crook and Woehr 2011).

In parallel with how corporate leaders try to convince politicians
about their corporate political preferences, they also work directly with
political and social issues in the form of corporate responsibility and
corporate governance. As a response to the growing critique of business, these managerial tools have been strategically advanced (Menon
and Menon 1997, Werther Jr and Chandler 2010), often framed
as a voluntary attempt to go beyond impression management and
make businesses trustworthy and responsible (Sanford 2011). Hence,
corporations' conscious engagement in environmental and social issues
has not been conceived as a form of disruptive activism but predominantly a strategic choice, executed at the top leadership level, with
the company constructed as a unit with the capacity to create 'organic
linkage[s]' between business and society (Frederick 2008:523).

In its most progressive version, these studies of stakeholder management and voluntary efforts position the company politically alongside other citizens within a wider democratic sphere, giving rise to
the notion of 'corporate citizenship' (Matten 2003, Moon, Crane
and Matten 2005, Crane, Matten and Moon 2008a, Graz and Nölke
2008). This framework makes it possible to study the corporation as
a legal entity next to other civil society actors, where the organisational unit is defined as 'a body separate in identity from its members'

---

[1] This has also been called 'corporate activism', for example in the book *The
new corporate activism: Harnessing the power of grassroots tactics for your
organization* (Grefe and Linsky 1995).

(Crane, Matten and Moon 2008a:3). This further enables analyses of how changing state–business–citizen relations affect corporate efforts to go beyond legal and regulative requirements to act in an ethically correct manner (Moon and Vogel 2008), stretching to notions of social activism and global citizenship – that is, taking responsibilities as a 'corporate citizen' in all the nations where the corporation is active (Frederick 2008). This movement has led to active interventions, for example by so-called community invest-ments or community lending (Kurtz 2008:250), and it has raised philosophical questions about how 'the people' is the basis for CSR (Horrigan 2010). Consequently, there is a tendency within the sphere of business to think of 'politics' as something more than a change-able structure or formal rule to be lobbied for, where studies of CSR have also been expanded to better include how corporate voluntary engagement is enacted through managers' personal values (Heming-way and Maclagan 2004).

The political engagement of corporations in social and environmen-tal issues has additionally given rise to the category of 'political CSR' (see Scherer and Palazzo 2007, 2011; for a comparison between the United States and Europe see Rasche 2015). Based on a Haberma-sian framework of deliberative democracy, political CSR normatively envisages a world where private actors – namely corporations and civil society organisations – intentionally and deliberately create the rules and processes of governance and regulation themselves, without the need for a sovereign state. Political CSR repeats many of the man-tras spawned in the 1970s when corporate investments were made in public relations and public affairs professionals. Whilst corporations at that time wished to gain 'freedom from government regulation' (Beder 2005:117), they have more recently framed the self-governance approach as a response to the increasing inability and unwillingness of nation states to govern and act (see further Moog, Spicer and Böhm 2015). It is a strategy that fits the diffused politico-economic land-scape of neoliberalism in which environmental and climate change governance has been embedded (see further Peck and Theodore 2012), leading to, as some authors argue, a depoliticisation that is at the heart of Habermasian consensus-building processes (Edward and Willmott 2013; see also Mouffe 1999). The trend seems to be that corpora-tions increasingly function as platforms for citizen/employee identifi-cation processes, self-regulation and responsibilisation (Fleming 2014,

Endrissat, Kärreman and Noppeney 2017), as authority is decentralised by the state and firms occupy ever more central places in society (Levy and Kaplan 2008).

1.1.2 Activism as Business Strategy

It is not only the boundary between the corporate world and formal politics (including legislation and implementation of deliberative democratic programmes) that is increasingly diffuse. Commerce has also offered a fecund platform for activism, where activism thrives on a disruption of boundaries between society and business (Soule 2012, de Bakker et al. 2013, den Hond, de Bakker and Smith 2015, Girschik 2020). This can be observed when companies increasingly collaborate directly with social movement organisations and NGOs, especially when aiming to address global environmental problems (e.g. see Doh and Guay 2006). Of interest here is how corporations manage environmental activists as stakeholders differently according to the reputation and status of the activist group (Bansal, Gao and Qureshi 2014, Perrault and Clark 2016; also see den Hond and de Bakker 2007; den Hond, de Bakker and Smith 2015). Environmental concerns can either be recognised and included in business decisions (Banerjee 1998, Banerjee 2002, Allen, Marshall and Easterby-Smith 2015), or activism can be treated as a threat to be smothered (Zietsma and Winn 2008, Hiatt, Sine and Tolbert 2009, Delmas and Toffel 2011). So-called corporate-responsibility-based activist groups have targeted firms with increasingly ingenious actions to advance corporate responsibility beyond private regulatory initiatives (Mena and Waeger 2014), and typical environmental pressure groups have had some success in holding businesses to account, pressuring them to change course on a range of issues (Bertels, Hoffman and DeJordy 2014). One example is Greenpeace's campaign against the Lego–Shell partnership, which was 'a textbook example of environmental activists using clever social media and protest techniques to raise the public's awareness about the environmental dangers involved in drilling for oil in the Arctic' (Böhm and Skoglund 2015).

Environmental NGOs can, in addition, go native by entering business. One example is WWF's Green Office programme, which seeks to disseminate knowledge and mobilise organisational members to act pro-environmentally (Uusi-Rauva and Heikkurinen 2013). Another similar case can be found in the environmental charity Global Action Plan, which entered a large British construction company to change the behaviours of the employees by making some of them into environmental champions (Hargreaves 2016). Even Greenpeace, seen by many as a radical NGO, has collaborated closely and extensively with a range of businesses (Yaziji and Doh 2010). These studies nevertheless draw an implicit line between the worlds of activism (often associated with civil society political action) and business (often seen to have a main interest in profit-making) (see Pacheco, York and Hargrave 2014).

To complicate the simplified view that activism is merely entering profit-hungry private corporations from the outside, there are other studies of how activism is becoming embedded and sustained within businesses or other types of organisations that deploy commercial operations (Girschik 2020). This includes a continuous enactment of gay and lesbian workplace rights (Raeburn 2004), gender and women's rights (Fondas 2000), and the transformation of feminism into femInc. ism (Ahl et al. 2016). Commercial activism has furthermore been attributed to a number of different but related people or groups of people, such as consumers (Brenton 2013), volunteers (O'Neill 2012), cooperatives (Schneiberg 2013) and passionate individuals (Kraemer, Whiteman and Banerjee 2013), one being Paul Gilding, the former director of Greenpeace (Wright and Mann 2013). Within commercial activism, we also find shareholder groups (Proffitt and Spicer 2006, Mena and Waeger 2014) and investors (Hoffman 1996, Perrault and Clark 2016), who wish to ensure a good return for their money. Returning to these in more detail later on, we will first engage with those who have been most noted in various media for breaking the confinement of activism to a place called civil society: activist entrepreneurs or enterprising activists, employee activists and CEO activists.

1.1.3 Activist Entrepreneurs

An early example of green enterprising activism is Mirvis' (1994) view of how progressive business should look. Mirvis showed that, on the one hand, an environmental agenda can be driven from the top, perhaps by an inspirational business founder or, on the other hand, from the shop floor, by the employees and workers. Analytical focus is thus commonly given to an individual with agentic capacities. One of Mirvis', and after him, many others' favourite examples of enterprising environmentalism in the form of an activist company is The Body Shop, established in the mid-1970s. The Body Shop was one of the first start-ups to have a clear environmentalist agenda, rolled out effectively by the late human and animal rights activist Dame Anita Roddick. The Body Shop has since been well known for running various environmental campaigns, targeting a rich variety of things from animal cruelty to sex worker trafficking (Muhr and Rehn 2014).

Dame Anita Roddick did, however, meet strong criticism for setting up her activism in the form of a business, and especially so when she sold it to L'Oréal in 2006. As a response to being called an 'ecocapitalist' (Hartman and Beck-Dudley 1999:255), she proposed to act from within, as a 'Trojan Horse' in a hostile environment (Cahalane 2006), and this is what she attempted, until her death a year later. In one of her last interviews, Roddick emphasised that she had no wish to be defined by business but to be remembered for her civil society engagement (Cahalane 2006). On a personal basis, she thus tried to keep up the common separation between the civil sphere and the business sphere, regardless of her work 'from within' in the latter.

Having failed to significantly expand the brand beyond its niche, and losing large parts of the customer base loyal to the environmental cause, L'Oréal later sold The Body Shop to the Brazilian company Natura in 2017. Yet some of Roddick's ideas were kept alive on the surface via brand activism and a belief in the customers as a force for good (Medium 2017). As a testament to its activist history, The Body Shop even developed a product line 'just right for guys on the go' called 'Activist' (The Body Shop 2020). The idea was to attract so-called consumer activists, individuals who attempt to use their purchasing power consciously and responsibly by being informed about the impact of the goods and services they wish to attain – in other words, consumers who vote with their money. By offering the signing of petitions online, and with the help of these socially and environmentally aware consumers, The Body Shop even suggested that their customers could accomplish 'change on an unprecedented scale' (Medium 2017). Brand activism as business strategy is consequently not necessarily dependent on an organisation being constructed as a unit filled with political agency, since the brand as image can be invested with such, regardless its organisational host. The Body Shop's activism could thus move on quite detached from committed organisational members who work for a cause. Nevertheless, The Body Shop, under L'Oréal, continued to suggest that activism was ingrained in the organisational culture, where campaigning for various issues was still proclaimed as an important part of the daily work of the employees (Medium 2017). To remain activist companies, and not just activist brands, business organisations thus seem to need a strong and authentic connection to their value creation, coherently represented by the employees and projected onto the brand.

Another popular 1970s example of an activist company that has enjoyed a successful mobilisation of a political image and brand is Patagonia. Patagonia sells outdoor clothing and is underscored by a brand that succeeds in merging a down-to-earth philosophy and nature protection with extreme sports. The company was founded by Yvon Chouinard, who has been acclaimed for practising what he has been preaching (Baldwin 2018). On Patagonia's website, under the heading 'activism', the company states that it is 'in business to save our home planet' (Patagonia 2020). The company does, however, apply both CPA and activism by merging legal and direct activist actions (Chouinard, 2016), one example being their targeting of the US government's rolling back of protection of national monuments. Patagonia changed its normally colourful website into one with a black background with the statement 'The President Stole Your Land' and took the issue to court (Wolf 2017). By using the silhouette of Trump's head profile, the company kept drawing attention to the offence, referring to how criminals had been brought to public awareness historically. This shows that activist companies of various sizes can play the same role as civil society movements when they attack oppressive state rule. Businesses, however, enjoy other means, for example monetary muscle and authority gained from market popularity.

From Patagonia's website, we additionally learn that they practically support community building and their employees' personal environmental engagement to keep up the activist spirit internally. The company openly seeks to nurture the political motivation and individual values of its employees, since they are convinced that this spurs creativity and brings in new ideas to the company (Patagonia 2018). They therefore actively encourage their employees to work as volunteers for two months with a salary, embedded within an environmental grassroots group. In comparison with The Body Shop, which mainly engaged their employees in campaigning, Patagonia thus comes across as a bigger supporter of employee activism.

The former major supplier to The Body Shop, the cosmetic retailer company Lush, also exemplifies how activism is brought in as a coherent strategy, all the way from the employee to the sourcing and selling. Lush maximises the ethical sourcing of their products by acting as activist consumers business to business (B2B consumer activism, see Table 1 in the Appendix), using their 'buying power to affect positive change in the world' (Levitt 2016). Illustrative of the mediatised 'political activism' at Lush, all earnings generated from the sales of specific products, such as the 'GayIsOK' soap and the body lotion 'the charity pot', are also given directly to grassroots movements (Levitt 2016). Similarly to the strategy of The Body Shop, Lush has also launched specific activist products. In 2013, the London riots spurred the creation of a Gorilla Perfume called Lavender Hill Mob: 'a calming incense to still the mind and remind us of the importance of community' (Lush 2018). Each product or product line is thus branded to effect a sense of political engagement that the consumer can tap into and display on the bathroom shelf. At the same time as the perfume is charged with 'the importance of community' (Levitt 2016), so too is the internal organisational culture, in popular commentary formed by 'an ethos and personality that's difficult to describe. It doesn't come directly from the founders, it comes from the organisation and it is something that you belong to. It is a company in the true sense of the word, as in a group of individuals' (Levitt 2016).

Repeatedly then, there is in activist companies an interpellation of community belonging, where the workplace is constructed to function as an open platform for the enactment of personal political preferences. As social and environmental issues are being hotly debated and campaigned for across all sections of society, it thus seems necessary to acknowledge boundaryless activism as something that not only permeates various organisations, including private corporations, but as something that is initiated, established and sustained by how enterprising activism offers employees and consumers the chance to co-create a 'community'.

In the wake of how activism has been taken into business, where even Greenpeace (2018b) has acted as a model for how to start a company, scholars have slowly begun to study how activists migrate over from civil society or social movement organisations in order to create new business opportunities, which they consider to be a more ethical way of mobilising markets for a specific cause (Dubuis-son-Quellier 2013). In close proximity to enterprising environmental-ism, we can thus find the notion of 'ecopreneurship', which denotes when sustainability or the environment motivates the business entre-preneur (e.g. see Pastakia 1998, Dixon and Clifford 2007). Here, the creation of alternative organisations by entrepreneurs who choose to solve a wide variety of political and social problems (Hockerts 2006, Bacq and Janssen 2011) stretches all the way from social and green enterprising and profit-making to 'community-based social initiatives' (Daskalaki, Hjorth and Mair 2015:421). To the extent that the entrepreneur conflates with conceptualisations of the activist (Barinaga 2013). The concept of 'entrepreneurship' has furthermore been detached from 'enterprising' (Hjorth and Holt 2016), to make sure its activist qualities can be properly observed, seen as an 'inher-ently *disruptive activity* with positive social change outcomes' (Dey and Mason 2018:85, emphasis original). This leaves 'activist entre-preneuring' to be all about truth-telling, generative of a removal of self-imposed limits for the release of collective imagination (Dey and Mason 2018:85). Based on the conflation of activism and business in practice, scholarship on entrepreneurship has with conceptual ease morphed into activism. With emphasis on how human relational-ity, community building and collective action are coupled to a non-instrumental entrepreneurial subjectivity. What happens to activism, conceptually, is however unclear.

1.1.4 Employee Activism

According to frequent media reports, business has in general started to recognise that external activism moves into companies with a rise in the number of activist employees (Calandro 2017). Instead of pres-sure from external sources, it is thus internal sources that are iden-tified to put pressure on the leadership direction of variously sized companies. Consultancies have accordingly set out to assess the levels of seriousness of employee activism in order to facilitate a transfor-mation of those employee activists who can be identified as on the edge of becoming 'pro' their employer. Here, activism is definitely not thought about as disruption, neither is it configured as an inter-nal bottom-up movement, but it is seen as a defence mechanism, where the employee protects the employer by becoming an 'advocate'

(Higginbottom 2014). In the view of business media, activist employees are therefore to be assessed and treated as stakeholders, managed and listened to, both to secure the company's reputation and to build an internal organisational culture that supports loyalty and creativity that is eventually assumed to result in sustained competitiveness and profits (Higginbottom 2014). As leading consultants in activism as business strategy repeatedly propose, embracing employee activism and community building is a way of 'seizing opportunity' (Shandwick 2016) and of becoming 'the employer of choice' (Higginbottom 2014, Crisafulli 2018:14).

This normative popularised business conception of activism as business strategy is tightly wedded to managerial tools such as 'employer branding', designed to socially steer employee activism. With the increase of environmentalism permeating organisations, major multinational companies have started to adopt Green Human Resource Management (HRM) practices to attract a younger generation, who are proven to be more interested in environmental issues (DuBois and Dubois 2012, Ehnert, Wes and Zink 2013, Renwick, Redman and Maguire 2013, Aust, Muller-Camen and Poutsm 2018). The emergence of the term Green HRM (Renwick 2018), which outlines agendas for how to train, manage, reward and lead employees with regard to environmental issues, points to an awareness of something like internal activism, conceived as enacted from within an organisation. If a phenomenon at work is worthy of attention from HRM, then it is arguably something of organisational significance. Given that internal activism can involve commitment, motivation, resistance and performance issues, it is obvious that HRM would be keen to manage employee activism. Green HRM is thus all about synchronising values between an organisation and its members – a process of becoming unified that is suggested to 'make the world a better place' (Sonenshein 2016:349). The reason for a business to exist should is thus proposed to go beyond the focus on maximising the wealth of shareholders and stakeholders and be tuned into the current challenges in the world, via the employees (Sonenshein 2016).

Activism has consequently been brought to the core of businesses that had previously been uninterested in internalising the political imaginaries of either the citizens or their own employees. This embracing of activism is not only pursued by strategists educated in business schools, where the Anthropocene epoch is digested and the irreparable effects of 'business' and 'management' are taught, but by employees who conceive of themselves as impelled to take action when they finally meet anthropocentrism face to face at work. These employees often explore opportunities to be social change agents who can influence their top management and direct the employer towards specific problems. While the active influence of employees on their employer in respect of social and green issues is relatively understudied by business scholars (however, see Hemingway 2005, 2013, Howard-Grenville 2006), it is a well-documented trend in popular culture and stories told by consultancies.

1.1.5 CEO Activism

In The Huffington Post, Calandro (2017) summarises a popular scientific assessment of activist employees, which suggests that it is millennials in management positions who seek to change their employers the most. Configured as a unified agent, that is, 'the employer', the public relations firm Weber Shandwick claims that businesses are guided by activist employees to 'humanise and unify their enterprise voice' (Weber Shandwick 2016:2), but it is mainly CEOs that are demanded to take a clearer stand on political issues and be the responsible face and moral model, internally and externally. This has led to a particular extension of how corporate leaders have previously engaged with politics (as described in the first part of this chapter), in that a distinctive type of CEO activism has developed in the twenty-first century, with the recruitment of millennials. These younger generations strongly wish for their employer to bring in social and political purposefulness at work, which results in intergenerational tensions. The CEO position is not only filled with responsibilities for business development but is at the forefront of social, political and environmental transformations. The CEOs, it is argued, can therefore no longer afford to be silent but have to speak up in line with their employee activists who, for example, may wish 'to align their retirement plans with their company's social commitments' (Calandro 2017). Activist employees who express such demands of their leader simultaneously construct themselves as followers of a specified CEO position, one which for them is filled with added capacities and 'power' to exert, outwards and top-down.

Despite this bottom-up demand to become an activist, some CEOs of large corporations have also taken trendy activism into their own hands, without visible demands from below (Chatterji and Toffel 2018). If CEOs were previously spoken about as 'sustainability leaders', they have thus become increasingly mediatised as 'industrious activists' (Gumbel 2005). Among these CEO activists, some may identify strongly with an activist agenda, while others may enjoy a looser connection to the political implications of activism. Those CEOs who only occasionally identify as activists at work can be recognised by how they play their political green or gender cards in relation to profit motives. Hence, the growing trend of CEO activism shows a clear continuum of political engagement, from those who are willing to disconnect from profit motives and make economic sacrifices to pursue their political imaginaries or ideals, to those who occasionally deviate or seek to perfectly align the profit motive with the political motive (Hinterecker, Kopel and Ressi 2018). Nevertheless, both aim to conquer a moral high ground.

In the few academic studies of CEO activism that exist, focus has been on a general trend for CEOs to act politically (Rumstadt and Kanbach 2022). CEO activism is often identified as disconnected from the core of the business, and political actions are thus to be taken in parallel with the business operations, for example defined as 'the practice of CEOs taking public positions on environmental, social, and political issues not directly related to their business' (Larcker et al. 2018:1). In these instances, the business becomes a communicative platform, suggesting that CEOs can influence political issues via their easy access to media channels (Chatterji and Toffel 2016). In comparison with the ability of governmental politicians to raise public awareness, CEOs tend to receive more media attention and have a greater effect on popular opinion (Chatterji and Toffel 2016). Importantly though, this conquering of a moral high ground is not a straightforward strategy (Branicki et al. 2021), as Starbuck's CEO Howard Schultz experienced when he was criticised for having imposed political standpoints on the baristas, who were expected to communicate 'correctly' with customers about race issues in the United States (Chatterji and Toffel 2015). Popular business media is likewise quick to question whether the 'moral leaders' generated in 'corporate activism' can really be fully trusted due to their inevitable connection to profit motives (Paulas 2017).

1.2 Critical Perspectives on Commercial Activism

What the presented examples of a boundaryless activism expose is the difference between (often smaller) companies that self-identify as activists and (often bigger) corporations that rather choose to speak about their engagement in CSR, stakeholder management and Green HRM. It is quite clear that Patagonia and the Tata Group in India differ in how they affirm social responsibility. While Patagonia is focussed on its core environmental message and community building, allowing it to say that 'rampant consumerism is not attractive' (Semuels 2019), Tata is a huge conglomerate of firms that aims to grow into one of the biggest companies in the world by embedding sustainability into its progress (Bonanni, Lépineux and Roloff 2012). The closer we get to a core business that relies on market segments that are pro-environmental, the closer we also get to expressions of green commercial activism, instead of just corporate responsibilities or initiatives.

Hessnatur in Germany offers another and much criticised example of how activism has gone into business and how business has gone into activism. Founded in 1976 on strong values and a business of organic and Fairtrade clothing aligned with a green organisational culture, there has been repeated questioning of Hessnatur's green authenticity. Commentators display a need to distinguish economic value creation from the creation of green and social values. Many wish the economic to be kept separate from the political, cleansing environmentalism from dirty capitalism. This tendency is often played out in relation to brand strategies, which have provided a fruitful focus for critical academic debates (Dauvergne and Lister 2013, Montgomery 2019). Interrogations about the green content in the brand function as a relay for criticism of profit-seeking businesses, which, it is argued, strategically hide under illusionary green façades. Hence, branding is judged differently depending on the context of the business operations and how the brand does or does not point to a gap in the everyday operations (Ottman 2011, Grubor and Milovanov, 2017).

Processes of green branding also show how brands are continuously co-constructed by a plethora of actors (see Hatch and Schultz 2008, Kornberger 2010), unable to be controlled by the branded organisation itself. Even Patagonia's branding strategy has been criticised from a leftist perspective as leading to unnecessary consumption and growth of the company (Dauvergne 2016). Hence, brands have been increasingly described and scrutinised as sources for value in the progression of 'globalised flexible accumulation' (Goldman and Papson 2006) and a so-called anti-brand movement has arisen, adding to constant tensions within branding (Holt 2002). Companies are then often left to evaluate how to keep up an authentic relation to green environmental concerns in a collapse of the boundaries between internal and external communication activities.

The media, environmental movements, state agencies, shareholders, consumers and employees all have an interest in constructing green brands, although this carries the risk of being called 'greenwashing'. No matter how companies and their employees contextualise themselves in relation to ecological complexities, suspicion prevails among consumers and critical scholars alike. This is perhaps not surprising, considering the rebranding of British Petroleum to Beyond Petroleum (Beder 2002, Christiansen 2002, Muralidharan 2011) and how 'star species', such as polar bears, have been utilised by various corporations in attempts to appear green (Yusoff 2010). To stimulate a positive impression internally and externally, companies are even making use of social and environmental atrocities without a direct causal link to their own operations (Muhr and Rehn 2014). Here, critical commentators, for example in debates about 'woke capitalism', imply that citizens' suffering is turned into a corporate asset (Rhodes 2022).

In contrast to the use of social and environmental atrocities, companies have also utilised co-branding strategies to position themselves in a more positive activist light. Cederström and Marinetto (2013) criticise such co-branding strategies by vividly illustrating how the ice-cream company Ben and Jerry's supported the Occupy movement, and how Mercedes-Benz mobilised Che Guevara to emphasise the potential of carpools and thereby property sharing. Perhaps to fuel debate, Mercedes-Benz substituted the star at the front of Guevara's hat with their own logotype in a commercial re-make of the acclaimed rebellion. There are numerous other examples of how the anti-capitalist Che Guevara has been utilised and exploited for capitalist ends, raising questions such as: 'So how did Che Guevara – the face of the Cuban Revolution – become CEO of corporate America?' (Davis 2016).

From a critical perspective, Che Guevara is here functioning as a model for the nomadic lifestyle inhabited by what Slavoj Žižek terms the 'liberal capitalist', someone who argues that there is no necessary friction between capitalism and the social good (Cederström and

Marinetto 2013). Giroux (1994:27) adds to this view by considering commerce as something that has taken over 'critical public cultures'. In comparison with the political landscape of the 1960s and 1970s, activism has been 'mainstreamed', and particularly so within the environmental movement (Jamison 2001:10), which suggests that NGOs are part of this mainstreaming due to their close acquaintance with business or implementation of business strategies. Furthermore, it has been shown that this position leads to a commodification of civic engagement and 'chequebook activists' (Hensby, Sibthorpe and Drvier 2011:809).

This is a criticism that results from an intellectual will to keep activism in an external strong position from which it can aim at its target more accurately. Social theorists have hence been historically sensitive to the potential compromising of activists' external positions – external in the sense of there being a clear dividing line between 'us' and 'them' – as 'mainstreaming' is assumed to result in a less radical political position. The German philosophy professor Peter Sloterdijk (2014) seems to agree, pointing out the loss of possibilities for critique, as activism is diluted by capitalism. He argues that conventional anger banks, such as political parties and social movements, have been partly replaced by all sorts of economic opportunism that affirms active or passive forms of aggression, enacted overtly or covertly. He further suggests that capitalism functions too well as a vessel for speeding up social change (cf. Sloterdijk 2014), where the inhumane rhythm, rather than just the dilution of activism, is considered a major problem.

The criticism of the boundaryless attribute of activism has, in addition, called attention to what is going on when corporations craft, facilitate or constrain citizenship from within the business sphere. At the same time as performative change can happen from within business, by various sorts of balanced confrontation and collaboration across hierarchies (Parker and Parker 2017), it has been suggested that there exists an abusive form of alignment between corporate interests and citizens' concerns about sustainability, insofar as corporations often try to incorporate and harness people's political agendas (Nyberg, Spicer and Wright 2013). Bridging the world of business and NGOs, for example, is often quite explicit in the renewable energy sector, as consumers are called upon to act, as moral citizens, to make the right choices (McEachern 2015). It has been argued that this results in a negative and crippling effect on people's political subjectivity (Kuhn and Deetz 2008), for example a confinement of people's capacity to believe in their own political power to accomplish various transformations.

In the case of climate change and efforts to accomplish a sustainable society at work, Taro Lennerfors (2013) nevertheless complicates this argument of simple corporate co-optation of the activist. According to Lennerfors, truths generated externally to an organisation can infuse the personal ethics of the individual employees to such a degree that they choose to live, machinated, in accordance with that specific truth. Here, employees are disciplined and governed through an organisational 'outside', rather than controlled and managed at an organisational 'inside'. Nevertheless, it has also been shown that employees or organisational members still experience 'some latitude to author their own reality, though always in ways shaped by the available social discourses' (Humphreys and Brown 2002:422).

Despite the acknowledgement of some 'latitude', this very 'latitude' has yet again been claimed to be a key element for how businesses draft successful empowerment games to roll out neo-normative control of their employees (Fleming and Spicer 2004, 2009). That is, when managers realise that it is impossible to align the core values of the organisation with a complex and heterogeneous workforce who may be increasingly cynical about such values, they instead aim for an existential empowerment of the employees, who 'should not be expected to share the organisation's values', but perhaps even oppose them (Fleming and Sturdy 2009:570). Business organisations that acknowledge the human to be inherently complex are thus strategically cutting their employees some slack to better manage and steer a multiplicity of passions and at times contradictory personal politics. This tension between activism and its management, bottom-up self-organising and supposedly functioning co-optation from the top, is, however, long-standing. Labour and union movements have always expressed their experience of struggles and strains in relation to top-down versus bottom-up organising (Dewey 1998, Marens 2013, Hampton 2015).

1.3 Conclusion

The examples of commercial activism explored in this chapter, found in various historical and international arenas, illustrate the fecund business paths taken by activism. The categories outlined are sometimes hard to keep separate, as they tend to merge and support each other. A common difference between lobbying activities and the engagement in formal politics by corporations, and 'activist companies' such as Patagonia, is the creation of a coherent value chain in the latter – a strategic coherence that spans from the activist entrepreneur to the employee activist and consumer activist, all offering to build a 'community' that bridges business and society. Even though it is difficult to draw clear scholarly boundaries between a commercial interest in formal politics via coalition building and grassroots tactics and commercial interests in activism *per se*, a corporate turn to 'activism' is important to acknowledge.

However, seen from a broader historical perspective, companies may perhaps always have been activists to some extent (Böhm and Skoglund 2015, Böhm, Skoglund and Eatherley 2018). Corporations have long needed to go beyond impression management to win the trust of others (customers, policymakers, employees and citizens) and make them truly believe in the positive effects of goods and services. Tellingly, when Henry Ford (1863–1947) paid three times more than the then average wage to his workers to bring automobility to the masses, perhaps he could have been regarded as an activist. When the Marxist and English craftsman William Morris (1834–96) created his home styling business, mainly based on a refined production of patterned wallpapers and materials, perhaps this was his attempt to counter capitalism in efforts to restore a sense of community and local connectedness. Commercial community building is still hard to disconnect from other types of community formation, located in civil society, as 'belonging' and 'togetherness' are equally seen to be facilitated by contemporary activist companies.

To have this broad perspective of activism in mind – with its historical roots in, and contemporary enrichment by, business strategies – will be of importance for the rest of this book. The sheer number of businesses that have invested in change, especially in relation to environmentalism, testifies to a boundaryless attribute of activism that is understudied. Rather than confining activism to actions pursued by civil society, we should acknowledge how activism has gone into business and vice versa. As argued by Sloterdijk (2014), commercial activism offers a significant change in speed and tempo, and the question is how climate activism marries with this sort of temporality and dynamism of technological innovation and entrepreneurial disruption (Glezos 2012). Despite a growing 'slow movement' in attempts to live more sustainably, perhaps acceleration will become increasingly alluring to the environmental cause and quests to accomplish social transformations aided by renewable technologies, 'here and now', in quick response to the climate emergency.

2 | The Activist–Business–State Conglomeration

Just as activism has gone into business, and vice versa, it has also permeated governmental bodies. Policymakers have turned their attention to 'the activist', and activists have moved in the other direction, to pursue their personal politics from within state and international authorities. Just as it has become futile to restrict activism to 'civil society' in order to set it up as an opponent to state and business, so too it has become impossible to keep it separate from governmental bodies, and especially so when looking at environmental issues (Hochstetler and Keck 2007, Olsson and Hysing 2012, Hysing and Olsson 2018, Abers 2019). As activism has multiplied through business strategies, it has also spread within the 'entrepreneurial state', a state that seeks to enable growth and lay out new technological paths by affirming high risks as much as citizens' aspirations and ambitions (Mazzucato 2015a). In light of this forceful boundaryless attribute of activism, this chapter continues to trace climate activism, with a focus on how it is becoming even more dispersed and diffuse when bolstered through formal political bodies, and what we call the activist–business–state conglomeration.

To better understand how the activist–business–state conglomeration is massaged and glued together, the chapter starts by situating the development of climate activism in relation to deliberative democratic programmes of participation and energy democracy – programmes within which the citizen category has been complemented by, or even swapped with, the activist. This is a shift in climate governance that is partly echoed in the turn to prosumerism in renewable energy policy discourse, a discourse that in the UK 'manifest[s] itself in a peppering of the words "local" and "community"' to tap into both renewable energies and people's energies (Walker et al. 2007:68). To prepare the reader for the empirical section of the book, this chapter thus touches on how, in particular in the UK political agenda on climate adaptation, consensual deliberation and a top-down creation of market pull have been slowly revised by a call for climate actions and community building, resulting in a bottom-up market push.

The brief summary of the UK renewable energy policy landscape is also complemented with a broader picture of how passions and desires to go green have been nurtured in a turn to prosumer activism. Particularly emphasised by the EU, citizens-turning-activists have been offered the chance to make green political changes their businesses, literally speaking. Despite the fact that parts of this policy vocabulary, with its abbreviations, funding schemes and elaborate subsidies will be repeated later on by our research participants, it should not be mistaken for a causal driving force of climate activism. After all, political programmes to activate citizens bottom-up rarely turn out as anticipated (Bäckstrand 2010, MacArthur 2016). Therefore, even though the policy environment of a country is undoubtedly an important, even crucial, factor (Mitchell and Connor 2004, Mitchell et al. 2013), we are more curious about the ways in which the policy context becomes embedded in the activist–business–state conglomeration. In the cases presented, the policies and subsidies are experienced as short lived and constantly changing. The formal political regulations are conceived by our research participants to offer more uncertainty and slack, rather than any detailed and austere advice about preferred paths forward.

While prosumer activism is directed towards, picked up and redesigned by citizens, there are two other forms of activism of interest to such an empirical focus: investor activism and insider activism. Investor activism is a type of commercial activism that creates bonds between investors, governments and intergovernmental networks to pressurise businesses in all sorts of directions. Despite looking like a clear-cut example of an 'outsider' form of activism, pursued by investors (including state institutions), this chapter illustrates how it has become a commercial form of activism that increasingly permeates business organisations due to the knowledge movement on climate change. Lastly, to grasp the extent of what boundaryless climate activism has become, we briefly summarise how green insider activism can be pursued by public servants, normally assumed to work apolitically as neutral implementers of decisions made by elected politicians (Olsson and Hysing 2012, Hysing and Olsson 2018). The reader can thus expect to meet prosumer activism, investor activism and insider activism later on, detailed and analysed in Chapters 5, 6, 7 and 8.

2.1 Deliberative Democracy – from Citizen Voicing to Activism

After World War II, proponents of democracy started to emphasise the need for democratic participation with the inclusion of citizens, communities and NGOs (Cooke and Kothari 2001). Governments subscribing to democratic rule accordingly highlighted the importance of a healthy civil society, 'free' to take 'action', which would lead to collective decision-making for local, national and transnational regulations on rights and justice, including environmental issues (Pattberg and Stripple 2008). In the associated policy literature, the broader category of citizen is thus commonly mobilised to facilitate public or private initiatives and drive compliance, in contrast with the narrower category of activist. At the same time, citizens with 'voice' are occasionally identified as taking disturbing counter-actions, sometimes challenging politiciams and businesses a bit too much, from the external position of civil society. Nonetheless, the underlying political approach to manage citizens, not just in general but also potential activism, within the democratic structures of a state, is 'deliberative democracy' (see further Talisse 2005). With roots in liberal thought, but renewed by the critical theorist Jürgen Habermas (Kohn 2000), deliberation has thus found noteworthy additional application in the governance of activism.

An example of the accentuated deliberative interest in the citizen–turning–activist can be observed in the political response to the so-called yellow vest movement in France (Chamorel 2019). Here, urban elites were accused of being out of touch with the wishes and needs of the non-metropolitan majority, which is why President Emmanuel Macron proposed the implementation of a 'national debate', in the form of a series of debating events, organised in towns and cities around the country, rhetorically claiming to give people a voice, and mandatorily adding that their voices of course would be listened to. Macron often referred to the 'yellow vests' as 'activists' and their radical flank even as 'terrorists', whereas his orchestrated national debates involved 'citizens', or even 'ordinary citizens' (Cole 2019).

At the same time as deliberative democracy is believed to facilitate and raise support for specific political projects among the population, it is also considered to be a bureaucratically effective way to respond to general problems with democracy – a political system criticised for being increasingly detached from the wishes of the people (Smith 2009). It can sometimes even be difficult to detect deliberative democracy, since states use it without overtly naming it as such (Ravazzi 2016). This results in a stark difference between democratic efforts that turn to expert or interest groups and democratic innovations that engage citizens more directly in decision-making processes (Smith 2009).

As is well-known, deliberative democratic processes have been broadly implemented in the energy transition to counter general resistance to environmental concerns (Smith 2003, 2009), climate scepticism (Myers, Ritter, and Rockway 2017), and NIMBYism [Not In My Backyard] (Devine-Wright 2014). Particularly when it comes to the installation of onshore wind turbines, NIMBYism can arise among local citizens who feel their landscapes or house values are being negatively affected. Far from the existential allure of infinity and hope, represented in the aesthetic dimension of our book cover, many thus still perceive these technologies to be oversized, alien industrial developments in the countryside (Devine-Wright 2014). Given the prevalence of substantial commercial interests involved in the installation of large-scale renewable energy projects, it is perhaps not surprising that some are prone to oppose them, as they often do not have a direct (financial) stake in them. To meet such resistance, town hall meetings can, for example, be held to channel citizen opinion and let people participate under the auspices of a democratic process. At other times, money is directly paid to those regions where the installations are made, to bring about citizen compliance.

The strong political belief in the importance of citizens' inclusion and active participation is nevertheless also one of the reasons why the literature on renewable energy policy has a tendency to repeat its focus on NIMBYism, diagnosed as more than a problem with payback schemes. That is, resistance to renewables is conceived to be a result of more general negative political tendencies based on unsuccessful democratic rule and lack of adequate participation processes (Sharon 2019). In this vein, citizens are imagined to host a potentially problematic political subjectivity, one that can counter and thwart what is considered the common good (Walker, Cass, et al. 2010).

The depth of citizen inclusion is furthermore identified as key for a successful evocation of awareness, participation and debate, so as to make diverse opinions heard, and by extension, governable (Hobson 2009). Policymakers not only wish to identify and include citizens' views by means of opinion polls to become updated about them, but also to use deliberation and participation to spread knowledge about such issues as environmental problems, leading to a knowledge process that governs people and the climate in tandem (Paterson and Stripple 2010, Stripple and Bulkeley 2013). The ultimate aim is to create knowledge processes that flow in two directions: from citizens to policymakers and from policymakers to citizens. To govern both the citizen and the activist, deliberation programmes nevertheless need to encompass as many negative 'anti' resistance movements as positive 'pro' movements.

One of these identified 'pro' movements is renewable energy action stimulated via communal ownership. It is 'communities', one exponent of deliberation argues, that need to be empowered by ownership, to endorse a feeling in people that they 'possess the power to set the agenda for the resource' (Sharon 2019:10264). An embracement of property mechanisms is common in the energy transition, here exemplified by how material possessions are seen to causally provide people with another 'possession' – political power. Aided by a material focus on renewables in the energy transition, democratic deliberation has thus intensified the level of inclusion by making the citizen into a proprietor – a figure made to bridge society and business through 'ownership' and 'action' rather than through 'inclusion' and 'participation'. Nonetheless, it is still a citizen who is assumed to lead the way from an external position, executing civil society influence on state and industrial affairs (Petschow, Rosenau and von Weizsäcker 2005).

The rhetoric of a more sovereign, rather than deliberate, form of rule has been revisited in parallel in political science, as expressed in conceptualisations of 'the entrepreneurial state' (Mazzucato 2015a) and 'Greenovation' (Fitzgerald 2020). A case in point is environmental technologies that demand extensive research and development, supported by complex state-subsidised innovation systems that are out of citizens' individual or collective budget reach (Foxon et al. 2005). In contrast to the bottom-up rhetoric of deliberation, transnational networks and state governments are tellingly also eager to take the lead on green innovations 'top down', nonetheless balanced by treating citizens as 'enlightened consumers' (Jamison 2001:125), or by win-win situations supported by the business sector, such as 'Growing Green' launched by the World Bank in their facilitation of climate action (Deichmann and Zhang 2013). Consequently, green deliberative democracy merges the quest to strengthen citizen participation with renewable energy commercialisation processes under an overt governance leadership of the state (Fast 2013).

The ongoing merger of overt and covert international and national stimulation of climate actions may, in the light of boundaryless activism, look relatively smooth. It is nevertheless a cocktail of democratic flavours that has been met with general criticism (Boggs 2000, Castells 2018), and particularly so in relation to local renewable energy deliberations. These often generate a mismatch between governance officials and citizens who 'talk past each other' (Fast 2013:94). Officials prioritise 'objective-world claims' and the construction of facts, with a focus on technical details and financing mechanisms, while local citizens prioritise 'social-world claims' (Fast 2013:94). Even though deliberative democracy, and deliberative activists, can challenge representative democracy, institutions and politicians (Ravazzi 2016), it is recognised as a top-down, technocratic and elitist tool that deadens politics via consensus and creates a post-political condition (Swyngedouw 2009, 2010). This is a condition that in turn has spawned calls for more authentic, bottom-up green radicalism that allows real participation and the inclusion of an increasingly diverse set of voices of 'the people' (Heyley 2014). For example, prompted by 'critical democracy' (Smith 2009:6), designed as a response to the conceived lack of plurality and passion in deliberative democracy policy programmes (cf. Mouffe 1999) that opens up for an inclusion of previously excluded voices.

According to Andy Stirling (2015), sustainability was originally initiated by such voicing, spawned by proper democratic struggle driven by subaltern interest before it was turned into a lukewarm, mainstream effort to manage the planet. The grassroots version, he suggests, wished to bring about a radical transformation of society in sustainability terms, while the managerial version, involving large public and private institutions, only showed an interest in incremental transition. Stirling's preference is for bringing about transformations that are created via tacit and embodied knowledge, leading to diverse and unruly forms of organising without known ends (Stirling 2015). Hence, a controlled 'transition' is evidently not the same thing as a dispersed and diffuse 'transformation'.

Ananya Roy (2009) has investigated differently the relationship between citizens' passionate calls for transformation and policymakers' instrumental calls for transition. She asks how citizen participation and inclusion are targeted when the citizen takes an activist stance and empirically affirms cases where there are already 'more rebellious forms of citizenship and mobilisation' present (Roy 2009:159). Instead of categorising how effectively self-regulation and responsibilisation conflate either via a bottom-up or top-down mobilisation of governing, Roy advances our understanding of political participation aided by spatial theory. The empowerment of personal politics, identities and certain ways of living should, according to her, not be seen as a bridging of the institutional level and the civic level. Empowerment attempts should not be misunderstood as resulting in compliance alone, but 'grassroots regimes of government both resist and comply with what may be perceived to be top-down forms of rule' to re-create 'the terms of rule and citizenship' (Roy 2009:160f). There are, in effect, unknown outcomes in the meetings between deliberation and activism, when civil society 'action' is stimulated and thereby becomes governed.

Garside (2013) aptly shows that environmentalists have sought to enter this questionable political space of deliberative democracy and argues that the aim of environmentalism should be to disturb the legitimacy of democratic decision-making bodies, and the limits they impose, to enforce alternatives. This argument, which further points out the limits to transformation via democratic means, is motivated by inspiration from the post-human turn, suggesting that to be able to end the oppression of biospheric life the human would have to create a more inclusive democracy, one that expands the 'sphere of concern' beyond what has hitherto been encompassed by liberal democracies (Garside 2013:256). The anthropocentric category of citizen, for example, would become an ecological category – dethroned to act as an equal in the ecological dominion. Not ecological as in a political flavour, but an 'ecological citizen' ontologically speaking. This would be a citizen inclusion as diverse as it is locally formed, spurred by bioregional imaginaries rather than political lobbying, recycling activities and ecological shopping (Garside 2013), showing that there are other possible aspects at play, in addition to the most obvious loci of intellectual interest – top-down politics, bottom-up self-regulation and capitalism.

It is not only bioregional imaginaries that have been proposed to be included in the sphere of concern, hand in hand with a deeper inclusion of the citizen–becoming–activist. Arjun Appadurai (2013:175) proposes that 'deep democracy' is growing in the light of the 'porousness of national boundaries' that erodes attempts to govern democratically within national borders. Democracy should consequently be constituted without borders but with cemented roots of 'intimacy, proximity and locality', universally underpinned by international class solidarity as suggested in early socialism (Appadurai 2013:176). To provide some sort of relevant collectivity, deep democracy thereby revises deliberative democracy to be shaped by horizontality as a fundamental quality of 'depth' to be accomplished via community partnerships (Appadurai 2013:176), leading to thoughts about a fruitful coupling between activism and community building with the aim to foster transparency and international outreach. In effect, from Andy Stirling to Arjun Appadurai, a boundaryless attribute of activism is endorsed, even though activism and its collective expression in terms of community is often still attributed to civil society, albeit extended to include some sort of ecological representation, biospheric affinities and green imaginary projected on to the citizen–turning–activist.

2.2 Deliberative Democracy, Renewable Energy Communities and Climate Activism in the UK

Interestingly, criticism of deliberative democracy seems to have hit home in some countries and international governmental bodies. It has, for example, been taken up by the UK government to complement climate adaptation with an emphasis on climate action. Over time, a shift has occurred in approaches taken by successive UK governments to get closer to the individual citizen's personal politics. The citizen is not only a potential sceptical adversary, but foremost an energetic resource and key for the utilisation of renewable energy sources (Walker et al. 2007). Policy espousal of 'the citizen' are getting closer to conceptualisations of 'the activist'. In the case of the energy transition, this is someone with environmental and/or technological passions, targeted as a person with the need to feel a sense of belonging, assumed to have a desire for social and political power through the capacity to possess material means, individually or collectively. This shift in policy engagement and rhetorical focus have thus had an impact on the way renewable energy technologies are experienced, adopted, diffused and implemented, as we will show in the four empirical chapters, with a main focus on the UK.

The environmental benefits of renewable energy were an important element of the civil society activism that emerged in the UK in the 1950s and 1960s, linked to broader civil rights movements and grassroots quests for increased democratic participation. Yet, for government, the opportunity for energy self-sufficiency offered by renewables would be the initial driver for action. The oil crises of the 1970s saw a quadrupling of crude oil prices, crippling economies around the world, including that of the UK, which was increasingly dependent on imported oil (although domestic coal remained important). The turbulence of this period prompted the Department of Energy (created in 1974) to explore alternative energy sources, including renewables such as geothermal and hydropower, as well as supporting a further expansion of nuclear power (Énergies 2015). Throughout this period, interest in community-based renewable energy began to grow at the grassroots level, linked to 'interest in self-sufficiency, local decision making and collective small-scale action; alongside a wider desire for more community engagement and empowerment' (Hoggett 2010:17). Yet it would take another thirty years before central government would explore the potential benefits of more distributed energy generation.

Although the UK, from the end of the 1970s onwards, enjoyed energy self-sufficiency thanks to North Sea oil and gas, UK governments were now eager to avoid the short-sightedness of the past. Renewables were therefore firmly on the agenda as a means of securing long-term energy supplies. In January 1981, the government made a modest £4.6m investment in the construction of a 60-metre wind turbine at Burgar Hill in Orkney (Wilson 2012). In the event, the Orkney turbine suffered commercialisation problems and turned out to be the last wind turbine of its era to be funded directly by the government (Wilson 2012). Having privatised large parts of the UK energy market for generation and distribution in the 1980s, the Department of Energy published *Renewable Energy in the UK: The Way Forward*, which called for a new, incentive-based scheme to promote the commercial development of renewable energy (Department of Energy 1988) – a methodology that would shape the policy of successive UK governments up to the present day (Wilson 2012).

With the Brundtland Report published in 1988 and the Rio Earth Summit of 1992, the environmental benefits of renewable energy, specifically in mitigating and adapting to climate change, were fast emerging as a driver for political change; energy self-sufficiency was no longer the only or even prime consideration. The summit specifically promoted increased inclusion of stakeholder groups and laypeople, with the wish to create win-win situations via the implementation of deliberative democracy and market-oriented incentives (Bäckstrand et al. 2010). The 1990 White Paper, *This Common Inheritance*, published in the final months of Margaret Thatcher's prime ministership, acknowledged climate change as a major global challenge (Department of the Environment 1990), and the 1997 Kyoto protocol gave the UK a new target for reducing greenhouse gas emissions, adding to the momentum of renewables.

For decades, the role of local communities in helping the UK develop its renewable capability was ignored in central government communication, but from the late 1990s, the benefits of more distributed energy generation involving local people and communities gathered momentum and support (Hoggett 2010). At the turn of the millennium, strategies to decarbonise UK national life took more diverse forms (see further Muinzer 2018), and bottom-up approaches began to be supported by government funding and awareness-raising initiatives, with key national policy documents, notably the 2003 Energy White Paper, which highlighted the benefits of community renewables for the first time. In March 2006, following the Energy Act 2004, the government launched a Microgeneration Strategy aimed at identifying obstacles to the creation of a sustainable microgeneration market and recommending ways to tackle these.

With ambitious new decarbonisation and renewables targets to meet – and despite the lip service paid to local-scale renewables and microgeneration in the earlier half of the decade – the Labour government chose to throw much of its weight behind large-scale offshore wind projects in which citizen groups had little stake. Later on, however, the 2009 Low Carbon Transition Plan released by the newly created Department of Energy and Climate Change (DECC) stated that community action was 'an integral part of the Government's Strategy'

(DECC 2009:92). DECC backed this up with the Low Carbon Communities Challenge (LCCC), offering local sustainable energy projects the chance to become test beds aided by seed funding. The 2000s also saw initiatives such as NESTA's 'Big Green Challenge' (2007–2010), which further boosted the development of community ownership within renewable energy, and 'Green Communities' (2002–2011), an Energy Saving Trust programme to help citizen groups deliver carbon savings and sustainable energy projects, which attracted over 4,000 members (CSE 2010). The investments involved were relatively modest: NEST, for instance, offered £1m to encourage community-led responses to climate change (Purewal 2013).

FiT (Feed-in-Tariff) was the first significant government measure to promote smaller scale domestic and business renewable electricity generation (Grover 2013).[1] This had an effect on how people could come together more easily via renewables, with a 2015 review (Nolden 2015:6) of the FiT scheme showing

that people have been directly empowered through the number of domestic installations. … Many more people have a direct stake in the transition to a low-carbon economy through participation in, and shared ownership of, school and community energy projects. (Nolden 2015:6)

The call for citizen climate action, rather than mere adaptation, has since then accelerated, particularly at local government level. By late 2018, 67 percent of UK local government councils had declared a Climate Emergency (Climate Emergency UK 2020), many of which took more seriously 'the need for urgent action to address the climate crisis' (Carbon Neutral Cornwall 2020). Up and down the country so-called

---

[1] In April 2010, the Labour government introduced the FiT scheme to support investment in small-scale renewable and low carbon electricity generation projects up to 5MW capacity. Householders and smaller businesses would now be paid per kWh for any renewable electricity (solar PV, onshore wind power, hydropower, anaerobic digestion and micro (<2 kW) combined heat and power) fed into the National Grid. The scheme was an immediate success with 71 MW of renewable capacity installed during the first nine months, and at its peak, in 2015, 1,738 MW was installed with 83 percent of this new capacity coming from solar photovoltaics. Uptake slowed markedly following the subsequent cut in subsidies, but by the end of May 2017, 902,560 installations had been supported, generating a total of 6,091 MW in renewable energy (BEIS 2018).

citizen assemblies took place to discuss concrete actions to achieve the planned 'net-zero' target 2050 (Parliament UK 2019). In a revival of deliberation, these assemblies brought together 'residents, community groups, businesses' and councils to materially realise actions on climate change, as exemplified in a policy report under the slogan 'involve – people at the heart of decision-making' (Camden Council 2019). Hence, the UK government increasingly recognises the power of citizens and consumers to actively contribute to climate action, although only some of the UK energy policy is banking on the hope that citizens will become more proactive 'smart' consumers and invest in the energy transition even as prosumers (Department for Business 2018).

2.2.1 Prosumer Activism

With the popularity of renewable energy, the concept of consumer activism has been easily extended to prosumer activism via the 'professional consumer', that is, lay persons who 'require close to professional grade products and services' (Kotilainen 2020: n.p.). Prosumer activism is an extra sibling in the commercial activism family that has matured into a richer and more knowledgeable character by combining traits of activist entrepreneurship, investor activism, employee activism, brand activism and consumer activism – all in one. The boundaryless attribute of activism is thereby enriched, and particularly so by assumptions about prosumers as an untapped resource for speeding up action in the energy transition. Already envisaged by Toffler in the 1980s, prosumerism builds on the spread of expertise through a decentralist philosophy and higher education, extended to the exploration of 'new technologies for environmental control, solar heating, or urban agriculture with the aim of making communities partially self-sufficient' (Toffler 1980:258). Prosumers do not vote with their money only in the final step of the value chain, in the consumption of a product, but in the very first steps of the value chain, with the production of electricity and heat, based on individual or collective ownership of the means of production. The ideal of self-sufficiency is thus merged with an ideal of ownership, with prosumerism endorsed via the capacity to possess renewable technologies.

Due to their early adoption of, and personal investments in, potentially disruptive, innovative, small-scale renewable energy solutions (Baker and Phillips 2019), active and knowledgeable prosumers have also been recognised by policymakers as the vanguard of the much needed, but heavily contested, restructuring of the energy system (Burke and Stephens 2017). Burke and Stephens contend that prosuming, as a grassroots movement driven by the human capacity to possess, follows an alternative path to the energy transition, one that goes against many established energy regimes due to the attempted decentralisation of both technical solutions and management structures. In their view (Burke and Stephens 2017), prosumer activism may be more effective in reaching an actual transition than centralised systemic changes, since decentralisation allows citizens to broadly experiment at the same time as social aspects are merged with technical change. Prosuming has thereby grown into a social movement that facilitates the transition to a sustainable energy system by realising a political change through the materialisation of a technological change.

Grassroots activists who oppose the dominance of fossil-fuel generation of electricity and heat, may, however, prefer to speak about prosuming as a form of energy democracy (Burke and Stephens 2017). They mix their call for social justice and economic equality in the energy transition with attempts to destabilise existing power relations and amend previous acts of dispossession and marginalisation. Prosumer activists are not only attempting to take total control of their own production and consumption in their practice of self-mastery. They also decide how to organise themselves, produce renewable power, distribute it and share the profits, as we will illustrate in Chapter 8 (Climate Activism via Citizen Groups).

However, a problem within prosumer activism is the reliance on 'buying power' to be able to be in charge of the revenue streams (Roberts 2016). It is also unclear how the 'selling power' will be channelled in the future, with a fully decentralised, two-way grid system (so far most grids are only one-way, i.e. people get their electricity and heat from centrally located power stations). Furthermore, there are no common rights established for energy prosumers within the EU, as Greenpeace and ClientEarth, a non-profit environmental law organisation with the Earth claimed as its main client, state in a report (Roberts 2016). Citizens can in addition only take climate action as prosumers in some EU member states. The discussion about prosumerism as a form of activism thus touches on unfair conditions in relation to established businesses. There are differences within the EU regarding how prosumers are supposed to tackle competitive disadvantages, given that they often need to follow the same rules, regulations and market circumstances as established energy companies. Hence, it has been argued that investment risks, technical incompetence and the threat of losing certain consumer rights on becoming a prosumer could thwart the movement (Roberts 2016).

Another problem that faces prosumers is the growing surveillance of their investment and consumption behaviour. Trans- and intergovernmental networks, such as the EU, have been quick to recognise prosumers as potential 'energy citizens' who are more active in the overall energy system and who can be monitored en masse by new technical possibilities of real-time data collection and analysis, via the so-called Internet of Energy and Smart Grid (Citizenergy 2018). According to InnoEnergy, the Institute of Sustainable Energy, this calls for technical innovations based on Artificial Intelligence (AI), implemented to make the huge datasets manageable for modelling and steering how we are to optimise the two-way production and consumption of electricity. Prosumerism is thus to be embedded in centralised digital solutions for decentralisation, whereby the former ideals of self-sufficiency and ownership quickly mutate into less activist circumstances.

This mutation is driven by novel political ideas behind the call for 'smart' solutions, which are supposed to empower citizens through education (Kandpal and Broman 2014), and thereby unlock the untapped potential of 'community energy' beyond the ways in which communities have emerged previously. That is, the so-called smart solutions are meant to stimulate a 'major energy democracy' that could 'boost renewables' as well as 'pave the way for alternative finance such as crowdfunding' (European Commission 2018a). According to the project description of Citizenergy (2018), not only are EU citizens to be enrolled in the investments, they will actively participate 'in the future of Europe's energy mix', and 'build the energy infrastructure [they] want', all by individually choosing which energy resource and solution to fund (European Commission 2018b). Common ownership is not only to be accomplished by sharing stocks in a jointly owned renewable energy company – such as Greenpeace Energy in Germany (2020)[2] – but the EU citizenry is also invited to

---

[2] Greenpeace Germany has run an energy cooperative since 1999, aiming to transform the energy system through prosumer activism. Radically promoting renewable energy solutions, Greenpeace Energy is mobilising the informed and

invest directly in shared machinery or more individual solutions for electricity generation.

The rhetoric used to speak about this as a green opportunity replicates civic activism with calls for 'Your power – take part in the green energy revolution' (Citizenergy 2018). At least 40 million euros have been invested in thirty-two platforms, fifty-seven projects and seventeen countries (Citizenergy 2018). Looking further into these platforms, they act as crowdfunding facilitators branded in different European countries as: WeDoGood (FR), GreenChannel (FR), Ecco Nova (BE), OnePlanetCrowd International (NL), Green Energy Cooperative (HR), Green Crowding (DE), BetterWest (DE), Energia Positiva (IT) and Abundance Investment (UK). This exemplifies how a new image of finance taps into voluntary labour in prosumerism, assumed to be pursued by citizens–becoming–activists in the energy revolution, and not just transition. Substituted by a more activist vocabulary, an 'energy transition' is thus no longer enough; a revolution legitimised by the EU is required. Consequently, with an affective activist dimension, there is an attempt to align the means of production with an expanded financialisation of the infinite renewable resources: sun, wind and waves (Citizenergy 2018).

2.2.2 *Investor Activism*

The conflation of power over one's actions and the power of money is perhaps best exemplified by what is called investor activism or shareholder activism. The organisation Activist Insight (2018), for example, sell 'shareholder activism intelligence' to clients such as lawyers, investment banks, proxy solicitors and hedge funds. These services are necessary, they argue in their 2018 review of activism trends, since there is an increasing amount of assets flowing to activist funds due to successful activist strategies (Activist Insight 2018). Other business consultants have cropped up to echo this trend, proposing that investor activism should be taken seriously, as a way to create more sound business operations and unleash opportunities of value creation. The Scandinavian investment company Skagen is at

concerned citizen to use their power to possess new renewable capacity as well as support the activist stance of Greenpeace.

the forefront, promoting their stimulation of investor activism and constructive investment engagement with the slogan 'activism is coming of age' (Skagen 2017).

Previously understood to be a minimal subversive phenomenon and a managerially neglected disturbance to corporate strategies, shareholder activism is increasingly recognised to be a 'social movement that has changed the balance of power in modern corporations' (Goranova and Verstegen 2014:1231). Investor activism is thus commonly described as a type of activism located on the outside of business organisations, enacted by commercially minded activists who target businesses by investing in them to then demand organisational changes (Rehbein, Waddock and Graves 2004b). Yet, in a thorough review of the development of investor activism, Goranova and Verstegen (2014) show the diverse forms and aims of this type of activism, including the enforcement of specific environmental or social causes. Investor activism can have a significant impact on getting businesses to change their environmental behaviour and performance. Perrault and Clark (2016), for example, show how firms respond differently to investors' environmental activism depending on the status of an activist group, in addition to the threat that the activism incurs. Activists prefer to hunt down specific industries and companies, commonly those that have a huge impact and can lead to irreparable effects, since these are the most visible and thereby questionable (Rehbein, Waddock and Graves 2004a).

An example of how money can be used to buy you power to take climate action was played out in 2021, when the activist hedge fund Engine No. 1 gathered their forces with others, such as Vanguard Group Inc., and made it possible for Kaisa Hietela, a Finnish renewable energy strategist, to enter the board of ExxonMobile (Pohjanpalo 2021). With a Master's degree in Geophysics as well as Environmental philosophy, Hietela mobilises different disciplines to accomplish change, known for her abilities to generate a smooth alliance between business logics and green logics (Belfiore 2021).

Another example is the UK bank Barclays, which has been targeted by climate activists, forcing it to 'beef up' its climate actions by investing less in carbon-intensive industries and 'publish "transparent targets"' (ClientEarth 2020). Some investors, worth about $200 billion in assets, have similarly supported a shareholder motion to urge Japan's Mizuho Financial Group to cut its lending for coal and other fossil fuels. According to Reuters in Tokyo, it 'marks the first time a Japanese publicly traded company has faced a shareholder climate change resolution' (Sheldrick 2020). Investor activism has also been pursued by Norway's largest pension fund and life insurance company, Kommunal Landspensjonskasse (KLP) and Storebrand ASA (STB.OL), as well as Denmark's MP Pension. These have connected increasingly with traditional activist organisations such as Greenpeace. To collaborate 'with shareholder activists all over the world to turn their voices into megaphones' is even part of Greenpeace's (2018a) outspoken strategy, a strategy supported by a wider fossil-fuel divestment campaign, as we will empirically touch on in Chapter 5 (Climate Activism at Vattenfall). The divestment campaign has used activist methods to put a direct stop to polluting activities, but also to bring about radical shifts in financial convictions and investor behaviour.

The fossil-fuel divestment campaign, which does not have a unified organisation but exists in many guises and organisational forms around the world, exemplifies how investor activism strengthens affinities between individual investors, NGOs, state agencies and climate activists within businesses. The idea and hope is that joint action across organisational boundaries will, given the financialised nature of today's economy and the power of money (or in this case divestment), create significant ripple effects to change business behaviours (see Gillan and Starks 2000, Proffitt and Spicer 2006, Kurtz 2008). The logic is here that, while in the past social change was brought about by action on the streets, social and environmental problems can now be addressed by infiltrating business (Guay, Doh and Sinclair 2004, Grewal, Serafeim and Yoon 2016, Perrault and Clark 2016, Sullivan and Mackenzie 2017, Cundill, Smart and Wilson 2018).

Clearly, investor activism is not only used to further climate or other environmental goals. Before the explosion of activist rhetoric, similar processes were used to bring about wider social changes. An early example was Margaret Thatcher's privatisation waves of the 1980s, which saw large parts of the UK's hitherto public services being turned into private companies (Dobek 1993). One logic was that this would turn citizens into shareholding investors, making companies more agile and entrepreneurial (Musacchio, Farias and Lazzarini 2014).

This logic has developed at different speeds around the world, one example being the growing phenomenon of shareholder activism in Japan. Prime Minister Shinzo Abe was himself labelled a 'shareholder activist' by *The Economist* in 2015, as he came around to the idea of using investors and their influence for significant corporate governance reform in Japan (The Economist 2015). Activist investment has since then increased, with reports of how pro-activist shareholders seek to influence Japanese managers (Uetake 2018). Exported to Japan from the US, mainly by Daniel Seth Loeb, investor activism is here concerned with freeing unnecessarily large sums of cash hoarded in corporate treasures, improving margins, cutting costs and making the economy more agile (Rice 2014, Silver Greenberg 2018). The idea is that money should circulate between actors more swiftly to infuse the stalling Japanese economy, and thereby serve the social welfare of the citizens. Since it is the dividends that should increase to reduce the corporate treasure and throw money back into the market to speed up transactions, turnovers and a fast-consuming lifestyle in general, shareholders and governments have happily joined forces.

The main point of interest is that investor activism is used for transformational action, in this case, to release monetary resources for shareholders and by extension, society at large. As illustrated earlier, the same logic can be applied to gear action towards environmental activism. From a conventional view on activism as enacted in civil society, often against capitalist forces, investor activism may however look like a bastard sibling who suddenly pops up, claiming rights to be related to civil society activism, purportedly in support of public benefit. Looking at investor activism differently, however, namely as a sign of how activism is becoming boundaryless, may help us to accept the bastard sibling into the by now quite diversified family of activism. So, everybody who is engaged in this type of activism supports the emerging activist-business-state conglomeration.

2.2.3 Insider Activism

Activism, in its diverse forms, seems to know no boundaries, even taking root at the heart of the state. The term 'insider activism' has been developed for understanding activism pursued at work within state authorities. Olsson and Hysing (2012, Hysing and Olsson 2018) open up the black box of the state, arguing that government employees have increasingly deployed a personal political position, which, however, is not necessarily seen as legitimate, given the ethos of political neutrality that the state bureaucracy deployed by the civil servant is supposed to maintain.

Olsson and Hysing observe four trends that characterise the emergence of the 'insider activism' phenomenon: first, more ideational flexibility has been given to individuals both within and outside the public sphere; second, increased engagement with civil society and citizens as participants has facilitated the mobilisation of key individual actors within the public sector; third, the dissemination of knowledge and fostering of 'expertise' in policymaking has mobilised more than 'technical experts' – it has demanded 'problem solvers'; and fourth, with weaker democratic party politics but stronger bureaucracy there follows a deepened political position of public officials. Even though the roles of 'deliberative practitioners' (Forester 1999), 'street level bureaucrats' (Fineman 1998), institutional activists (Abers and Keck 2009) and 'policy entrepreneurs' (Kern and Bulkeley 2009) have been known for some time, Hysing and Olsson (2018) have clarified and reappraised their activist position, of importance to our understanding of how environmental policymaking and implementation can be influenced in surprising ways.

Hysing and Olsson (2018) emphasise 'an everyday perspective' among public officials who act openly or subversively to explain policy-driven climate actions 'on the ground'. An insider activist is thereby identified as a public official who is connected to civil society organisations, and who acts intentionally and strategically to enact change in policymaking in line with personal politics (Olsson and Hysing 2012). Consequently, insider activism is a testament to how personal preferences, shaped by normative formations of knowledge, for example about sustainability and climate change, come into play through everyday actions and self-regulation across organisational settings. We can thus expect that environmentalism not only exists in public institutions but within a whole range of organisations, whether they are pursuing public or private values.

An accentuation of how formal political bodies call for 'action' may in addition have affected insider activism in still unknown ways. Starting in early 2019, many councils from around the UK declared a so-called climate emergency (Climate Emergency UK 2019) to support a planet-wide campaign for local governmental bodies to become a 'powerful catalyst for community-wide action if paired with a clear action plan' (Cedamia 2019). These 'climate emergencies' are no small thing: majorities of actual councillors had to vote for quite a radical motion. Some of the votes were close; some were lost. Thus, formal political struggles are taking place inside these councils, and this is, of course, part of the point: to encourage this agonism to come out into the open; to get politicians and council workers to argue with each other about important environmental issues. It is nevertheless unclear how this affects insider activism, as we shall empirically investigate further in Chapter 7 (Climate Activism in Governmental Authorities).

2.3 Conclusion

Tellingly, in processes of deliberative democracy, the citizen has been easier to mobilise than the activist. The reason for this is that, historically, activists were not considered to be representative of the citizenry in general, but were conceived to be a problematic and unruly minority – a minority unfit for self-regulation via soft empowering and in need of more aggressive measures by states. This conventional separation between citizen and activist, and the ways of deliberating citizens when it comes to their environmental concerns does, however, differ in the case of climate activism. In comparison to the French 'yellow vest' movement in 2019, the worldwide Occupy movement sparked in 2011 (Jaffe 2016), or in the 2013 immense street demonstrations infused by *O Movimento Passe Livre* (The Free Fare Movement) in Brazil (Holston 2014), climate activism inevitably provides deliberative democratic proponents with challenges. These three cases all share the attribute that they are easy to spot. They also share the conviction that they speak for and represent a broader mass of people than just those that make themselves into visible targets out on the streets. In contrast, boundaryless climate activism is less easy to spot, although it also seeks to speak for, or perhaps rather to, a broader mass that has not yet understood the importance of climate action. Consequently, due to the less aggressive and more embedded everyday and dispersed outlook of climate activism, it could be governed very well in less counter-aggressive ways, with soft empowering approaches that seek consensus, change of behaviours, and climate actions taken in good faith, especially via hopeful renewable energy community building. However, we can also assume that climate activism – because of its characteristics of being less obvious and less aggressive, more about community relations than demonstrations in the street – can find alternative ways to reproduce and prosper, before becoming governable anew.

The policy shift from climate adaptation to climate action, and from deliberative democratic consensus processes to the empowerment of passions and desires to go green via capitalism, shows that states are not only becoming more entrepreneurial (Mazzucato 2015a, 2015b), but they are also becoming more favourable to activism. That is, instead of only accomplishing the energy transition indirectly via deliberation, enabling states are now governing the population through activism, to encompass both potentially unruly citizens and to bring about citizen–activists. This intensification of citizen inclusion, and a formal political turn to 'the activist', differs greatly depending on region and cultural context, economic means and social ends, as we discussed in relation to the EU. By extension, social and environmental transformation have been differently speeded up by the emerging activist-business-state conglomeration

Green investor activism is, for example, growing strong in the Nordic countries and in Germany, where Greenpeace uses the power of monetary investment to bring about radical actions to stop commercially polluting activities. It is testament to how climate activism and its correlating collective action is animated by the power of money. Money is no longer just an end but has become a means to achieve wider social and environmental goals, pursued via citizens' rights to possess property as climate investor activists or prosumers. Hence, the activist–business–state conglomeration is speeding up energy transitions in a turn to affluent transformations by the EU, even sanctioned as a financialised 'revolution', in mutual efforts to turn climate adaptation into climate action.

Tensions between deliberative democratic processes and what is believed to be a more personal, autonomous and authentic environmental politics are mirrored in tensions between economic and social/ environmental value creation. That is, while many large-scale renewable energy projects are dominated by considerations of economic or even corporate value, grassroots renewable energy initiatives are often portrayed as driven by social and environmental values. As we will discuss in the next chapter, the former has historically been harder to connect to the political subjectivity or identity of the activist than the latter. Activism, and its associated political subject who invests morally in the self, has therefore mainly been empirically and theoretically disassociated from capitalism and its reliance on economic subjects who invest monetarily in themselves. However, the former separations between citizen and activist, as well as between activism and business, have been destabilised in practice, and complicated by studies of prosumer activism, investor activism and insider activism.

3 | Activism and Its Collective Force

Although activism has been observed in a broad range of empirical settings, as illustrated in Chapters 1 and 2, theories of activism are commonly based on empirical studies of contentious struggles and actions that are located in, and taken by, civil society. Scholars with a focus on social and environmental movements have nevertheless started to slowly problematise the empirical, and consequently theoretical, confinement of activism (Soule 2012, de Bakker et al. 2013, Weber and King 2014). Activism has been rethought with a trans-valuation of politics. Studies of activism, formerly framed with keywords such as struggles, challenges and conflicts – with their rise explained by competing or contrasting views, ideas and visions – have started to expand and nuance the conventional framing of dissent and defiance. Politics has been explained in multifaceted ways by shifting attention away from abstract theory to empirics, particularly in studies of resistance or emancipation in digital activism and prefigurative social movements (e.g. see MacGregor 2019). This chapter continues to explore this intellectual release of activism, as well as the limits of its theoretical reach.

After a brief discussion of how the basic assumptions in studies of activism have undergone alterations, the chapter investigates old and new links between activism and community, as well as between community and business. Community is often invoked in the sustainability transition literature to infuse localised ties and thereby counter modern forms of state rule, individualisation and capitalism (Van Der Schoor and Scholtens 2015). Situated within an ethics of care, Curtin (1999) discusses 'ecological communities' in the context of clashes between Western forms of knowledge and local knowledge cultures. Within an ecological community, citizenship becomes distanced from the nation state and liberal property rights, as horizontal and bottom-up relations between people are emphasised and nurtured (Crane, Matten and Moon 2008a:152–162). Community is thus a political imaginary that has been widely seen as a normative force to accomplish sustainability transitions through intimately connected people, embracing a biospheric vitality and deeper relation to the Earth. Ecological communities, sometimes called 'ecocultures' (Böhm, Bharucha and Pretty 2015), bring the interconnectedness of life to the fore, configuring environmental politics as spanning across business and society.

One way in which activism has become increasingly boundaryless, mobilised by the activist–business–state conglomeration, is via calls for action and a rejuvenated affirmation of solidarity, loyalty and community relations, often by various sorts of business activities. However, the question remains open as to how boundaryless activism can be thought of in relation to community formation, when the notion of civil society is slowly becoming redundant and affinities with nature are emphasised. If community formation was previously used to distinguish and identify activist movements (Christensen and Levinson 2020), this may be difficult in a study of climate activism, with its commercial footing and dispersed community relations. Just as the figure of the activist is becoming indistinct, so may the collective form and force of activism. Hence, the already existing empirical scope as well as theoretical reach of activism will have reconfigured the link between activism and its collective movement – but how?

3.1 Activism in Transition

There are at least three basic assumptions in theories about activism that have played a vital role in the way activism is thought of, both in academia and among political practitioners. First, a specific conception of political subjectivity, or activist identity, underpins most understandings of activism. Second, activism is mainly thought of as driven by political agency and resistance, proven by contentious counteractions with *in situ* notable or long-lasting implications that lead to material transformations. Third, activist identity and actions have been coupled to a particular understanding of collectivity, coming together and community experience (Christensen and Levinson 2020:xxxi–xiii). The activists and their actions are consequently configured as gathered in 'activist communities' or 'intentional communities' (Simon and Herring 2020). How the basic assumptions behind activism intermingle has nevertheless shifted over time, much depending on novel enactments of activism and conceptualisations thereof.

3.1.1 Activism as Identity Work

It has been uncontroversial to explain activism by tracing and identifying its source or origin in an intentional individual activist or collective of activists, with the assumption that the creation of a certain activist identity is crucial (Eleftheriadis 2015). Some even dare to stipulate that 'organizing *is* politics *is* identity' (Reedy, King and Coupland 2016:1553, italics in the original). From a more collectivist identity to an individualised one, an activist identity is suggested to be formed via 'associational ties' (Haug 2013:707), in attempts to accomplish 'political self-actualisation' (Yates 2015:7), or autonomous selves (Reedy, King and Coupland 2016). These are taken as proof of an activist identity and political subjectivity that serves human agency formed around 'resistance', as observed, for example, in the Occupy and environmental movements (Jaffe 2016, Daniel 2006). Social movement studies have been particularly keen to make actions in the form of resistance against a clear 'anti' their main interest (Dixon 2014:28), and, like studies of resistance to hierarchical structures within a particular organisation (Alvesson and Robertson 2015), analyses of activism in civil society have prospered hand in hand with knowledge production about identity work and its politics.

Some political resistance movements have made tentative efforts to go beyond the notion of counter-actions, which has resulted in a scholarly critique of the taken-for-granted aggrandisement of individual or collective heroic identities (Bobel 2007). This intellectual post-heroic stance repeats findings about gender in activism (Katzenstein Fainsod 1998), which in parallel have been complemented by a growing interest in how radical activists can engage in smaller acts and micro politics (Jacobsson and Sörbom 2015), suggesting that activism can be executed differently, depending on new forms of coming together (Davis and McAdam 2000), collective participation and rule-creation (Kokkinidis 2015), communal leadership (Sutherland, Land and Böhm 2014) and anarchistic forms of organising (Land and King 2014). All this is understood to be an active attempt to loosen up the strict view of what activism is, how it can be performed and by whom.

3.1.2 Activism as Action

If action was first foundational for liberal ideas of human freedom and tolerance, Karl Marx connected action to a physical concentration of people with a shared grievance (Jasper and Poulsen 1995:494). Political subjectivity and an activist identity have since been understood through action conceived as an utterly human capacity to self-master and committedly bring imaginations to fruition through the materialisation of alternatives. Studies of activism promote a realisation, often judged according to a sensed materiality – a materiality that is embraced analytically both for a better understanding of how the actions are taken and for an evaluation of their effects. That is, activist actions are recognised as 'actions' depending on their material impacts, for example a successful disruption of structures or a coup d'état. This analytical focus on the cause and effect materiality has, in the case of environmentalism, been stretched to include all sorts of bodily mobilisations, from cycling in efforts to decarbonise (Horton 2006) to ecoporn and Fuck for Forest (FFF), an environmental organisation that funds its activities through the dissemination on its website of sexually explicit photographs and videos (Măntescu 2016). These examples suggest that human imaginaries are best triggered and materialised by bodily encounters.

The priority within activism of physical–mental contact through direct material encounters is based on an assumption that re-invokes the dualism of talk/action similar to the lyrics of the song 'A Little Less Conversation', originally performed by Elvis Presley in 1968. When political changes are wished for, these are rhetorically demanded to come about with calls for less talk and more action (Mieder 2009), or, as two well-known sayings suggest, 'walk the talk' or 'actions count, not words'. Just as a separation of talk/action has dominated ideas about activism in popular culture, so studies of 'actions' often rely on an ontological position that separates talk from action (Bracken 1994). Words are required to be acted upon (with body parts other than the mouth), as exemplified in the policy report titled 'Ending Violence Against Women: From Words to Action' (United Nations 2006). Words are neither conceived nor conceptualised as good enough in themselves, and 'policy' is obviously not enough for a realisation of 'politics', as the UN makes the reader aware of in their call for resilience under the slogan 'from policy to action' (United Nations 2018). In a very normative and causal way of thinking, words must lead to later actions that are consistent with the preceding talk (Olsen 2017). It is not until that point that politics, in any form, is repeatedly judged to be authentically executed.

The way in which politics has been made dependent on actions beyond text and utterings has nevertheless been rethought with more fine-grained empirical studies of activism. The separation between talk and action has also been ontologically questioned (Billig 1995, Felman 2002), for example by Judith Butler in her early conceptualisation of 'performative speech acts [as] forms of doing' that institute reality in uncharted ways (Butler 2002:113). According to Butler, although physicality may still provide actions that are multi-sensorially judged to be more potent bodily expressions of politics, actions can be constituted by words, for example in the form of hate speech (Butler 1997). In the book *Notes toward a Performative Theory of Assembly*, the merger of linguistic and bodily performativity is further elaborated (Butler 2015), which opens a way for analyses of a broader set of actions – actions that take us beyond a narrow interpretation of the activist category. The barking in the song 'A Little Less Conversation', in the line 'a little less bark', would then, after all, be possible to conceive as an action, inspired by the Kynics or 'dogs' in Ancient Greece (Foucault 1984/2011). Or as Bruno Latour points out, 'acting *and* speaking politically is something entirely different from acting or speaking about politics' (Latour et al. 2018:7, our emphasis).

3.1.3 Activism as Prefiguration

Attempts to broaden the basic assumptions in studies of activism have turned to 'prefiguration', Do-It-Yourself approaches and an affirmation of creative, everyday and mainly non-violent actions in the here and now (Epstein 1991, Maeckelbergh 2011). According to Carl Boggs (1977), prefigurative politics developed in the nineteenth century independently of Marxism as a critique of bureaucratic domination among anarchist groups, including syndicalists, council communists and the New Left. Boggs identified these alternatives to top-down organisation and dominating hierarchies to be 'prefigurative' if they displayed a vision of revolutionary democracy by embodiment. That is, if activists succeed in exercising 'the ongoing political practice of a movement', managing to build a working model for horizontal decision-making and benefiting society at large, this activism would be considered to be prefigurative (Boggs 1977:99). Studies of prefiguration are thus mainly interested in practices that are observable, performed as everyday actions, with a strong emphasis on embodiment.

The consideration of precisely what prefiguration is has altered over time (Polletta and Hoban 2016), but it is commonly conceived to merge activism with a 'fostering [of] alternative and radically democratic practices' (Cornish et al. 2016:116). In the 1960s, prefigurative politics expanded from the concern for workers subsumed under factory production to more general political themes, such as feminism and environmentalism. This shifted the focus of the 'doing' of prefiguration to more personal, everyday lifestyle issues, which were to be collectively embodied by the movements. Instead of hardcore actions of resistance, prefigurative politics came to offer softer, non-violent actions of co-creation, or, what Judith Butler (2017) refers to in a video-recorded talk at the University of California Los Angeles (UCLA) as a way to act that does not reproduce a violent world, but instead enacts the principles that it wishes to establish. Carefully scrutinising the 'how' of how radical acts are deployed is important, she argues, since '[t]he methods we use carry the burden of prefiguring the world in which we want to live'. We should therefore not forget that the acts we use carry our 'aspirations, images and visions of the world that we seek to bring into being' (Butler 2017:0:53–0:56). At least since Carl Boggs, prefiguration is thus an attempt to reconstruct the world as it should be in the here and now, making the acts more inclusive of those who are either repelled by, or lack the physical capacity to practise, muscular violence or loudness. In effect, prefiguration opens up for a more affective and reflexive relation to the self, at the same time as it implicitly requires an unbroken connection between thought and action, or a 'realised' unity of the mind–body. That is, a seemingly rational confessional coupling that can be challenging to consistently live out and sustain in everyday actions.

Since prefiguration affirms less aggressive everyday mundane actions, and a more generative coupling of thought and action for the crafting of a politically coherent identity, some have viewed it with suspicion. Clear and visible antagonisms, and a radical activist identity or subjectivity, are still conceived to be the beating heart of an authentic, true, political activism. The political subject of prefiguration, on the contrary, has been suggested to fall into the grip of the post-political condition, with its non-radical, ostensibly rational form of movement that easily spills over into processes of depoliticisation (Smith et al. 2017). Prefiguration has consequently ended up in the same basket as deliberative democracy, critiqued for 'the increasing evacuation of the proper political dimension from the public terrain as technocratic management and consensual policy-making has sutured the spaces of democratic politics' (Swyngedouw 2010:214). Accordingly, although prefiguration is often conceptualised as a form of decentralised organising, or radical democracy, secured within social movements instead of being seen as something that could happen anywhere, this does not protect it from processes of depoliticisation. From a critical perspective, it has even been argued that it is the generous production of a less aggressive political subjectivity that has come to constitute a new threat to 'politics' (cf. Smith et al. 2017). Prefiguration is held responsible for producing a subjectivity easily co-opted by expertise and governing through behavioural nudges, which have made human psychological complexity their target in efforts to grapple with the last remnants of irrationality (cf. Leggett 2014). Nonetheless, such irrationality is in other theory on activism talked about in terms of affect and emotions (Gould 2010, Jasper 2011).

3.1.4 Activism as Emotional Work

It is not surprising that emotions have been an area of interest in analyses of activism, considering the very strong imagery that exists around conventional depictions of activism as protest (Gould 2010): clenched fists, demonstrative bodies, hopeful messages, stern faces and tears; and the conventional interpretations delivered on top of these depictions about the existing anger, despair, dissent, hope, passion, desire and strength gained from togetherness. This mix of positive and negative emotions has been used to explain how action is energised (cf. Jasper 2011:291) and partly explains why struggle is assumed to be better than smooth encounters. Struggle is conceived to induce excitement that opens a way for new states of mind, spurs affects, teases out capacities to imagine things differently and spawns new worlds. There is thus an important chain, it seems, from action *against* something, which is experienced as a more or less thrilling struggle, yet to be enjoyed in togetherness. Descriptions of activism have thus emphasised an emotionally driven autonomous individual, mixed with an assumed human craving for collective emotional experiences (Jasper 2011). The individuality created by notions of an intentional activist is thus conveniently balanced by highlighting desires for belonging and friendships, for example conceptualised as a social movement constituted through 'affective ties' (e.g. see Farias 2017). A 'movement' is thereby as much a moving gathering that unfolds processually as it is a gathering to be moved by (cf. Pedwell 2019), especially when fighting for one's life (Gould 2009).

The contrasts between positive and negative emotions and affects have nevertheless changed with environmentalism (Seymour 2018). People are on the one hand having negative experiences due to stressful environmental problems, and on the other hand having positive experiences due to enjoyable human–nature affinities. Environmental activists are met by hatred and cynicism (Seymour 2018), that they often have to respond to, just as they perform emotional work when they turn self-resentment into more positive self-mastery. The love of nature, biospheric care and empathy with animals, instead of anger and actions directed towards certain humans and organisations, have prospered hand in hand with a desire to turn around negative human impacts in the here and now (Roth 2010). Accomplishing a direct positive emotional effect in the present, instead of arguing about negative path dependency, is a growing characteristic of environmentalism, driven by a sense of belonging to the whole Earth. This re-wilded human who seeks togetherness with nature is equally mirrored in action-based ecological pedagogies and a theoretical refusal of disembodied knowledge production. Hence, 'gut level understanding' (Roth 2010:81), or even poetic 'yearning for interconnection' with nature serve as a 'fundamental link between emotion and environmentalism' (Ottum and Reno 2016:1–2). Consequently, with the transformation of environmentalism, action has become less 'anti' and leading to struggles, due to an increased recognition of pro-environmental thinking and activism underpinned by positive emotional affinities and excitement towards nature.

3.1.5 Activism as Community Formation

Coupled to an activist identity (political subjectivity) and actions (material realisations and embodiment) are conceptualisations of 'community', understood broadly as the coming together of a group of people, including wishes for 'a people' to come (Goh 2006). Empirical investigations of activism in social movement studies often mix and merge the rich literature on community and resistance eclectically to better understand community formation in activism. Religious communities, for example, historically founded on specific sacred languages for their coming together and sense of belonging (Anderson 2006), may become more activist through disruptive actions and 'prophetic activism' (Slessarev-Jamir 2011), including engagements with environmental and social movements (Smith 1996). A community identified as non-political, with a focus on a certain set of affinities and social interactions, may thus be transformed into an activist community, where social movement theory offers a range of political terminology with which to understand this process. It is therefore important to distinguish between community activism, mainly developed by social movement theorists, and 'community' as more generally studied with roots in anthropology (Vered 2002), sociology (Appadurai 1996), and political philosophy (Esposito 2010).

In the case of climate activism, this sort of morphing between non-political and politicised understandings of community seems to be particularly prevalent, specifically in the UK, with its Transition Towns and history of village communities and local marketplaces that have undergone considerable change in tandem with the environmental movement (Leach and Scoones 2015). The historical sense of an active village community, while still very much visible, has increasingly been affected by decentralisation efforts (Jamison 2001) as well as individualisation and heightened mobility among the population, which have all affected communities throughout the country (Morgan 2005). Over time, this loosening of community, as traditionally formed, has merged with how democratic deliberation has left its idealised and instrumental view of citizens, and tuned into the political passions and citizen–activists 'on the ground' (as discussed in Chapter 2) (cf. Walker et al. 2007). To better understand climate activism in this reformation of what 'community' has become, it is thus helpful to trace and reinvigorate the theoretical assumptions that bridge the domains of activism and community formation, after which we will investigate the increasingly prosperous surface of contact between activism and community formation within business.

3.2 Community Formation

At least since Plato's *Republic* and other writings on a just society, based on equality within hierarchy, a collective of self-renouncing equals and a harmonious whole has been ethically prioritised over individual freedoms (Rancière 1992/2007:73–75). The community has since become known as a unit that hosts some sort of commonality based on mutual agreements about what is proper and improper – an understanding of community formation that brings the inclusion of certain people at the cost of excluding others (Etzioni 2004), be it via the intentional sharing of ideas and ideals, friendships and affinities, or through habits and rituals. Explanations of community formation and the human will to come together have also, due to these basic assumptions, been richly problematised, for example by Jean-Luc Nancy, in *The Inoperative Community* (Nancy 1991) and Giorgio Agamben in *The Coming Community* (Agamben 1993). Jacques Derrida even stated in an interview that he does not 'like the word community', emphasising that he was 'not even sure if he liked the thing' since he 'always had trouble vibrating in unison' (Caputo 1996:25).

3.2.1 Community and Togetherness

Contemporary studies of communities often take the community itself for granted as a pre-existing unit that hosts very human capacities, from thoughts and visions, to relations and specific ways of living. This is perhaps inherited from Robert A. Nisbet's essay on community in his 1967 book *The Sociological Tradition* (Asplund 1991:37), where 'communal life' was defined in relation to a group of households, geographically close to each other and being functionally dependent on each other (see also Crow and Allan 2014). Community relations, in their closeness and functional dependency, thus differed from similar interdependencies that have been shown to exist in relation to other groups of individuals as well as society (Elias 1987/2001). From early sociological perspectives, functions thus defined the community and were conceived as shaping the individuals by offering them specific modes of being and relating to themselves and others.

From this perspective, a different version of tensions between the individual and the collective arose. Either, there was an emphasis on how community formation could be planned by individuals, or how it could result from a collective mind (*anima*), where the individual plays no part at all, but where a historical movement, pantheism, determines the changes that occur. The sociologist Norbert Elias (1987/2001:5) was nonetheless questioning how individual actions with goals and purposes could be explained as resulting in social formations, as they were either seen as 'anonymously mechanical or as supra-individual forces based on pantheistic models'. Community, on the other hand, could thus be theoretically advanced as a third alternative, a middle ground between the individual and the group, positioned to grapple with the unsolvable questions of individual–collective nexuses of causes and effects, and conceptualised as something that rather encompasses the individual and group in togetherness. In more practical terms, community can consequently be conceived to arise through shared beliefs or interests that drive the formation of togetherness, where the common denominator of togetherness within the group can be refined and also change over time, just as individuals do.

3.2.2 *Community and Nihilism*

To complicate this view and advance the problematisation of togetherness in the individual–collective nexus further, Roberto Esposito (2010) traces the etymology of community and philosophically interrogates basic assumptions in studies of communities. Historically, he argues, community came with an obligation, an 'office', and was thereby the opposite of being immune. That is, etymologically speaking, the *munus* (a gift given to you to be given away, which therefore requires reciprocity and mutuality) shared by the *communitas* creates a lack of mastery (Esposito 2010:5):

In the community, subjects do not find a principle of identification nor an aseptic enclosure within which they can establish transparent communication or even a content to be communicated. They don't find anything else except that void, that distance, that extraneousness that constitutes them as being missing from themselves; 'givers to' inasmuch as they are 'given by' a circuit of mutual gift giving. (Esposito 2010:7)

What is expropriated in the process of giving is the very subjectivity that constitutes the 'proper property' (Esposito 2010:7). In other terms, the proprietary subject is decentered, which results in a commonality based on what is improper, rather than proper. In this process, one is forced to remove oneself from oneself, and alter oneself, in relation to an 'outside'. In a very negative sense, Esposito (2010) concludes that the community, etymologically understood, does not nurture a collective bond, recognition and a mutual identity, but an exposure leading to spasmic dizziness and unending alterations of the self without any refuge in a fixed identity.

Following this historical perspective of how community as gift-giving affects the individual–collective nexus, Esposito (2010) continues to investigate contemporaneous claims about community as a response to nihilism: the thing versus no-thing. He unifies these previously separated notions, thing and no-thing, to enable their philosophical coupling. In opposition to other conceptualisations, he suggests that these notions come together, although they are not becoming the same, by how they thrive on a common surface and are thereby mutually constitutive of each other. Community is defined by its non-thing, a diffusion from within, where the 'inter of community cannot be joined up except through a series of "exteriors" or "moving outside", through subjects open to what is properly outside of them' in a subtraction of their own subjectivity (Esposito 2010:139). Hence, in stark contrast to anthropological, sociological and social movement studies of community formation, this particular philosophical exploration exposes a different function of community, and perhaps Esposito's exposure of how a sense of community infiltrates self-mastery explains why Derrida found it difficult to vibrate in unison (Caputo 1996).

The link between existential nihilism and community is repeated differently in other theorisations of community formation. In contrast to Esposito's conception of the constitutive relation between nihilism and community, Goh (2006) suggests that community, in the works of Deleuze and Guattari (1988), is anything but nihilistic. Even though Deleuze and Guattari omit 'community' as a concept, their image of a 'nomadology' offers 'the chance of the future event of a community-to-come [...] always open to something new, always forms itself anew, which as such guarantees its future, and even promises a radical future unrestricted to its present form' (Goh 2006:226). It is suggested that what was originally an anti-community thought in Deleuze and Guattari, one that conceived of community as a negative unity of confinement, is undone by a deterritorialisation where socio-materialities move across space (Goh 2006). Constructs that are more about movement, dispersion, disorganisation, montage and collage allow an understanding of community formation that is based on unexpected outcomes of social and material flows. With an emphasis on multiplicity, which points to the need to understand sociality and materiality together as a multiple event that cannot be compressed into preconceived signifiers, community is thus about a togetherness radically open to futures, and future selves.

In the book *Commitment and Community: Communes and Utopias in Sociological Perspective*, Rosabeth Moss Kanter (1972) traces the link between group formation and ideals of utopia. An imaginary society is from her perspective fundamental to the formation of a community. Dreams, high aspirations, spiritual forces and desires are conceived to be basic elements of human life that can coalesce harmonically, resulting in community as a response to existential nihilism – a nihilism that is furthermore assumed to be annihilated by how utopian communities seek to materialise a political ideal that is often positive or 'pro' a specific alternative that is yet to be realised. From domestic, agricultural and entrepreneurial to political and religious communities, various communities-to-be have, with varying success, replicated this – often based on the belief that it is a materialisation to be accomplished by a human who is naturally drawn to harmony and mutuality, instead of competition and exploitation. The common denominator in strategic community building across this spectrum, according to Kanter (1972), is group solidarity and self-determination of values to follow, established by the nurturing of ideas and attempts to fulfil these by specific practices and ways of living.

Hence, in the 1970s, when Kanter laid forth her sociological study of community building, it was common to point to a community as a distinctive unit, positioning it in relation to society at large, but still making it possible for individuals to conceive of themselves as 'individuals'. Business organisations, however, were typically considered non-utopian and non-communal, since membership required skill, dependency and coercion, rather than voluntary individual commitment and desire to belong to a specific group (Kanter 1972). From this perspective and at that time, the basic assumption about communal ways of living relied on the idea that humans were committed to their fellows yet also dependent on the availability of sufficient resources and security, in accordance with Hobbesian thought (Hughes 1998).

While this entails a certain sense of harmony, which many still wish to be at the heart of community formation, Alinsky (1971:120) suggested, in the 1970s, that in order for a new community to take shape, the existing society first needs to be disorganised. An element of controversy and disorganisation is depicted as fundamental for infusing people's will to take action and change the current situation by community formation. As in scholarship on activism, this reliance on struggle has nevertheless been seriously questioned by turning to other ontological assumptions about human ethical relationality, asking whether authentic human nature is not more 'pro' than 'anti' (Hughes 1998).

3.2.3 Community and Locality

Besides a preference in community studies to point out the human need for togetherness and visions of better futures, influential explanations of community formation often concentrate on the importance of locality, either by looking at the invocation of belonging or sense of closeness, or by focussing on existing social groups created by interactions and mutual aspirations (Appadurai 2013). In this strand of literature, a place is assumed to host a certain type of identity formation, where the loss of togetherness is often linked to the loss of belonging to a specific location and community as host. Togetherness is consequently made dependent on localism, and with territorial dispossession comes an assumed dispossession of a sense of belonging. This loss of possession over land in tandem with the loss of localism as togetherness, collective self as well as individual identity, has especially been pointed out in criticism of globalisation trends. With calls to rebuild lost community belonging and localism, it has nevertheless been shown that people who stress the loss of social ties, for example in areas that undergo material change, potentially start to create a mutual understanding of what is going on, which in turn regenerates social ties and community belonging (Lewis 2016). This suggests that geographical determinants, previously of relevance for contextualising community formation as localism, are less useful if a sense of belonging is to be understood, and especially so in highly mobile societies, where the notion of a 'community of interests' has become more useful (Alinsky 1971:120). As summarised in the introduction to the first ever encyclopaedia of community published in 2020:

Traditionally, human community has had a geographic base: To be a community, people have needed to be physically near one another. Today, however, many people find the strongest sense of community within groups that are not geographically based. That is possible because community is a cultural construct that can be conceived in an almost infinite variety of ways. Even hermits, we are told, like to think that they belong to the Community of Eremites. There is a dynamic relationship between the need for people to belong to community and the extraordinarily varied ways in which that need is met. (Christensen and Levinson 2020:xxxiii)

Sarah Pink empirically investigates the link between locality, community and activism further. Starting in studies that have shown that urban activism in the UK is becoming more engaged with, and entangled in, formal politics and bureaucracy, and is increasingly based in legal activities enacted by a middle class, she locates the agency of activism in local committees and projects (Pink 2008:165). Pink analyses activism in the case of the UK network of the international Cittàslow (Slow City) movement with the wish to go beyond the notion of community by turning to 'activist agency' in relation to sociality and place-making (2008:165). In contrast to seeing the community as an agent that drives change, she argues that the 'Cittàslow activism is better understood by analysing how agency is produced through actual local embodied social relationships' (Pink 2008:163). Instead of making community into an organisational unit that gives rise to resistance, she questions how both practical actions and imaginations are generated through social relationships. The origin of a specific community is thereby explained with a focus on how sociality and experiences lead to certain actions and imaginations that are connected to a more abstract conceptualisation of place-making. Of importance for conceptualising activism in place-making is the notion of 'gathering', that is, an assemblage of time, space, persons, objects, sensations and sentiments (Pink 2008:166). To gather, the basic activity of coming together, is hence the very source of agency and activism, where relations developed in Cittàslow towns lead to actions (Pink 2008). It is by doing certain activities, and experiencing them together, that people are enabled to talk about and imagine a community assigned to a specific location that hosts a designated people.

3.2.4 *Community and Capitalism*

Community, and specifically the expansion of social cooperation, has perhaps most famously been emphasised by Hardt and Negri in their conceptualisations of 'empire' (2000), 'multitude' (Hardt and Negri 2005) and 'commonwealth' (Hardt and Negri 2009). Based on the etymological and historical connections between community, commons and commune, they develop a theory of 'communism' with hopes to fit the global capitalist reality of the twenty-first century. Empire, in this *oeuvre*, continuously aims to expand its frontiers with the help of a decentred form of rule over social life, involving manifold deterritorialisations and globalisations. The 'common', on the other hand, not only encompasses the Earth's resources, but the processes and outcomes of human relations and creative engagements. In their analysis of capitalist development, new forms of labour arise with immaterial production dependent on intrinsically driven wishes for creativity in combination with a more knowledgeable citizenry. The division of work and life is thereby not as distinguishable, given that labour is carried out in a wider variety of spaces, which complement or substitute the factory or workplace, where 'capitalist work arrangements have succeeded in appropriating the discourse of communism' (Guattari and Negri 1985/2010:27).

In other words, community and its creative potential are part and parcel of the global capitalist regime that is empire. Community arises out of how people seek encounters that are joyful and meaningful, which results in an optimistic view of a multitude of productive potentials (Ruddick 2010). Yet this very creativity also keeps empire afloat. In Hardt and Negri's view, it is the historical task of the multitude to redirect this creativity to better ends; that is, a people 'capable of autonomously constructing a counter-empire, an alternative political organisation of global flows and exchanges' (Hardt and Negri 2000:xv). Pointing to the 1970s anti-nuclear and ecology movements, Guattari and Negri (1985/2010) illustrate how revolutionary processes led to an alternative programme where ecology was less about nostalgia and protest and more about new types of action and uses of science (also see Eyerman and Jamison 1991). It is here, they argue, that the communist programme develops with '[s]truggles against the labor process and its overcoding of time; struggles for alternative housing arrangements and for another way of conceptualising domestic sociality, neighborliness, and cooperation between segments of the socius' (Guattari and Negri 1985/2010:73). Being inspired by the seventeenth-century Dutch philosopher Baruch Spinoza, collaborations between humans are thus conceived as fundamental for 'potentia', the power to act, where a co-producing collectivity respects, acknowledges and co-creates the individual, or singularity, and not the other way around (Ruddick 2010:22). It is between these poles, singularity and collectivity, that the so-called communism of capital balances:

In this respect, the problem of distinguishing between the 'common', the ethico-political whole constituted by singularity and produced by the making-multitude, on the one hand, and the 'communism of capital', the form of capital accumulation and the symmetrical representation of new processes of social and cognitive production of value, on the other, no longer exists. In this context, any action aimed at securing a higher level of necessary income and any reference to financial capital have to do with exchange value and exchange value only, with commodities and commodities only. Identifying an alternative to the current character of the world of capital, the so-called communism of capital, is no longer possible at the level of wages and welfare in general. (Balibar et al. 2010:315–316)

3.2.5 Community and Business

In contrast to these politico-philosophical discussions about the relation between community and capitalism, studies of business organisations have also honed in on community, albeit under a different guise. A famous historical example of corporate community building is the inclusion of human life-optimising agendas at work in Henry Ford's creation of Fordlândia, a utopian village erected in 1928 after clearing 10,000 square metres of Amazonian rainforest around the Rio Tapajós in Brazil. According to a number of academic studies and other documentaries (of various trustworthiness and quality), the village was perhaps more of a personal, political aspiration of Henry Ford, than an economic gambit. The production of cheap rubber for car tyres was not to be secured just by an extended family, but the founder of the car company aspired to help others to manage their way of living. From the introduction of health regulations to the construction of a hospital, and from specific ideas about child education to the building of a school on the corporate premises, Henry Ford entered the 'industry of building men' to accomplish his 'work of civilisation' (CGTN America 2015). The workers later rioted against the strict rules and medical treatments that were supposedly to secure their health, but instead had made them sick. An alternative 'community' or 'gathering' unfolded, as the employees got together to enact other values and wishes about ways of living. They revolted against the corporate community building from within, and the experiment had to be dismantled.

Other examples of historical 'community firms', or *kigyo kyodotai* in Japanese, have been under scholarly attack due to their patriarchal order and psychological contract that seek to nurture loyal employees, from birth to cradle (Inagami and Whittaker 2005). A 'community of fate' is fostered in these traditional Japanese firms, in a way similar to how groupism underpinned community formations in the eighteenth-century agricultural villages (Inagami and Whittaker 2005:10). There are thus, undoubtedly, historical similarities between the Japanese and Western examples of corporate community building if we consider the extended familialism at play. The early concepts of community firms seem to have relied heavily on embodied states of dependence between a host organisation and groups of people who were fundamentally economic subjects and thus prone to be steered by values and rules to survive. Just as the Japanese community firms often build on what in Japanese is called 'ie' – that is, Confucian familialism based on parent–child power relations defined by senior authority (Inagami and Whittaker 2005) – Western community building firms also relate to employees as if they were dependent children, especially so when coinciding with colonial ambitions and the spread of educational agendas via business operations. Henry Ford has consequently been accused of megalomania and Japanese managers of paternalism.

The fostering of employee loyalty, linked to offers of safety and security via a commercial organisation and strong value-laden employer, has, with cultural and political differences, been a broader historical phenomenon richly observable in various societies. In less critical terms, it has been suggested that companies-as-communities are based on an organisational focus rather than a market focus, whereby the employees are increasingly managed as members instead of workers. This echoes Kanter's (1972:3) definition of a community: 'it operates to serve first and foremost its own members; any benefits it provides for the outside are generally secondary and based on the need to support its own' members. Ideal corporate community building, as exemplified in Japan, also attunes to commitment and harmony via an abundance of resources and security, rather than coercion and exploitation, which Kanter (1972) pointed out to be the main difference between a utopian community and a business organisation. Consequently, choosing the right cases and applying certain conceptualisations of community formation make it possible for researchers to describe some businesses as communities.

With early works on social responsibility and business ethics, such an analytical community perspective of business grew (Solomon 1993:150). Solomon suggested an analysis of the corporation, not as a legal or monolithic entity consisting of flowcharts, or an anonymous bureaucracy and statistical representation of expenses and turnovers, but as a gathering of humans. By affirming a view that a corporation is constituted by the humans it consists of, he argued that it would also be easier to understand the corporation as an organisation made up of human relations:

The concept of community also shifts our conception of what makes a corporation 'work' or not. What makes a corporation efficient or inefficient is not a series of well-oiled mechanical operations but the working inter-relationships, the coordination and rivalries, team spirit and morale of the many people who work there and are in turn shaped and defined by the corporation. So, too, what drives the corporation is not some mysterious abstraction called 'the profit motive' (which is highly implausible even as a personal motive, but utter nonsense when applied to a fictitious legal entity or a bureaucracy). It is the collective will and ambitions of the employees, few of whom (even in profit-sharing plans or in employee-owned companies) work for a profit in any obvious sense. (Solomon 1993:150)

Perhaps inspired by the history of community firms, as well as the academic analytical view of the corporation seen through the eyes of the sociology of communities, business managers have been implementing such thoughts to craft a community at work and instrumentally create an extended family, friendships and social security for their employees. As long recognised, this makes a separation of the private and professional difficult (Kanter 1977), and with time it has resulted in even more diffuse boundaries between work and leisure time with an advancement of corporate optimisations of 'life itself' (Rose 1999, Fleming 2014). This is especially visible in regions where sustainable development proponents intervene to alleviate poverty through calls for entrepreneurial self-reliance (Duffield 2010). Peredo and Chrisman (2006) further show how such calls seek to sustain communities via community-based enterprise. By utilising cultural and social capital, these communities are to act 'corporately as both entrepreneur and enterprise', 'managed and governed to pursue the economic and social goals of a community in a manner that is meant to yield sustainable individual and group benefits over the short and long term' (Peredo and Chrisman 2006:310). Hence, in addition to how business organisations have been thought of as communities, the logic of business has now also been imposed onto stakeholder communities. The authors not only marry business and community as a way for capitalism to enter and enrich a pre-existing (poor) unit located in a specific geographical spot, they also rely on an important ontological assumption about how life is to be kept meaningful, via 'community'. Community relations are thereby monetarily augmented. Instead of being polarized, money and meaningfulness are in the literature on community-based enterprise often merged into a harmonious whole, or what Kanter (1972) spoke about as a curing of nihilism and existential despair.

Key in the making of communities into businesses is the targeting of the identity work that is supposed to be the creative source of poor people's prospective process towards collective self-reliance. Contingent identities are to be formed in relations between individuals and their surroundings to enliven untapped affinities and potential friendships among people or employees who then gather and mobilise themselves in self-organised ways. Hence, alternative forms of entrepreneurship, such as ecopreneurship or sustainable entrepreneurship, repeat old school business ethics in how the 'alternative' is underpinned by revived conceptions of the community as a fecund test-bed to attach to and grow on (Shepherd and Patzelt 2010). Notably, community is, just as activism, located within civil society, treated as a unit that can infuse social transformation (Daskalaki, Hjorth and Mair 2015), but also extended to conceptualisations of 'hybrid organisations', that is, organisations whose core operation is based on a merger of economic and environmental or social value creation (Alnoor, Battilana and Mair 2014). With this hybridity, a broader variety of exchange relations and gift economies has been analytically affirmed, which also relates to our discussion about boundaryless activism in Chapter 1, and the interest among some entrepreneurship scholars to withdraw from studies of business, to rather focus on organisational disruption and collective actions.

In comparison to a growing scholarly debate that is interested in the entanglement of community groups and business organisations, these are in public discourse commonly depicted as separate, polarised entities. Community groups are a generous expression of human relationality and business organisations an expression of human utilisation and logistical command. Looking into the legal forms that exist for the coming together via business activities, a more complicated picture nonetheless arises. The most common form, an incorporated company, which perhaps has issued shares (*Aktiengesellschaft*), is clearly profit-driven and bridges between business and society. Public-benefit corporations have been around for a long time, mostly set up by governments to run specific services for the benefit of the wider public. Here, the main bridging is made between the state and society. The specific entity 'community', has furthermore been bridged to business with other juridical forms, ranging from non-profit enterprises to charities and community-interest companies. These are often very clearly commercially run, but with operational profits that are reinvested into the organisation and the purposes the organisation serves. There has also been the rise of so-called B Corporations, which is a private certification scheme for for-profit companies, assessing their social and environmental performance. In fact, B Corporations are said to 'form a community of leaders and drive a global movement of people using business as a force for good' (Certified B Corporations 2020). All these juridical organisational forms suggest an increased blurring of community and business, which also has grown with organisations that engage in 'grand challenges' (George et al. 2016).

3.2.6 *Community and Neoliberalism*

Late modernity has repeatedly been suggested to bring about an increased individualisation, that is, a separation and distancing between people. This is due to a waning influence of institutions that are based on social solidarity, such as churches, unions and political parties (Bennett and Segerberg 2011). As briefly mentioned earlier, it has been popular to consider community formation as a response to this individualisation trend. As Rose (1996) argued already in the 1990s, however, we need to take a historical perspective of the discourse on community into consideration. 'The community', he suggests, cannot be disconnected from the rise of neoliberal governance. Hence, if social statistics and the social sciences in general have established 'the social' as a reality, then community has complemented that reality, becoming 'a new spatialization of government: heterogeneous, plural, linking individuals, families and others into contesting cultural assemblies of identities and allegiances' (Rose 1996:327). Rather than governing people directly through public institutions, underwritten by notions of society, 'the community' has emerged as a complementary vehicle of indirect governance and the stimulation of self-regulation.

Regardless of problems with governing at a distance through the allure of togetherness in community, it is necessary to somehow acknowledge that many people living in 'actually existing neoliberalism' (Peck, Brenner and Theodore 2018) have found comfort in the everyday experiences of togetherness, spoken of as formative of a community, or various communities, be it at work, home, online or in the neighbourhood. As globalisation and mass-society have been shown to result in an ever increasing individualisation of society, creating a range of negative social effects, such as mental health and well-being problems (Veenhoven 1999), talk about the importance of community relations has provided a useful patch for an open wound. If not a promise of care, community building has created a sense of safety and security for people, similar to the function of enclosed suburban neighbourhoods or even gated communities (Sakip, Johari and Salleh 2012). The call for people to engage in communities has thereby agreed with the will of the state to make people more responsible for their own lives, without overt, visible oppressive measures.

Communities are not only conceived as malleable units, a piece of clay to form and govern, but are 'a means of government: its ties, bonds, forces and affiliations are to be celebrated, encouraged, nurtured, shaped and instrumentalised in the hope of producing consequences that are desirable for all and for each' (Rose 1996:334). Especially in the UK, the mother country of neoliberalism (Harvey 2007), there is thus a proliferation of community rhetoric: there are community homes, community care, community hospitals, community schools, community interest companies, police community support officers, community farms, community supported agriculture schemes and so on. There is no shortage of community organisations in the UK, some of which have developed from the 1970s onwards in top-down manners (e.g. see Willmott 1989), to replace receding social welfare systems whose state institutions were originally created for mass population management. Aiming to address the shortcomings of large-scale, bureaucratic social welfare systems, which often created inhumane and regimented approaches, the idea of community has promised to cultivate smaller-scale solutions, nurturing personal interactions between people and putting humanity at centre stage. Through community, 'power to the people' has thus seamlessly been merged with 'individual responsibility'.

It is important to acknowledge this historical context of neoliberal governance through community, which has been accompanied by the dissemination of knowledge about climate change and its solutions. In some ways, one can argue that the environmental crises have led to even more inventive governance and self-management techniques (Darier 1999, Dowling 2010, Lövbrand

and Stripple 2013), which have recognised the need for community building. Before, various decarbonisation diets called for people to 'do their bit', as illustrated in detail by Paterson and Stripple (2010:341). They argued that climate change had been appropriated 'for an individual, almost narcissistic subject, who thinks of "his or her emissions" and his or her responsibilities regarding them' (Paterson and Stripple 2010:341). Nevertheless, although this subject was inevitably nurtured as narcissistic, it was also 'forced to problematise his or her practices through peer pressure, comparison, and communication' (Paterson and Stripple 2010:341), but not necessarily in close relationships of community type. Around this time in the knowledge production about environmental problems, individual actions were increasingly connected to lifestyle choices and a personalisation of quite political topics, such as climate change and labour standards (Bennett and Segerberg 2011). Over time, new types of interaction between personally concerned individuals nonetheless mobilised a personalisation that differs from the activist saying 'the personal is political'. The personal was rather seen as enmeshed in specific forms of knowledge and expertise produced externally from the 'personal' (Bennett and Segerberg 2011). In other words, in contrast to the narcissistic subject of carbon diets, emerges a more knowledgeable and productive subject. One that is open for a coming together based on new ways of knowing – an epistemic community.

3.3 Conclusion

To be able to understand what constitutes climate activism, and how people come together under the new circumstances presented in Chapters 1 and 2, we have in this theory chapter discussed the basic assumptions attached to activism as well as community, with a focus on how these are related to politics conceived as individual action taken to a collective form and force. It becomes clear that activism has been conceptually broadened, theorised with the help of a plurality of perspectives, which has left a unified and neat conception of activism behind, and opened a way for multiple forms of activism and ways to study its boundaryless attribute and collective force. The autonomous individual, assumed to be found in expressions of activism, has notably been differently balanced by a collective formation of togetherness. The above summary points to seemingly crucial elements for the human – how activism as a collective force thrives on togetherness, individual emotions and collective affects, nihilism and utopias, local self-sufficiency as well as extended familialism and security, for example in so-called community firms. These aspects are all important as a backdrop to the four empirical chapters, as they help us to explain what is happening to political subjectivity and relationality in commercial activism, from CEO activism to employee activism, investor activism, insider activism and prosumer activism.

However, there are still a few things missing in this chapter for the creation of the analytical shift needed to trace boundaryless activism when climate change is becoming a climate emergency, adaptation is extended to actions, and civil society is surpassed by the activist–business–state conglomeration. What perhaps has reconfigured politics the most in activist community formation is the outspoken call for more thought and awareness leading to actions by an abundance of actors who have been educated about and learnt its practical importance for the unfolding of an authentic political movement – not for erecting new structures in the existing world, but for engaging in novel and alternative organisational forms in attempts to enliven new worlds. Understanding community formation in relation to a movement of knowledge, or what we conceptualise as a wide 'epistemic community', which includes knowledge about various political practices, is thus crucial for our wish to create an analytical shift in the study of boundaryless climate activism.

4 | *Epistemic Community*

Analytically focussing on the knowledge movement that feeds bound-aryless climate activism and gives the activist–business–state conglom-eration its fuel stems from an interest in the dissemination of realities generated by natural scientific simulations and explanations of climate change. These realities effectively permeate, question and sometimes even disrupt previously socially constructed boundaries – territo-rial, organisational and individual. The will to find truth has been surpassed by the will to take action in response to the omnipresent climate emergency. Since this natural scientific priority of the material condition of climate change is taken for granted, why would humans as problem-creators and problem-solvers not get an accentuated sense of actions, all inspired by the expert emphasis on human dominion and material effects?

As mentioned earlier, this does not seem to be the case, consider-ing the desperation with which the complexity of challenges, present crises and future disasters have been communicated. This complexity previously required responses in the form of mitigation and adapta-tion, but somehow the shift to a climate emergency has made things more presently urgent, perhaps even felt. Based on the intensified reality of climate change, climate adaptation has forcefully been extended to action (Deichmann and Zhang 2013), with international authorities that speak openly about the problems to incite action via policy (United Nations 2018). Activists across the generations agree (Thunberg 2019), and businesses are slowly realising that conven-tional corporate engagement in politics is futile, which is why they empower or employ activist employees (Rauwald 2020), as a response to the lack of visible actions that produce human impact and material effects in the right direction.

In contrast to the repeated complaints about a lack of human climate action, it should be clear by now that this book traces how this identified lack has been responded to. Intensified calls for action have undoubtedly had an effect on the outlook of climate activism and its collective organisational form and force. Simply calling for action is a fundamental part of this activism, which also is complemented by an emphasis on authenticity and causal coherence – what is said needs to be backed up continuously with what is done. In the process of making humans aware, not only of their responsibility for potentially irreparable effects on the Earth but also for their political abilities to responsibly take actions and collectively respond, knowledge has become crucial. This chapter advances the concept of 'epistemic community' to craft an analytical position that can trace how knowledge movements underwrite the boundaryless attribute of climate activism and facilitate human relations, for example, relations that glue together the activist–business–state conglomeration. It is thus an analytical position that is equally interested in questions of human relationality and subjectivity.

Climate activism especially is supported by the making and spreading of knowledge, conceived as something that should be made to stick to sustain, designed to be internalised and materially acted upon, facilitated by technical and financial solutions such as renewable energy technologies and European Union-sanctioned crowdfunding platforms. The epistemic movement fortified by science on climate change thus encompasses more than a scientific episteme; it also vitalises a specific way of knowing, via the two other Aristotelean categories of knowledge: *techne* (practical knowledge) and *phronesis* (judgement). Scientific knowledge turned into applied knowledge among laypeople is not necessarily meant to result in totally correct usage; rather, it should produce a noticeable change of behaviour in line with the newly acquired knowledge coupled with self-reflection, an intensification of relationality and collective action, be this knowledge of nature, plants, interest rates, how to install your energy gadgets, or knowledge of ethics and politics.

As outlined in Chapters 1 and 2, and as we experienced in the field, all these aspects are explicitly merged in people's efforts to respond holistically to the call for actions. Tellingly, the knowledge movement has not only been deepened by criticising human existence on Earth to create concern and awareness, but it has also been effectively broadened. Therefore, instead of emphasising an expert position in a demarcated epistemic community (Haas 1992, 2015), we will in this chapter extend this concept to encompass a broader knowledge movement, one that explores how the activist-business-state conglomeration and boundaryless activism enrich practices of self-critique and the conviction that one can alter the world by altering oneself as well as others. Hence, reflection upon the potentially erroneous human and ethical implications of individual actions underwrites the epistemic community and creates a positive but potentially blind force for action that it is necessary for the community to repeatedly reflect upon anew. For instance, who can, in advance and with lay knowledge, see potentially wrong technical solutions coming? In comparison with previous studies, which have emphasised the inclusion of ethical experts (Moravec 2017), we thus aim to show how 'the expert', as scholars of epistemic communities knew them, have been re-positioned in relation to the activist–business–state conglomeration. This book seeks to build not only on previous insights about epistemic communities but also to move away from their over-reliance on identifiable experts, including the inclusion of specified activist groups or stakeholders who are already sufficiently invested with academic attention within political science. Instead, we turn towards the activist–business–state conglomeration, equally partaking in knowledge, as a movement of understanding that advances *Bildung* processes and enables ethical contemplation, actions and relations.

Even though previous efforts to study knowledge movements and changing political landscapes have made impressive efforts to include soft and dynamic aspects of activist practices and social life, similarly to Haas' conceptualisation of epistemic communities, these follow explanatory routes that need to be re-thought. If looking at these routes critically and in relation to historical notions of community, they seem to follow a focus on instrumental relations, with academic devotion to formal political processes. A result of this academic bent is a limited conceptualisation of epistemic community, construed as belonging more to the historical conceptualisation of society (*Gesellschaft*) and not community (*Gemeinschaft*) (Tönnies 1957/2002).[1] We thus revisit this conceptual pair to better acknowledge how the contemporary call for action is assisted by a will to form togetherness in search of greener futures.

---

[1] In German, the word *gemein* shares roots with the Latin term *communis*, but in some languages a distinction between the two notions, *Gemeinschaft* and *Gesellschaft*, is harder to discern (Asplund 1991:8).

The chapter starts by addressing the contemporary limitations of what an epistemic community can be conceptualised and considered to be, to then present the main relevant ideas about *Gemeinschaft* in Ferdinand Tönnies' work – a work of its time that undoubtedly also includes dated ideas about structures that have already been left behind. Despite Tönnies' now quite dated work, we are interested in what is left of his conception of community when looking at the dispersed, sometimes messy and even unplanned, actions and relations between people. Advancing the concept of epistemic community can thus help us to zoom in, from the details of boundaryless climate activism, to the relational particularities of how renewable energy actions bridge business and society.

4.1 Communities of Expertise

Studies of communities of expertise often share an interest in the dissemination as well as the usage of natural science, which has led to important insights about how this specific type of knowledge production has made technology a dominant element in the stimulation of collective action (Haas 2015). These so-called epistemic communities build on compromises between short-term and more long-term commitments and concerns, sustained by a continuous dialogue between scientists and policymakers (Haas 2015). It has been suggested that prosperous epistemic communities rely on policymakers who play a part in more than one institution, and on scientists who are open to collaborations outside a specific research group. There are, however, limited discussions about the relational element in this boundary spanning since the epistemic movement is mainly positioned at the level of manageable causes and effects in political decision-making (Haas 1992).

Other political scientists have been equally curious about causal explanations for the development of political processes and authority, for example analysing 'discourse coalitions' and linguistic regularities of language-in-use (Hajer 1995, Hajer and Versteeg 2005); or investigating 'strategic action fields' with the inclusion of social movements (Mey and Diesendorf 2018); or exploring 'instrument constituencies' in an attempt to understand how 'specific models of governance gain momentum as they link up academic research strategies, new business opportunities or political agendas' (Simons and Voß 2018:15).

The intended audiences are clearly policymakers, which is why the explanatory focus is located in the changes of policymaking rather than changes of human relationality, community formation and activism – a tendency additionally seen in the study of 'advocacy coalitions' (Sabatier 1988) and 'advocacy networks' (Keck and Sikkink 2014). Similarly to strategic action fields and instrument constituencies, these coalitions or networks re-assume the existence of basic separations between civil society, business and formal politics. They often include a strategic element, for example by demanding an analytical focus on 'networks' or 'specialists' who are seen to gradually learn how to best attain a certain policy direction.

The interest in the efficiency of policy and political decision-making, from its potential deviations to its well-designed influence, are investigated through a focus on how specific policy objectives are to be reached and how specific actors are strategically targeted to be transformed (Haas 1992, 2015). It becomes clear that compared with the problematic personal political position of insider activists in state agencies (Olsson and Hysing 2012, Hysing and Olsson 2018), it is legitimate to infuse policy with personal engagement if this engagement is based on scientific expertise. Policymakers are to be smitten by scientists' personal engagement in scientific expertise, which is suggested to nurture long-term relationships between scientists and policymakers (Haas 2015). Devotion and commitment are thus important for securing a unified momentum and ideas that can be sustained over time. 'Knowledge', in the natural scientific view of fact delivery and truth construction, is not only there to show the correct content on which policies should be based, but also, 'knowledge' about politics is there to infuse the human will to form collective movements that correspond to a specific content. Policymakers, unsurprisingly, have been inspired both by natural science and political science.

Legitimacy is moreover to be gained in the epistemic community by the settled and mutually agreed upon ideas that have been transparently obtained by consensus (Haas 2015:177). According to Haas, epistemic communities do not form around negotiations of 'social facts' but rely on less social topics, one example being the ecological epistemic community, created by 'hybrid and brute facts, where claims about physical phenomena may be evaluated by recourse to mechanisms independent of the subject of study' (Haas 2015:177). Hence, the epistemic community shares 'tangible understandings', where ecological facts, for instance, are to be merged with public policy (Haas 2015:177). This slight recognition of how scientific knowledge movements are inseparable from more general movements of knowledge through time, with their correlating subjectivities and relationalities, is partly why epistemic communities is still a useful concept for our shift of analytical focus – away from formal politics to boundaryless activism; away from civil society to the activist-business-state conglomeration; and away from adaptation to action.

As an extension of Haas (1992), self-organised epistemic communities have also been illustrated to unfold when knowledge dissemination is effective and leads to a spread of uses in society (Davis Cross 2013). Instead of targeting a specific actor to be transformed, the knowledge movement, or epistemic community, seeks to reframe a chosen topic. One example is the movement that counters increasing scientisation (McCormick 2006). Knowledge movements thus include struggles – not as we have first and foremost been used to making sense of protests and demonstrations in studies of activism, but as 'epistemic struggles' (Icaza and Vázquez 2013). These struggles could, for example, involve opposing ethical positions and opinions about what is good, bad and feasible with renewable technology, followed by an active mobilisation of a quite technical topic that materialises change, or a 'transition' of the energy system. Debates about 'deep decarbonisation' bring this type of struggle to the fore (Maize 2017). Epistemic struggles can also relate to diverse opinions about commercial methods and their positive or negative consequences, extended to the invention of new distribution models, gift economies and profit-sharing.

Epistemic communities can equally be haphazardly shaped by digital technologies that facilitate collaboration and coordination of actions between individuals, a bridging between various organisations, as well as diffusion of knowledge beyond the closest community (Bennett and Segerberg 2011). The social network thrives on the technical network provided by digital technologies, whereby instructions for actions can spread transnationally at scale. This knowledge dissemination about specific topics can result in disorganised and unintentional actions scattered horizontally, questioning the very rationale of how actions have been granted political status only if a self-mastering individual stands causally behind them. Furthermore, these haphazard, scattered actions have been shown to be constructively 'pro' rather than 'anti' (Byford and Wong 2016).

Knowledge is thus recognised as that which performs the boundary spanning, and which can even disrupt and infuse discontinuity. If national scientific capability and causal paths for policymaking dominate Haas' original definition of epistemic community (Haas 1992), other formations of expertise have thus proliferated. In these, expertise comes across as more feral, pursued by any citizen as a scattered way of living that embraces the possibility of exploration and disruption (Garside 2013). If an imaginary citizen (for example in novels) creates new worlds with words, a *flâneuse* prefigures these worlds with walks (see also Benjamin 1997). Both are moving about according to a grounding curiosity about the unknown, which results in interventions in the far too known. Despite a possible individual imaginary nationality or an individual disruptive moving about in the world, it is a way of living that can be shared and catalysed in meetings between individuals, their fantasies, inclinations and interrogation of the status quo.

In so-called 'close communities', experts have been found to *flâneur* and wander between organisations that are constructed to have boundaries, moving from one place to another, for example seeking to work with the same environmental issues in various host organisations (Harrigan, Achananuparp and Lim 2012). The close community of professional wanderers do more than mere 'boundary spanning', that is, linking organisations with external sources of information (Tushman and Scanlan 1981). These wanderers are facilitating the establishment of close communities across organisational boundaries. Studies of close communities are thus of special interest since they have illustrated how individuals come together and relate to each other stimulated by a common cause. Similarly to an interest in communities of practice, studied as processes of becoming (Wenger 1998), attention is given to how people collectively engage in the same practices and shared goals, with a focus on how relations between people unfold. Such practice- and cause-based close communities have been identified in countries with limited population numbers where everyone knows, or knows about, everyone else (Guy and Shove 2000:19). However, it has also been suggested that close communities arise within highly populated countries when people share a high degree of education and political engagement in a geographical location that is isolated, be it in island regions or remote places. Studies of close communities are thus curious about the relationality infused by the locality of professional activity, while studies of communities of practice concentrate more on shared knowledge and subjectification thereto.

There are similarities in how close communities, communities of practice and epistemic communities are conceived to rely on and co-produce knowledge and expertise, and how all of these can have transnational effects (see Haas 2004). If not wandering themselves, spanning individuals within these communities provide routes needed for others to engage across domains, supporting the creation of novel relations, which is crucial for the fostering of any collective movement. In the case of climate change and the energy transition, we thus expect to encounter spanning individuals who seek to animate relationality, to stimulate others to engage in renewables. The common denominator for contemporary epistemic communities is in our view their capacity to bring a personal knowledge position to the fore, releasing it into a dispersed knowledge movement for others, with unknown effects.

4.1.1 Epistemic Community and Action

Based on Immanuel Kant's (2013) answer to the question 'What is Enlightenment?', the role of knowledge has been debated and coupled to freedom and processes of becoming a human subject who is able to take action, one who is mature and civilised rather than immature and uncivilised (Kant 1899/2003). The alternative is to rest in immaturity and let oneself be lazily guided or even ignorant, as exemplified earlier in the scholarly criticism of community firms and their role as paternalistic guardians. To create understanding citizens, rather than robots who thoughtlessly repeat information and uphold the status quo, has, supported by the Enlightenment ideal, been pointed out as crucial for functioning democracies (O'Brien and Penna 1998), as exemplified in Chapter 2 (The Activist–Business–State Conglomeration). As previously illustrated, more localised interconnectedness has been emphasised in the energy transition literature (Devine-Wright 2014), with rich examples of how participation has been enabled and accomplished:from online tools, such as internet forums, to public information meetings, door-knocking, face-to-face meetings, interactive poster sessions and open talks from a stage followed by questions. Yet a mere dissemination of information about the need to decarbonise collectively via individual engagement has been deemed ineffective. The information needs to be seriously picked up and to become internalised as knowledge. Hence, to go beyond an intellectual uptake of information and transform this into knowledge in the form of a secular understanding and, in our case, green awareness, has been seen as crucial for the courage to take individual action (cf. Kornwachs 2000). Getting informed should be transformed into a mental state of being engaged, which requires more elaborate human tools.

Overcoming the problems of bringing knowledge to the level of 'understanding' and in-depth awareness has been argued as crucial for preventing climate scepticism and converting climate deniers (cf. Stevenson et al. 2014). However, even awareness has been deemed inadequate for reaching the whole way if correct actions are to be taken (Norgaard 2006, 2011). Despite massive public and private investments in higher education across the Western world, pursuing knowledge as 'understanding', it has been acutely realised that the human is still too slow to take action to meet the crises of climate change. Hence, in order to mitigate ignorance and passivity, citizens have been increasingly offered the chance to activate themselves, invited to take part in the production and dissemination of not only expertise but also the practice of deliberation itself – to empower fellow citizens in a combined decentralisation of the energy system and democratic enrolment via renewables (Valentine, Sovacool and Brown 2019). Knowledge dissemination about climate change, renewable technology and investment opportunities has deepened or even left deliberative democracy behind in a turn to knowledge co-production and voluntary experiments to breed an interest to act, not only by people's own choices as techno-optimist citizen consumers (Walker et al. 2007, Leach and Scoones 2015), but also, as our empirical chapters will show, foremost by citizens-becoming-activists through their own will to repent, alter themselves, make new friends and even re-invent others. The participation in deliberative democracy has been advanced to relationality in knowledge co-production, especially in business start-ups.

4.1.2 *Epistemic Community and Co-production*

Due to the difficulties of succeeding in bringing the citizen on board with deliberative democracy alone, and transform knowledge beyond understanding to reach relationality and engagement, deliberation has been advanced to empowerment through an intensification of knowledge co-production (e.g. see Valentine, Sovacool and Brown 2019, Norström et al. 2020). In contrast to positioning the origin of co-production of knowledge within the creation of effective responses to emerging challenges and increasing complexities (Norström et al. 2020), it should be clarified that co-production follows from a much longer tradition of knowledge production in the social sciences and humanities (Chandler and Reid 2019). This knowledge production has, since Kant, seemingly been enriching practices of self-critique, with elaborate attempts to mobilize reason and create prioritised 'meaning' for humans. However, if these practices of self-critique are based on repetitive reflections about the present condition and its shortcomings, then it becomes difficult for a knowledge co-producer to think in a radically transformative way. That is, the transformative thinking would still be predetermined by what counts as knowledge production, and thereby as 'knowledge' or not (Chandler and Reid 2019).

How the conceptualization and implementation of co-production could overcome this paradox is also unclear if looking at it historically. Rather than being a recent social innovation for how to best respond to emerging challenges in the Anthropocene Epoch (Norström et al. 2020), co-production has long played a fundamental role in the human sciences (Hansson, Hellberg and Stern 2015). From being a legitimate ambition of categorisation and ordering of things (Foucault 1966/2002), it has been brought into the realm of 'the human' and its willpower (Foucault 1978/1997), with attempts to include each and every individual in self-referential truth-seeking processes of knowledge production (Foucault 1980). Co-production of knowledge has since then become equally popular among social movements who wish to craft political influence (Mitlin 2008), as it has become among other actors who regulate social activity through education, such as museums (Graham 2012). It is not possible for us to delve further into the impact of the co-production trend, executed by very diverse actors, from para-ethnographic scholars to nursery pedagogues, here. It is enough to say that co-production has always been constitutive of knowledge but is now outspokenly and conceptually affirmed, taken for granted as fundamental to the knowledge movement itself. Epistemes are thus utterly human inventions pursued with exclusively human tools, diverse theories and methods, that change over time (Foucault 1966/2002). This leads to the view of epistemes in epistemic communities also needing to be reconceptualised into an analytical tool apt for exposure of how humans are engaging in old and new practices of self-critique, seemingly exceptionally well in the case of boundaryless climate activism and its collective organisational form and force.

4.1.3 *Epistemic Community and Bildung*

The understanding that the human subject can change the world, or rather 'others', by changing the self, takes its cue from *Bildung* (human formation), developed in late eighteenth-century German pedagogy. If *Bildung* was first used to denote wisdom and long-term knowledge progression under Enlightenment ideals of perfection, it has, with an exhaustion of the educational subject in late modernity, come to represent 'processes of transformation with unknown outcomes' (Reichenbach 2002:411). Historically, *Bildung* was underpinned by life-long personal perfection and a belief in self-formation and one's own mind, that is, subjectivity rather than objectivity. This is an assumption that brought with it a certain belief in intellectual equality, obtained in the way people can turn inwards, mainly to interact with each other, the world and nature, defined by 'openness, endlessness and independence' (Rönnerman and Salo 2017:458). The ideal was that anyone interested in or having time for introspection could seek the company of others to collaboratively realise their inner potentials under critical self-reflection and freedom from constraints, be they political, social or cultural.

This ideal concept of an unencumbered self and human relationality has been deployed in higher education, especially in the Nordic countries, where *Bildung* became a bridge between humans and society, under the assumption that it is the formation of humans that is to transform society (Asplund 1991). By virtue of notions of life-long learning and self-development, *Bildung* is still about nurturing specifically human qualities, for example, those of active citizenship and leadership (Rönnerman and Salo 2017:458). It thereby functions as a concept that extends communities of expertise or epistemic communities, and how these are connected to more than scientific knowledge and professional contexts. *Bildung* brings together the personal and professional in reflexivity and is less about specialisation and fragmentation, with a shift in interest to solidarity, relations to others and the sharing of knowledge.

This remnant of *Bildung* brings to mind the focus on human relationality in Ferdinand Tönnies' exploration of *Gemeinschaft* (community) and *Gesellschaft* (society), including his interest in the creation of public opinion via increased civic education (Tönnies 1957/2002). Public opinion in the late eighteenth century was mainly a normative construct that belonged to the middle class, which is why it is worth repeating Tönnies' general conception of the links between subjectivity, relationality and action:

Human wills stand in manifold relations to one another. Every such relationship is a mutual action, inasmuch as one party is active, or gives, while the other party is inactive, or receives. These actions are of such a nature that they tend either toward preservation or destruction of the other will or life; that is, they are either positive or negative. This study will consider as its subject of investigation only the relationships of mutual affirmation. Every such relationship represents unity in plurality or plurality in unity. It consists of assistance, relief, services, which are transmitted back and forth from one party to another and are considered as expressions of wills and their forces. (Tönnies 1957/2002:33)

After introducing the basic element of human willpower, getting along and gathering in the creation of positive reciprocity and gift-giving, Tönnies continues to clarify that *Gesellschaft* is based on knowledge while *Gemeinschaft* is more open to imaginings. *Gemeinschaft* includes thoughtful bonds to the Earth and other beings, while *Gesellschaft* nurtures instrumental relations – 'All intimate, private, and exclusive living together ... is understood as life in *Gemeinschaft* (community). *Gesellschaft* (society) is public life – it is the world itself' (Tönnies 1957/2002:33). The former, *Gemeinschaft*, is filled with a more connected version of humans via a transformational work on 'the self', and the latter involves a disconnected relation between ethics and actions, or thoughts and the effects of actions (Asplund 1991). How thought and action are connected thus differs between *Gesellschaft* and *Gemeinschaft* in Tönnies' theory of agency. In *Gemeinschaft* there is a deep connection between thought and action – they work as an organism with organs – while organising in *Gesellschaft* is driven by a mechanism, a detached thought that precedes a calculated action (Tönnies 1957/2002:33). *Gemeinschaft* as 'community' constitutes a core that unifies thought, action and the effects of this action, analogously explained as a natural process of how organs function.

The connection to *Bildung,* appears here, since the immanent connection between thought and action in 'community' leads to a person being simultaneously shaped by their ethical work on the self and actions, geared towards the promise of a future result – a *telos*. *Bildung* came to replace religion and beliefs, which previously had supported the formation of *Gemeinschaft*. In relation to a broader dissemination of knowledge and correlating norms, *Gesellschaft* did not, however, close off the various class layers in society but was, according to Tönnies, open: 'its ideas [could] be shared on the level of the whole nation' (Warland 2012:5). At the same time, the ideas did nonetheless originate in the elite, and the educated classes were increasingly inspired to spread their knowledge to the masses, whereby *Bildung* grew in importance as pedagogics for the link between a developed, creative and ethically reflective mind and sufficient action.

The *Bildung* movement was assumed to provide pedagogic tools that nurtured not only rationality but also critical thought, for example in relation to an overtly oppressive state. *Bildung* came to encompass a sense of obligation to fulfil one's duties at work, at home and in *Gesellschaft* (society) (Warland 2012). As a clear trace of the Enlightenment, Tönnies thus nurtured *Bildung* as a form of knowing deeply connected to values and judgement. Without necessarily opposing *Gesellschaft*, he attempted as a social reformer to counter the excesses of *Gesellschaft* by supporting more cooperative organisational forms (*Genossenschaften*), for example via partnerships between families. These insights in Tönnies' work on human relationality came to support the development of sociology as a discipline, spreading well beyond Germany (Asplund 1991, Inglis 2009), and as a binary pairing, *Gesellschaft* and *Gemeinschaft* have effectively serviced opposite ends of many sociological categories: egoism versus altruism; cosmopolitanism versus localism; contractual relations versus relational belonging; exchange versus unconditional giving; and competition versus friendship. In some languages, this polarisation is still evident, while in other languages the difference between community and society is hard to make out (Asplund 1991).

Bildung has also undergone a transformation since Tönnies' ideals, shaped in his time, suggesting that with an exhaustion of the political subject in late modernity, *Bildung* as a process can only offer an uncertain end goal or *telos* (Reichenbach 2002:413):

[I]t is not possible to ascribe a common telos to processes of *Bildung*. Many processes may well lead to increasing autonomy, competencies, sovereignty or even happiness (whatever that may be), but other processes may also end in increasing dependency, incompetence, a feeling of lacking sovereignty, and unhappiness (which may also correspond to a false 'disillusionment'). There is no real reason to look at processes of *Bildung* only in an 'optimistic' or 'positive' way, unless theories of *Bildung* are only to be formulated as driven by the wish or the *Sehnsucht*, the longing for *Bildung* [itself]. (Reichenbach 2002:413)

Bildung, emphasised as an important learning process and experience of praxis rather than an attempt to preach and reach a specific end, has also been discussed in relation to 'phronetic actions', that is, actions that are self-constitutive in relation to specific situatedness and a becoming world, often without tangible outcomes (Chia and Holt 2009:134). Actions here come about in a world that is rather loose and open for continuous redirection, where '*Bildung* are perceived as processes of transformation with unknown outcomes, not as processes of perfection (Vervoll-kommnung)' (Reichenbach 2002:411). It thereby becomes clear that *Bildung* is still formative of human relationality and the will to gather and take actions, linked to more dispersed and diffuse knowledge movements, such as the epistemic community in boundaryless climate activism.

4.2 Conclusion

As concerns about the power and reach of global capitalist mass society began to arise in the 1960s, it is perhaps not surprising that the concept of community (*Gemeinschaft*) grew in popularity. The aim of the renewed bearing of community was to stimulate bonds between humans, and to accomplish some isolation of groups from the mass, in the provision of more relation-based security. As well as being a counter to globalisation, a morally invested community was supposed to balance the decline of the welfare state and the accelerated commodification that fed an amoral market. This destiny of community has been well rehearsed and debated from various angles, as we laid forth in Chapter 3.

With scientific knowledge about climate change, however, globalisation has been reconfigured. In a reality dominated by carbon dioxide (CO_2) flows and a climate emergency, the global interconnectedness is unassailable, leading to the conventional notion of a community, separated out to host certain individuals, so to speak, becoming less tenable. It is of course still spoken into being in many places where self-sufficiency is to be stimulated, especially via renewable energy technologies. However, what we wish to theoretically emphasise, and analytically investigate, is an even more powerful version of community. Just as activism is slowly leaving the notion of civil society behind, theoretically and empirically, in its boundaryless becoming, so too has community gone through a fundamental shift. Community has not been surpassed, as we argue that civil society has. It has rather come to host the leftovers of what had anyway never agreed to be confined to 'civil society', now in the potent form of an epistemic community. It is thus still important for humans, it seems, to self-transform and gather collectively to 'get along' based on manifold human wills, to paraphrase Tönnies (1957/2002:33), though mainly driven not by an awareness of civil rights but by green politics in the taking of climate actions.

This has led to a growth of reciprocal knowledge processes, established via deliberative democratic programmes and the increasingly popular idea of empowerment through the co-production of knowledge. Knowledge has historically been, and seems to still be, linked to individual action. However, as this chapter has sought to clarify, knowledge is, in the energy transition, stimulating self-transformation, relationality and collective action at a deeper level, aided by a *Bildung* process entangled with renewable energy technology. In our view, knowledge processes and climate activism are thus increasingly merged in the formation of a knowledge movement that we wish to study through a re-conceptualisation of epistemic communities.

To grasp the necessary shift in thinking about community formation based on knowledge movements, it is still important to acknowledge Tönnies' ideas about community as an other-than-economic organisational force, merged with how ideas about *Bildung* have been renewed in the expansion of societies, economies and policies driven by knowledge (cf. Haas 1992, Knorr Cetina 1999, Powell and Snellman 2004), facilitating a conglomeration of the climate activist-business-state. By making the existing concept of epistemic community more inclusive of *Bildung*, as a process that secures human relationality as well as unknown outcomes, it also becomes more useful for a study of boundaryless activism. Hence, just as political theorists have argued that the citizen should be seen as a full human, expected to behave more like an agonistic activist with a complex set of qualities that would quickly exceed efforts to rule via unifying efforts of consensus, epistemic community also needs to be extended to host such a potent plurality of expressions and expectations on life. To be at all academically useful, epistemic community is thus expanded to analytically serve studies of a diversity of political collectivity, on the face of it present in boundaryless activism, of which climate activism and its knowledge movement are an example. As suggested by others (Zito 2001, 2018, Davis Cross 2013), by expanding Haas' conceptualisation of an epistemic community, we aim to follow both easily identifiable esoteric groups as well as more diffuse and dispersed gatherings. However, in comparison with these previous studies, we are not making any presumptions about the existence of causal relationships, available for policymakers to push and pull. If we narrowed in on such ideas among specific actors and networks, we would not be able to acknowledge the haphazard forcefulness that seems to come with climate activism. Hence, it makes it much more analytically sensible to follow the epistemic community without assumptions about causality, static networks with actors, as well as predetermined organisational boundaries or separations of domains. It is not until we follow epistemic communities as a broader knowledge movement that it is possible to understand how it unites, rather than splits, different domains.

By this extension of epistemic communities, we aim to capture the ongoing transformation of political subjectivity and relationality, to understand the bridging between business and society via renewable energy actions. We will do so in the next four empirical chapters by conceptually focussing on epistemic community, defined as a collectivity or movement formed when people share, reflect and co-produce knowledge about environmental degradation and climate change as well as further this knowledge by hands-on action via work with renewable energy technology. We initiate our analysis of climate activism by being attentive to current imaginations of 'power to the people' as well as 'individual responsibility', and how these two thrive on how *Bildung* processes foster self-transformation and a coming together. By tracing how knowledge about, and solutions to, climate change have been disseminated, we thus hope to better understand how people, wherever they happen to be located, engage, increasingly collaborate and bond, often horizontally, via renewable energy actions. Turning to theories that go beyond concepts of deliberative or radical democracy, energy justice and ecological citizenship in the energy transition, the empirical chapters thus explore the details of how boundaryless climate activism is pursued by the activist–business–state conglomeration.

To clarify our fascination with the boundaryless attribute of activism, we still see its collective form and force as an artery for political moments. By tracing its channels, diagnosing its winding routes, diversions, twists and turns, clogs and expansions, we can explore what is going on hand in hand with economic calculations and managerial logistics, acknowledging the political and activist dimensions of the everyday, potentially anywhere. This allows us to go beyond a fixation on civil society and rather affirm what Rancière (1992/2007:63) calls a '"reasonable" nostalgia' of community:

[W]e still take it to represent something we would not like to lose, namely a particular configuration of being-together without which thought and action are bereft of the virtue of generosity which distinguishes the political from mere business management.

5 | *Climate Activism at Vattenfall*

Corporations that operate within the energy sector are particularly sensitive to what has conventionally been seen as external activism and civil society activity in studies of CSR, corporate environmentalism and corporate political activity. Nevertheless, in this chapter, we will encounter CEO activism, brand activism and, particularly, employee activism. The chapter will thus illustrate empirical details of boundaryless activism, as presented in Chapter 1 under the heading 'activism as business strategy'. With the boundaryless attribute of activism, it becomes clear that activism has gone into business, and business has gone into activism, especially at the energy utility company Vattenfall, 100 percent state owned by the Swedish citizens. Vattenfall are thus formally representing a conglomeration of citizen-business-state, and their operations often secure this organisational form. However, when the citizen becomes activist, new things happen at Vattenfall. The employees mobilise their professional expertise hand in hand with their extensive concern for the environment and wish to take action, at work, often in response to a lack of visible material actions in the right direction. Vocal Swedish politicians and citizens support the need for this trend, while Vattenfall struggle with their commercial and green positions. Difficult decisions have to be made about possible future economic value creation, which is increasingly dependent on being accepted by a market and state with green priorities. This leads to corporate strategies and employee efforts that sometimes merge in building relations with others to speed up the energy transition by means of the mobilisation of an epistemic community at work and beyond.

5.1 The Greening of Vattenfall

Before we narrow in on what it is like to work with, and be personally engaged in, renewables as an employee at Vattenfall, a short introduction to the multinational corporation's greening efforts is needed.

Even though Vattenfall have a long historical trajectory of balancing acts between energy security and environmental and social aspects, for example in the north of Sweden where indigenous people and nature have had to give way to huge hydropower stations (Össbo 2018), their green profile grew quickly under CEO Lars G. Josefsson, who was in charge between 2000 and 2010. He was occasionally identified as taking a strong and politicised environmentalist position (Gumbel 2005) and was even labelled as an 'industrious activist' by Time Magazine's European Hero award in 2005 (Gumbel 2005). The change exemplifies not only Vattenfall's ambitions but also a more general will to mediatise and establish CEO activism in relation to sustainability and climate change. Since then we have in general witnessed increasing constructions of CEOs as models and hosts for vanguard positions, assumed to be important drivers or so-called influencers of social change. Their authority as leaders is used to make moral statements on how the business world is to behave better.

During Josefsson's time as CEO, Vattenfall incorporated climate change as both a green and a social issue, often mentioning a future generation as a loose way to talk about when certain goals were to be met (Skoglund 2014). Inspired by generational shifts and tensions, which have been fundamental to a sustainable development agenda (Skoglund and Börjesson 2020), Vattenfall still argued that fossil-fuelled power plants are necessary into the near future. In 2008, the Vattenfall group produced the main part of its electricity by burning fossil fuels (75.1 TWh), and it was made clear in the corporation's Annual Report that Vattenfall were both one of the largest electricity producers and one of the largest emitters of CO_2 in Europe. This was mainly due to Vattenfall taking over various European fossil fuel operations from 1999 onwards, which included East German lignite-based power stations, some of the dirtiest and most carbon-intensive in Europe. In Sweden, in contrast, Vattenfall mainly produced, and still do, carbon-free electricity and heat by hydropower and nuclear power.

In the slow turn towards climate change mitigation, Vattenfall invested more in hydropower, wind power and biomass power and were, in the early twenty-first century, deeply engaged in the research and development of carbon capture and storage (CCS) in collaboration with Norwegian attempts to capture and store CO_2 underground. In his new year speech in 2005/2006, Norwegian Prime Minister Jens Stoltenberg portrayed CCS as a Norwegian 'moon rocket' since the new business opportunity could eventually be important for the already existing technology, investments and experience in the oil industry. The idea was to transport CO_2 in vessels and pump it far underground into rock structures that used to house oil and gas. The cooperation eventually failed when the Norwegian project incurred excessive costs. Vattenfall, nevertheless, pressed ahead, inaugurating a CCS test facility at its East German Schwarze Pumpe site in May 2006 (Vattenfall 2017). At the Jänschwalde 1,600-megawatt power plant, where 80,000 tons of lignite was combusted each day, similar attempts were made.

CCS was heavily criticised at the time, with many climate activists calling it an attempt to 'greenwash' coal, one of the dirtiest and most carbon-intensive ways of generating electricity (Pearce 2009). Equally, studies showed that CCS was too expensive for individual companies to develop and implement and that governments would have to heavily subsidise this new, untested technology (Stephens 2014). In Vattenfall's public communication, however, the cost was not cited as a critical issue. Instead, CCS was presented by the company and the wider industry as a 'bridge technology', enabling and legitimising the continued use of lignite and coal for at least another thirty to forty years.

The backlash by the Swedish media and beyond was fierce (European Greens 2009, Sveriges Radio 2010). It heavily critiqued Vattenfall's greenwashing attempts (Climate Greenwash Award 2009, European Greens 2009). Vattenfall were more or less forced to respond with a press release, saying that there will be 'carbon free coal power plants' in the future and that CCS is a short-term solution in the wait for renewable energy technologies to become more viable (Vattenfall 2009a). Yet, in accordance with previous decisions and established long-term strategies, Vattenfall kept investing in old coal power plants as well as in the construction of new fossil fuel power plants, justified by the promise of large investments in the technical development and implementation of CCS. Clearly, Vattenfall had to do a lot of explaining to a sceptical public, and it took until 2018 for CCS to be seriously proposed again as a carbon mitigation technology, this time in the context of burning waste (Simon 2018).

Acknowledging a general political will and growing public wish in Sweden to mitigate climate change in the early twenty-first century,

Vattenfall pledged in 2007 that they would reduce their carbon emissions by 50 percent in comparison with a 1990 base. To initiate more extensive changes beyond the corporation as such, Vattenfall also established a global industry network, consisting of forty-two companies, called 'Combating Climate Change (3C)', launched via a 'pan European multi media campaign' (Vattenfall 2007b). The initiative pointed out that policymaking was lagging behind, whereas technology and financial issues could be solved by business. Vattenfall confidently concluded that '[c]ombating climate change must and will be a part of everyday life all over the globe', arguing that 'action' is needed by both politicians and consumers (Vattenfall 2006:2). The citizen-owned energy utility company is thereby taking it upon itself to augment and spread a certain way of thinking and acting in relation to climate change worldwide. Another example is Vattenfall's children-focussed advertisement campaigns and the social experiment One Tonne Life (OTL 2011). In close collaboration with the National Geographic Society, Vattenfall have also taken it upon themselves to educate school pupils on climate change in five European countries, asking and encouraging them to innovate for the future (Vattenfall 2007b: also see Figure 5.1). The original thinking about future generations within sustainable development is thus advanced by Vattenfall, who bridge the gap between business and society via a pedagogic turn to the competent child (Skoglund and Börjesson 2014).

To convince policymakers that action really was needed, and needed 'now', Vattenfall also launched the television campaign 'Sign up for the climate! Vattenfall Climate Manifesto' (Sveriges Radio 2010, and see the broadcasted commercial in Vattenfall 2009b). Deploying activist language, the 'climate manifesto' advertisement portrays a polar bear swimming around happily until a large ice block suddenly tumbles into the water. Next, a signature of a personal name appears, and it turns the sea surface back into growing ice, with the effect that the polar bear can escape the cold sea and climb back up on the recovered ice. The bear starts running, jumping and rolling around in the snow, reunited with its cub, with which it continues to enjoy the exploration of the snowy landscape. The TV commercial ends with an invitation: 'Discover what your signature can do for the climate'.

Figure 5.1 Front page of Vattenfall report (Vattenfall 2006)

By drawing on a petition approach, common within less violent forms of activism, the corporate TV commercial calls for the viewers' potential political agency. By the middle of September 2008, a total of 128,038 signatures had been collected, with all names easily accessible on the Vattenfall website. In addition to the act of signing, every signature was coupled to a suggested self-confession; that is, each person was, with their signature, admitting to being a cause of climate change. A reward for each person's signature was also provided in the form of a twelve-centimetre-tall baby-toy plastic figure (see Figures 5.2a and 5.2b). The confessions were thus mirrored in a materialisation, as the plastic figure was produced in Vattenfall's brand signature yellow colour, finally promised to be sent around the world to places where policy decisions were to be made. Ahead of the 2009 annual shareholder meeting (presenting the 2008 Annual Report), the climate manifesto surfaced yet again in a newspaper advertisement together with an invitation to the event at the China Theatre at Berns

Figure 5.2a and **5.2b** Plastic toy produced by Vattenfall in its yellow brand signature colour to be sent around the world. Photo: Annika Skoglund

in Stockholm on 29 April. The advertisement promises that all your questions can be answered and that you can even pose them to the management of Vattenfall. The ad also makes sure to present the number of people who have signed the climate manifesto, which then had reached a total of 230,000 names (Skoglund 2011).

No matter how sincere the continuous attempts to bond with citizens and clean up Vattenfall's operations may have been, for Josefsson the efforts to take Vattenfall towards a greener position backfired. In 2009, four masked activists sneaked into the Berns venue in Stockholm, where the annual meeting, open to Swedish citizens, was held. Screaming 'bullshit' and 'climate justice', they popped up behind the chairs, and the CEO was aggressively attacked as the activists threw capsules containing a green-coloured substance, hitting Josefsson's white shirt. At about the same time, a website was launched, rewarding Vattenfall with the 2009 Climate Greenwash Award. The organisers accused the energy utility company of hypocrisy, portraying itself as a climate change champion while lobbying to continue to use coal, legitimised by pseudo-solutions such as CCS (Climate Greenwash Award 2009).

Other environmental groups, such as Greenpeace, increasingly put Vattenfall under intense pressure, exposing their double standards: a low-carbon image at home in 'green Sweden', on the one hand, and in reality, one of the dirtiest and most carbon-intensive operators abroad, on the other hand.

This polarisation of Vattenfall – the polluting operations versus the environmental ambitions, were increasingly difficult to communicate legitimately about, and make sensible, to the Swedish electorate, the ultimate owner of Vattenfall. The company's environmental record became headline news leading up to the 2014 general election in Sweden, when all major Swedish parties promised to support a ban on new lignite operations. Big utility companies typically have a thirty- to forty-year time horizon in mind when making investment decisions. Yet in 2015, only about fifteen years after acquiring the dirty lignite business in Germany, Vattenfall decided to sell off these carbon-intensive operations (Vattenfall 2015). As the documents in Figure 5.3a testifies, the lignite operations would only be sold together with hydro operations in East Germany, probably to ensure that someone would take on the declining profitability of the lignite coal operations. In an interview with us in 2015, Andreas Regnell, Senior Vice President of Strategic Development, confirmed the fact that there was simply no future value in lignite.

Who, then, was going to buy Vattenfall's lignite operations in Germany if the writing was on the wall for 'dirty coal'? Vattenfall were not alone in realising that it would be very difficult to make any money with coal in the future. RWE (Rheinisch-Westfälische Elektrizitätswerk) and E.ON, two of the largest European energy utility companies, both with sizeable coal operations in Germany, have seen their share prices drop rapidly, prompting them to embark on a complex asset swap and refocus their businesses on renewables (Vaughan 2018). Iberdrola of Spain and Italy's ENEL have also gone through major strategic shifts towards more sustainable energy production (Orihuela and Reed 2018). Perhaps it was not surprising then that the sale of Vattenfall's German operations was quickly picked up by Greenpeace (see Figure 5.3b), which expressed an interest in taking over the generation in Boxberg, Jänschwalde and Schwarze Pumpe, as well as the lignite mining activities in Jänschwalde, Nochten, Reichwalde, Welzow-Süd and Cottbus-Nord. Their aim was not to continue business as usual, but instead to close down these facilities.

Vattenfall AB: Sale of Vattenfall's German lignite and hydro activities

Vattenfall AB and its affiliates (the "Seller") intend to divest their German lignite activities and contemplate to potentially divest their Eastern German hydro activities in an open, transparent and non-discriminatory process (the "Transaction").

The Transaction includes the shares held in the Seller's German lignite activities ("Lignite") and may also include the shares held in the Seller's Eastern German hydro activities ("Hydro") with the primary objective to divest Lignite. It is not an option to acquire Hydro without Lignite.

Lignite includes the lignite power plants Boxberg, Jänschwalde and Schwarze Pumpe and the corresponding mining activities Jänschwalde, Nochten, Reichwalde, Welzow-Süd and Cottbus-Nord as well as block R of the lignite power plant Lippendorf.

Hydro includes ten hydro power plants in Thuringia, Saxony and Saxony-Anhalt (seven pumped-storage and three run-of-river power plants). In the financial year 2014, Lignite and Hydro generated revenues of approximately EUR 2.3 billion and EUR 0.2 billion, respectively. The transaction perimeter also includes other assets such as gas-fired assets and real estate assets.

Interested parties are requested to contact the individual stated below and register their interest by email by no later than Tuesday 6 October 2015, 12:00 noon (Berlin Time) in order to receive further information on the process for the potential acquisition of the Seller's lignite and hydro activities (the "Process").

The Seller reserves the right to amend the Process and/or to amend the scope of the Transaction and/or to discontinue the Process.

Contact Person
Nicholas Blach-Petersen
Director
Citigroup Global Markets Limited
Power & Utilities Investment Banking
Tel.: +44 20 7986 5884
E-Mail: Vattenfall.GermanLignite@citi.com

VATTENFALL

Figure 5.3a Invitation to submit interest in hydro and lignite

The takeover bid put forth by Greenpeace was rejected by Vattenfall, who questioned its seriousness and responsibility to the workers and their families dependent on the income from the business. The Czech utility company ČEZ, the German energy company Steag, the Australian investment fund Macquarie and the Czech mining company Vršanská uhelná were among others showing a supposedly more serious interest. In the end, it was the Czech investor company EPH, together with a private equity group, that bought Vattenfall's German operations in 2016, making Vattenfall once again one of the greenest

Nicholas Blach-Petersen
Director
Citigroup Global Markets Limited
Power & Utilities Investment Banking
E-Mail: Vattenfall.GermanLignite@citi.com

October 6, 2015

Letter of interest

Dear Mr Blach-Petersen,

Greenpeace hereby wish to express our interest to acquire the German lignite
business that Vattenfall is planning to divest, as outlined in the document
"Vattenfall AB: Sale of Vattenfall's German lignite and hydro activities".
Please send us further information on the process for the potential acquisition of the
Seller's lignite and hydro activities. Naturally, we will respect the need for
confidentiality and non-disclosure as appropriate.

Yours Sincerely,

Patrik Eriksson   Annika Jacobson
Greenpeace Nordic   Greenpeace Sweden

Njalsgade 21G, 2.sal 64,	Stora Robertsgatan 20-22 A	PB 6803, St Olavspl 1	Rosenlundsgatan 29B, Box 151
2300 København S	00171 Helsinki	0130 Oslo	104 65 Stockholm
Tlf 33 93 53 44	Puh 09-698 63 17	tlf 22 20 83 79	Tel 08-702 70 70
www.greenpeace.dk	www.greenpeace.fi	www.greenpeace.no	www.greenpeace.se
info.dk@greenpeace.org	info.fi@greenpeace.org	info.no@greenpeace.org	info.se@greenpeace.org

Figure 5.3b Response from Greenpeace

utilities in Europe (Sennero and Lopatka 2016). Financially, however,
this cost Vattenfall dearly, as the company had to pay an additional
1.5 billion euros to close the deal, and LMMG (Lausitz Mongolia
Mining Generation), who were excluded from the bidding process,
submitted a complaint of discrimination and lack of transparency to
the European Commission (Zachrisson Winberg 2016).

With Germany's Energiewende – its energy transition policy – in full
swing, the German market situation consequently changed radically,

with subsidies now fully focussed on renewables. It thus made strategic sense for Vattenfall to refocus their business operations. Yet internal and political pressures certainly played a significant role in Vattenfall's strategic U-turn. It seemed increasingly difficult for the company to continue with its double-tongued internal and external communications. It had to make a strategic commitment to decarbonise, for example by the investment in the construction of DanTysk, an offshore wind farm in the North Sea, complemented by another large investment, Sandbank. Together these two wind farms were designed to deliver electricity equivalent to the annual consumption of 400,000 households (Vattenfall 2019a).

Vattenfall's strategic U-turn, away from coal and towards renewables, was helped by the company acquiring the Dutch energy utility company Nuon for 10.3 billion euros in 2009. With this deal, Vattenfall took over large wind power development projects in the UK, but in the process it almost drowned itself in debt. Vattenfall's employees have since had to experience repeated organisational turmoil and regular announcements that the company needs to reduce its workforce, mainly at its headquarters in Solna, Sweden. Nevertheless, the turmoil did eventually settle with a decisive shift towards a market focus on renewables in 2016. New investments were made in the UK, where Vattenfall became the second largest generator of offshore wind power, which secured some positive cash flow within the otherwise bleeding organisation. This commitment to renewables nevertheless required repeated heavy investments and, as is often the case, resulted in clashing organisational cultures due to new encounters with joint venture partners. However, the U-turn and strategic investment in the UK, at that time politically favourable for large-scale offshore wind power, secured Vattenfall's market position within renewables, gave positive economic results (Vattenfall 2019b) and made it possible to speak anew about decarbonisation in terms of 'fossil free living within one generation' (Vattenfall 2020) aided by a 'roadmap to fossil freedom' (Vattenfall 2021a). In 2020, Vattenfall also made a clear statement on the intertwinement of economic results and sustainability, as these aspects are more clearly co-reported in the annual report titled 'Annual and Sustainability Report, Progress for the Climate – It Happens Now' (Vattenfall 2021b). Conclusively, the organisation has also gone through a major transformation with a clear shift in focus on their human resources, raising more complex questions about whom they should recruit, and why, in response to the increased pressure posed by the citizen, and employee, as a potential activist.

5.2 Working at Vattenfall

What is it like to be employed by a heavily criticised carbon-emitting company where your work practices are shaped on the battleground of various sustainability quests – personal, political and corporate? At the end of 2007, the 'Vattenfall song' was launched on YouTube (Vattenfall 2007a), perhaps as a response to a media storm of complaints in Germany, but mainly used by Vattenfall internally. A corporate anthem can, after all, spur togetherness as well as build bridges. The song and video feature Vattenfall employee-workers in uniform yellow T-shirts and helmets, singing, dancing, jumping and playing air guitar in between film clips of white smoking chimneys, wind power plants, nuclear power plants and board members (mainly employee-managers) who were laughing and 'digging' the music. The lyrics begin by poetically stating that Vattenfall is:

> A European source of energy,
> We are Vattenfall and we are proud to be,
> A leading company, empowering society,
> Deliver, good heat and good electricity.

In this song, the workforce is shaped into a collective force, pictured as being filled with pride for enriching society. Their pride is emphasised by the portrayal of mutual enjoyment, as the camera only focusses on happy and satisfied employees, including members of the board of directors laughing and digging. The lyrics go on to list the different activities of the corporation, from hydro and nuclear power to wind power and research projects, ending with 'that's our accountability'. This is later followed by a competitive note: 'It doesn't matter if it's sun or rain, we're active all along the value chain, It improves our effectiveness, A benchmark for success', followed by the refrain 'deliver good heat and good electricity', as well as an accentuation of the collective force by more group dancing and close-ups on smiling faces.

In addition to the business reasons for making Vattenfall into a prosperous and secure employer, the lyrics emphasise how the collective (work) force is connected to personal political objectives and individual action through the giving of 'voice':

> It's openness when we communicate,
> In every person there is something great,
> Take part now and give your voice,
> To make us the employer of choice.
> We're working hard and we are having fun,
> Our goal is always to be number one,
> For customers, society, and environmentally.

Combined with a democratic agenda of sharing one's voice, the employees are thus further assumed to have needs other than those of a purely economic nature. The purposefulness offered is consequently an outspoken bridging between business, society and the environment, where the three are brought together into a unified goal of merging both hard and fun work, as well as market success and moral success. The enthusiasm for the employee and for the seemingly amazingly transparent work environment is to result in an extended enthusiasm, reaching that which is 'external' to the organisation. The strategic communication embedded in the song works actively with these boundaries, since the problem is, for many companies, that these boundaries can hardly be considered to be embodied by any employee. Employees cross organisational boundaries every day, going from diverse family constellations to work 'organisations', perhaps via public transportation, another sort of 'organisation'. These 'organisations' are evidently nothing like separate units with their own minds and agencies, even if such a reality sometimes is spoken into being. They can aso be seen as made up by how the Vattenfall employees engage and mobilise themselves, as 'a person' , which even the Vattenfall song asserts.

Importantly, in comparison with the internally communicated image created in the music video and Vattenfall song, we experienced both support and critique of Vattenfall's environmental engagement in the six offices that we visited for ethnographic encounters (four in the UK and two in Sweden) (also see Skoglund and Böhm 2016). We were frequently told that Vattenfall appreciates employees who work autonomously, take their own decisions and come up with creative and, it is hoped, functioning solutions. This capacity is needed due to the different circumstances in the various countries, projects and joint ventures. As one ocean analyst in the London office emphasised, no one is 'hovering' above you to control what you are doing, as in other companies, but there is trust among colleagues. Another employee spoke about how surprised he was when first starting in the London open office. There was no overt yelling and disagreement, as he had experienced previously in UK business culture. For him, the atmosphere was grounded in the Swedish consensus style of communicating, which created work conditions, which he compared to experiences of being in a library.

5.3 Working at Vattenfall Wind

The policy context, to which Vattenfall has had to adjust in tandem with their lobbying activities to steer policy paths, naturally takes different shapes in the various countries where Vattenfall operates. A project manager in wind power development thus has their professional responsibility highly influenced by political decisions, future policy scenarios and sudden changes in political rule. Nevertheless, the actual work tasks during wind development projects follow a quite standardised process. A wind power development project manager will, in the planning phase, commonly make sure that the experts keep to the budget and time frame. A so-called environmental house, a company that focusses on producing environmental impact assessments, will provide the necessary experts: an ornithologist, ecologist, peat slide risk assessor and acoustic specialist. These experts are normally not Vattenfall employees but will do the surveys and then write a report under the supervision of a Vattenfall project manager. The report is later used for all the permissions needed, which is a difficult task for onshore wind in comparison with offshore, where there is less involvement of both landowners and local councils.

There are also internal expert environmental managers at Vattenfall who work more directly with environmental surveys and licence conditions for contractors to reduce the expenses that arise with external environmental consultants. Their main responsibility is to assess and control the waste management plans for the sites, making sure that the vessels of the contractors comply with the stipulated conditions. There are, in addition, various method statements that have to be in place for later communication back to the governmental agencies that approve Vattenfall's licences. Sometimes licence conditions also need to be challenged in the planning phase, as in the case of updated legislation. When Vattenfall made environmental management an internal organisational responsibility, the projects became much more aligned not only with issues of carbon reduction but also with broader environmental problems, such as oil spills. When the responsibility rests on the individual employee, instead of being sorted out contractually with an external consultant, the environmental scope may take more personalised routes. The employee is after all thinking, and sometimes too much:

I thought that offshore wind was a good industry to get in to, and I was a bit surprised really that environmental management wasn't as important as what I thought it would be, considering that it's [offshore wind] being done to protect the environment. [...] But again, it's something that the guys in Sweden have really pushed so it's increasing a bit now. [...] I'd love to get more involved in our travel and I'm trying to get more involved in waste management and things but CO_2 would be, well trying to see how much fuel we use and things like that. [...] I think with environmental [issues] you have to push it a bit more and I definitely have to push it on to our contractors more as well. (2014, Environmental and Contents Manager)

Work with environmental surveys and reports is mainly considered to lead to expenses, where the licences and permissions are often approved after complementing surveys have been performed and more money has had to be spent. Environmental NGOs are also involved and invited to comment on the Vattenfall reports. In the UK, for example, the Royal Society for the Protection of Birds (RSPB) and the Marine Management Organisation (MMO, a non-departmental public body) often pose objections that are hard for the project managers to oppose. Even though Vattenfall employees express a strong belief that the environmental assessment they have produced via experts is more correct, they lack resources to constantly battle with, and respond to, the NGOs. The NGOs are instead taken very seriously, also due to their authoritative articulations on environmental topics that obviously are not the core competence of the Vattenfall employee and project manager, who is mainly in control of technical knowledge.

Technically, the project manager has internal support from colleagues who work with the grid, aviation, wind resources and Geographic Information System (GIS). An internal quality manager is in control of all the different components that are being fabricated across

Europe, with inspection and factory tests before assembly and erection at the site, and the main task for the project manager is to be an intermediary between different solicitors, to translate the juridical aspects into more realistic hands-on practicalities to be negotiated and implemented on the ground. The project managers are thus juggling with multiple knowledge perspectives as well as content, and they become professional mobilisers of knowledge, knowledge that spans organisational boundaries.

Except for an internal controller and general economic assistance during the project planning, major economic calculations are performed before the actual investment. These calculations are continuously updated depending on subsidies and fluctuating market prices. An employee with both technical and financial expertise will calculate the 'levelised' energy costs, which means that Vattenfall calculate how much money they will spend on building an asset, and how much money they are going to spend to maintain and operate it during its total lifetime. Then the calculation continues by dividing these expenses by the number of hours' power that can be sold from it. This exercise means that Vattenfall will be able to anticipate how much it costs to produce one megawatt hour of electricity, which can then be compared with the selling price. The difference between these figures, the expense and the income, provides the information for the projected profit.

As these financial calculations were explained to us, we were also told that it is very expensive to build offshore wind power parks due to the number of cables needed to export the power from the site at sea to the connection point onshore. Another added cost in comparison with land-based wind power is the required digging into the sea bottom for the foundations. As a result, the maintenance costs rise, and as we were repeatedly told, without subsidies, it would not be such a strong business case. At the time of these conversations with the UK employees, the subsidies had been decided by the government in alignment with EU targets and promises to Brussels. As a Vattenfall financial expert explained, since 'subsidies are the money the UK government is giving us [Vattenfall], it could always be discussed whether this is the best way of using the government's money. It could instead go to homeless people and they wouldn't need to be homeless any more' (2014, Senior Commercial Manager). Another, even more senior, manager adds provocatively that it is questionable how much of the UK subsidies should actually be pumped into the

Swedish economy via the profits made in the UK. Even when Vatten-fall produced negative financial results, the UK wind operations were suggested to be one of the strongest revenue streams, now securing both the green reputation and incomes with respect to the Swedish citizens as owners and taxpayers.

One of the quality managers, who has worked on large-scale off-shore projects together with many European nationalities, illustrated further the cultural complexity at play related to renewables as cash-cow. He clarified that the environmental engagement tasks faced by the employees also differ between the onshore and offshore wind projects. If you work with onshore wind, which has been around for longer, you will meet more 'greeny persons from the early days' (2014, Quality Manager). In offshore wind, however, the engineers have a different background. They often come from huge construction projects, some-times with experience from the oil and gas industry, which is consid-ered to be in the same offshore industry. Since it is their professional and technical experience that is mainly required, they have

no particular allegiance to being in a low carbon business, they are just there because they see it as an opportunity of a growth business to be in and they could quite happily switch back to working in oil or gas or nuclear engi-neering or coal [...] it's not the same as in onshore wind where people are often really motivated by doing something really good for the world. (2014, Quality Manager)

Another employee, however, added that engineers in offshore who are experienced technically really appreciate the work of the envi-ronmental managers, since they have seen with their own eyes how damaging offshore constructions can be to nature. The engineers and technical experts are thus prone to listen to the internal envi-ronmental expert, who is also considered to be better at creating compromises than external experts. One environmental manager, for example, was asked to change a condition in one of the evaluations so that the construction could start and electricity could be delivered as soon as possible. She refused, however, and was listened to, by both engineers and other managers. From her expressed experience, we can learn another important difference between using external environmental consultants and using internal employees who are able to take various perspectives and create a balance between envi-ronmental realities and economic priorities:

[T]here was one time there was like a spawning season for a species and it was going over 2 months and the construction team said that's when we want to construct and you need to remove that condition and I just held my ground because I said that I don't want to challenge that because there's a reason that's in place. [... And] when I do raise concerns I think they usually are listened to because I don't raise that many. I think if I was constantly, which I think is a problem with environmental consultants, they maybe are too vocal about everything so then you forget what are the most important bits that you are trying to protect really. (2014, Environmental and Contents Manager)

5.4 Working beyond Environmental Management

In our interviews with several environmental managers at Vattenfall, both positive and negative experiences of the corporation cropped up. One manager who works in offshore environmental management mainly spends time on writing environmental assessments and negotiating with various stakeholders regarding specific environmental issues. The desire is to be in control of potential environmental impacts in the construction and maintenance of wind power parks at sea, which is why the work includes impacts on fishermen. This means that the environmental managers have to integrate social aspects into their daily work, and during the planning phase, this mainly means being onshore to communicate with locals. The mission is to explain what Vattenfall are planning to do, to nurture general public involvement and thereby, it is hoped, come up with solutions that are initiated bottom-up, by the future users of the areas that will be affected the most by the wind power park. The locals need to have an understanding of why certain actions are necessary, for instance, the laying of the main connection cable in an area where they are used to fishing, or where some locals may live. At first, the locals are often afraid of change, but with time and correct 'management' we were told that many are eventually convinced that the offshore projects can have a positive impact, in the present as well as in the long run. To accomplish this consent, it is thus key for the environmental and so-called consent managers to engage early and be transparent with both local authorities and local citizens:

They just say how we are ruining their livelihoods, impacting everything, but the only thing is that we haven't got any evidence that we are ruining their livelihoods and we do pay them [the fishermen] compensation for the periods that they can't work. So it's a tricky one. I think it just needs to be well managed. I think that's the problem, there have maybe been other developers who haven't been maybe as open in communication with them but I think we're, Vattenfall are really good. We let them know everything that's going on ahead of schedule so they have time to plan. So I think we are just trying everything we can to make sure it's ok for them. (2014, Environmental Manager)

The main reason for being open and transparent is to gain trust, 'because you are never going to be trusted at the first meeting, you are just another big developer coming in' (2014, Senior Development Manager). It is, therefore, an advantage for the company to become as local as possible, for example by enrolling employees who originate from that geographic area and who speak the dialect, which has proven especially important for approaching the local population in the north of Sweden. Another way that Vattenfall communicates is by finding ways of allowing the locals to understand the process better, for example by bringing acoustic specialists, as well as engineers who design the cables, with them to public information meetings. They can then reply to potential worries about the health effects of sound waves and magnetic charges face to face. The knowledge exchange also works the other way around: as the locals are understood to hold important information about the human and biospheric life in the area, Vattenfall feeds this into their process. They can, for example, be asked to hand in reports of raptors, bats and golden eagles. As several employees testify, Vattenfall is, in comparison with other utility companies, more inclined to work closely with locals, to get them on board and included via co-production of knowledge in the planning process. Nevertheless, it was repeatedly suggested that, at the end of the day, this extra effort of bridging between the domains of business and society is the workings of capitalism:

We have to avoid impacts and reduce impacts as much as we can. There is so few companies that will choose to be green unless they have to be. Making money drives them. We are in a capitalist society where money drives everything. I am lucky that I work in an industry where I can make money for the company and stick with my values. (2015, Consent Manager)

This emphasis on personal values is taken to the next level of collective values by another environmental manager who tells us that, in comparison with his previous employer, Vattenfall is better at fulfilling their promises to locals. At Pen y Cymoedd in Wales, Vattenfall has, for example, constructed a mountain bike track as part of a community benefit. These things are important for local governments, too, as some of them wish to push community ownership. Vattenfall is taking that on board and looking at ways of creating win–win situations: 'It's commercial, but obviously on the flip side they are not just doing it for themselves, it's a way of looking at how we can meet our internal targets as well as helping the government hit their targets' (2014, Senior Development Manager). The Scottish government did, for example, support a highly contentious Vattenfall wind power project in Aberdeen. The government saw it as an economic as much as an environmental investment for the region, while the opposition considered it aesthetically polluting to the view of a golf course. The strong opposition, fuelled by Donald Trump, delayed the project for several years and made it an expensive affair for all involved. It was opposed in court three times before finally being approved:

[T]here's a lot of up-front consultation, about 2 years of consultation before you get consent for a project. We did have an Aberdeen project that was, I don't know if you heard about that with [the opposition from] Donald Trump, that's probably the most contested project that we've had offshore. (2014, Environmental and Contents Manager)

There are also well-organised local and national anti-wind campaign groups, such as the Country Guardian (2018) and the National Opposition to Windfarms (2018), both based in the UK, as well as the organisation for landscape protection (FSL 2018), based in Sweden. These are harder to manage and convince than the local authorities and citizens, as these groups have an *a priori* opposition to wind power, considering wind turbines aesthetically polluting. After meeting these resisting groups during visits to potential wind power sites, the Vattenfall employees often need to debrief each other. There is no specific internal support from human resources (HR), or other training, to handle the often strong counteractions taken by such groups. The employees are instead left to their own personal devotion to wind, which is one of the qualities investigated during recruitment, both in the UK and in Sweden. Being personally engaged in and convinced about the green value of wind power is assumed to be the only successful way in which you can muster enough mental power for the hardships of the job:

I guess I never feel threatened but sometimes I do feel like I'm being, like maybe I'm taking the brunt of it for the whole project, or for the whole of offshore wind farming in the UK, yes, they can get quite angry but it's never aggressive, I think I've heard worse from other industries, like maybe in Sweden. (2014, Environmental Manager)

It is an explicit strategy to recruit not only those with technical competence and managerial skills but also those with personal devotion. This can be seen in the Vattenfall leadership by looking at Piers Guy, who has extensive experience in responding to anti-wind power groups. Piers Guy was an early adopter of wind power on his own farm in South England and later became an influential manager of Vattenfall's offshore wind power operations. In the early days, he handpicked his employees for their passion for wind power, many of whom still work for Vattenfall today. His vanguard implementation of wind power and struggles with anti-wind power campaign groups can be seen in the documentary made by Spanning Films, released in 2009 (Spanning Films 2009).

   In comparison with managing consent in the UK, we also experienced first-hand how Vattenfall carefully crafts consent in Sweden. At a public information meeting in a small village in south Sweden, inhabitants in the area were either farmer families who had been living there for generations or summer house owners, Swedish as well as Danish. The information meeting took place in the community hall,[1] an old wooden house painted in the typical Swedish Falu red colour and with white frames. The meeting was held in the assembly hall, where events needing a stage were normally held. In the mini-kitchen, coffee and a home-made cheesecake were prepared, which would be used to extend the formal meeting with an informal discussion. Vattenfall had employed for the meeting a moderator who was theoretically and practically educated in methods of deliberative democracy and citizen dialogue. She had asked Vattenfall to place the chairs in

---

[1] Community hall is a translation from 'bygdegård', which can be better understood as a local venue. The notion of community, furthermore, does not exist in a direct translation to Swedish, since it denotes a regional office in Sweden, i.e. 'kommun'.

the hall in a wide circle, where all the participants from the area could be seated. Looking across the room, there was a whole range of ages present, for example, a grandmother with her grandson.

The meeting started with an introduction from the Vattenfall project leader, a woman in her thirties with young children at home. She described the history of the planning process of the wind power park, emphasising that there have been numerous project leaders involved from Vattenfall, and problems with the retention of project managers, adding that she would try to do her best to follow up on the previous work in a good way and stay devoted to the project and mission. She was also transparent about the fact that she was well aware of the local resistance to wind power in the area and expected to pick up on the counteractions that her previous colleagues had to endure. Residents had already sent her letters, she continued, stating that they were particularly worried about sound waves related to health issues. She thus had decided to bring with her an acoustic consultant with expertise in wind power park vibrations and sound waves.

After the sound expert and the other consultants involved in the planning process had presented their work on the development to the audience, a discussion, led by the moderator, unfolded rapidly. The dramaturgy of the moderator intensified the rhythm. She positioned herself in the middle of the circle of chairs, starting off in an energetic, almost explosive, way by asking a few provocative questions with a challenging tone, to get the debate going. There was little need for her to force a debate, however. One after the other, people raised their hands, expressing their strong dislike of the plans and the project. It soon became evident that the only one who would really benefit from the development was the landowner, while those living at the perimeter of the planned wind power park would be disturbed by the turbines. Those who expressed the strongest dislike were the Danish summer house owners. They argued that the reason they had invested in a house in Sweden in the first place was the unpolluted landscape and beautiful lack of wind power. Denmark and its countryside, meanwhile, were according to them full of aesthetically polluting wind power turbines. Now they wished to protect the picturesque and billowy Swedish landscape and their private investments, non-polluted by the 'tall machines'.

The moderator tried to make sure that everyone who wished to could express their criticism, and she meticulously collected these opinions while trying to keep the most agitated participants calm. If someone got too upset and disturbing, she walked up close to them and tried to meet their complaints by slightly leaning over them. She was mobile and standing, while they were immobile and seated. She demonstrated her courage firmly, showing with her whole body that she was not afraid of their verbal attacks, and she ended each argumentation by affirming the general right to think differently, especially here in the seated ring of deliberation.

5.5 Personal Politics and Passion at Work

During the five-year-long Vattenfall research project, we found very few common historical denominators among the employees who acted out their environmental engagement at work. They all seemed to have been inspired by different sources and heterogeneous backgrounds. The expected stereotype would perhaps be the young employee educated in an environmentally aware family setting. One of the environmental managers, indeed, told us that she had become interested in environmental problems already as a teenager, inspired by her closest family. At home, they always recycled and grew their own vegetables, and she subsequently worked actively for Greenpeace. Since then, she has joined other sustainability organisations and tells us that she takes pride 'in the fact that it [her work] contributes to a wider good' and that, in the end, it is about producing clean and sustainable technology. A general green interest can also be observed among the Vattenfall employees in how they express passion, both regarding their jobs in general and about their specific projects. Often, they do not consider a project to be Vattenfall's project but see it as 'their own project'. It was pointed out to us that their personal engagement is key to success in a project's development phase, particularly when various stakeholders and people who oppose developments need to be convinced of their benefits:

I found it interesting because I thought that environmental management is something that's going to, that sort of affects people, I've always wanted to have a job where I'm having to work with people all the time and the project I did in my degree was like in Africa, building like fish farming things for communities there and you could see like that depended on the marine resources. (2014, Environmental Manager)

Another environmental manager illustrated how she was previously engaged in an NGO that initiated marine research. She helped out as a volunteer on Saturdays, doing fishery surveys that contributed to a bigger research project that aimed to inform where protected areas should be created in the UK. It also included beach clean-ups, something that she has taken into Vattenfall UK as a collective, voluntary endeavour among colleagues across the organisation. This exemplifies a more conventional activist position, which is also embraced by a colleague in another office who has been active in the Transition Town movement. Before he became a senior manager at Vattenfall he worked actively for 'his town' for two years, which included the organisation of film screenings, support of a local market and planning for the introduction of a local currency called the 'green pound':

We've had this culture of just grab the money here in the UK in the 80s and 90s after Margaret Thatcher and everything, and I think with this recession now, right across Europe people are reassessing now their life values and I think we are going back a little bit now to more of a community and care for a communal view rather than just for the individual which is where we were for a while. (2014, Quality Manager)

In his case, however, very little of the expressed community experience has been translated into his current work practices within Vattenfall, although community thinking is suggested to play a larger role in general. Others at Vattenfall who are equally devoted to decarbonisation explain why it may be a problem to disrupt the boundaries between the business as an organisation and civil society movements:

We've got good relationships with a lot of these bodies but in some instances we'll all go on the other side with them like RSPB for example, obviously I love birds, I've done wildlife and things but I wouldn't join RSPB because you wouldn't know when I'm going to be one side of a table arguing for a wind farm and they're going to be on the other side objecting and I just don't want, not that it would matter but that membership as such. I like to read what they are saying and take it on board but I've not joined any. (2014, Senior Development Manager)

Significant for the green engagement among the employees is also their level of education or hobby expertise on sustainability. A senior manager described how he was inspired by an interest in landscapes, outdoor life and hunting. As a father, he became a mature student in the field of environmental management, which was the university degree most closely related to his interest in wildlife that he could find. In a different way, another employee mentioned that it was not until he became a father at a late age that he started to reassess the world and think about the future differently. He then started to read up on sustainability on his own and discovered various topics related to sustainability. He nurtured a private interest in issues such as population growth and the peak oil argument, which has driven him to work for a transition of the energy system ever since. Another more senior employee also emphasised that among his colleagues who are interested in climate change and the reduction of carbon emissions, most are highly educated on the topic, suggesting that 'gone are the days that it's all tree huggers and hippies that run about' (2014, Senior Development Manager). In one of the smaller offices in the UK, less derogatory terms were, however, used to describe the 'hippie' times that they feel are long gone.

Far from the hippie position are also expressions that affirm energy if it is produced in the correct way. Instead of thinking that the historical and current use of energy is negative, one employee suggested that we should embrace how much energy helps us in our daily lives and how it facilitates logistics, movement and life in general, from getting to work to cooking and heating our homes. With this sense of progress in mind, he even clarified that 'we should maximise using it as much as possible if we can produce it in an environmentally friendly way' (2014, Senior Commercial Manager). In comparison to how other employees saw this position as connected to modernity and dangerous growth ideals, this employee is driven by how renewble energy supports a new vision of progress, much aligned with what Vattenfall has expressed at a corporate level.

Others considered the difficulties of going through a transition, referring to the German way as 'brave' but inevitably problematic (2014, Quality Manager) and proposing that more governmental regulations are needed if environmental compliance from Vattenfall is to be truly accomplished. There is also a policy and lobby unit internally at Vattenfall, mainly consisting of communication experts and more senior staff, who are schooled in political processes. To support this lobbying activity, Vattenfall has also added younger colleagues with experience of the hardships of field work in wind power development projects. And, in addition to the normal corporate political activities undertaken by this group, collaboration with Renewables UK and other trade representative bodies has been emphasised to create a common voice for the industry. These do, for example, produce press releases informed by Vattenfall's communication people, showing that there are some types of stealth movement, where the industry comes together to have a combined voice against what they conceive to be a powerful anti-wind or anti-renewables lobby.

5.6 Epistemic Community and Employee Activism

Vattenfall's efforts to become greener, and to be seen as greener, have been influenced by a mix of trends, be they technical, political or communicative. When we look back at Vattenfall's internal and external communications – the TV commercial with desperately swimming polar bears, the climate manifesto, yellow plastic toddler toys and the Vattenfall song – the corporation at that time comes across as confused. However, imagine how it must have been to produce the Vattenfall corporate anthem. A high level of consent to being filmed and screened must have existed. In other words, it would be very hard to find employees – workers and managers – who would happily dance and sing along, smiling energetically, if they were not convinced about the green agenda of their employer and themselves. There is, in other words, no sign of cynicism that we can observe on the surface, but seemingly an expression of co-productive playfulness, togetherness and enrichment. The dancers and singers are not musical artists; they are just willing to make Vattenfall, themselves and the world greener.

However, as illustrated previously, the employees reacted, some of them quite strongly, to their experiences of a gap between the corporate communication efforts and the actual operations. This sort of discrepancy has been discussed at length in organisation and critical management studies, for example in relation to branding and stakeholder management, as briefly outlined in Chapter 1 on boundaryless activism. It is also a gap commonly addressed in the literature on sustainability and HRM, but an aspect that is largely overlooked by most companies that engage in sustainability (Ehnert, Wes and Zink 2013). The reason for the prevalent disconnect between strategic corporate visions on sustainability and everyday HRM is the clashing time and location categories between these two, sustainability and human resources. Corporations such as Vattenfall, with a strong focus on the green environmental element in sustainability, emphasise the far future and long-term thinking regarding their (polluting) impacts on an external reality, with effects on society and economy. HRM, however, focusses on health and safety in the present reality of the internal work environment, the social aspects of a specific location and employee experience of a 'here and now'. These two, green sustainability and the social work environment, were merged in the Vattenfall song but, according to Vattenfall employees with whom we conversed, often unsuccessfully so.

How the workforce experiences environmental and sustainable management is one of the main topics in Green HRM (Renwick 2018), a field that complements green mainstream management literatures, such as green marketing, green accounting and green retailing, by exploring how employees are more satisfied at work if their personal wishes comply with those of the organisation (Renwick, Redman and Maguire 2013). This was also expressed by many of our research participants who confirmed that a mix of job security and an outlet for their personal environmental engagement and extensive professional environmental knowledge made them feel satisfied at work. The merger of an economic rationale with a green politics is not expressed as a major struggle for the employees who work in the area of renewable energy, some were explicitly 'pro' progress, and others mentioned that economic growth needs to be fought and capitalism transformed.

Other, more visible 'epistemic struggles' were enacted in meetings between employees within the various units at Vattenfall (cf. Icaza and Vázquez 2013). Here, the struggles refer to strongly differing opinions about the energy resources exploited, from nuclear to lignite, and from wind to hydropower (Skoglund and Böhm 2016). Consequently, we can see how an epistemic community is shaped at the Vattenfall wind units by the way in which renewables are spoken about on a daily basis and verbally constructed in clashes with other knowledge formations and concerns. As we learnt during the ethnographic shadowing sessions, it is an epistemic community within which the employees define themselves and their position in relation to other Vattenfall units, and in relation to their meetings with the general public, family and friends (Skoglund and Böhm 2016). Hence, the epistemic community is formed around a collectivity or movement of employees who acknowledge, negotiate and share knowledge about environmental degradation and climate change, and their hands-on actions with renewable solutions in the office and beyond. Many are explicitly interested in stretching their professional actions outwards and therefore enhancing a wider relationality beyond the daily work in the office. The personal is inextricably linked to the professional (Kanter 1977), and *Gemeinschaft* to *Gesellschaft* (Tönnies 1957/2002). To use these often polarised categories analytically when looking at our empirics is thus increasingly untenable, and it becomes obvious that it is a dated theoretical separation. At the same time, perhaps there is still some sort of presence of both individual 'personal' action and other-than-economic togetherness and generous relationality (*Gemeinschaft*) that we can note.

Only occasionally do the wind power employees meet like-minded colleagues across the units, which makes the internal environmental movement primarily quiet and covert, with a few attempts at taking overt collective actions that are also supported by Vattenfall's official CSR agenda or environmental management approach. Normally when employee activism is played out within a larger corporation, it exemplifies a minority politics (Creed and Scully 2000, Scully and Segal 2002), but in the case of Vattenfall, this looks a bit different. Even though positioned as underdogs (Jacques 2006), a green personal politics is not coupled with a specific minority subjectivity, but rather with a dispersed global knowledge movement (cf. Taro Lennerfors 2013), which is why Vattenfall's 'tempered radicals' engage in struggle differently in comparison with political minorities (cf. Meyerson and Scully 1995). The Vattenfall employees ponder their position inside and outside the organisation and mobilise boundaries for various reasons (Langley et al. 2019), some exemplifying a wish to erect organisational boundaries, and others working in the opposite direction. A common denominator is nevertheless their expression of devotion to the knowledge movement on climate change, including devotion to their mutual co-production of possibilities of taking action at work, and thereby accomplish the energy transition in an environmentally friendly way together. In comparison with tempered radicals, their everyday jobs and practices are already geared towards collective transformative actions. These employees who work with wind power, environmental management, or consent and public deliberation processes do so because they think a transformation can be speeded up via their profession and employer. Importantly, though, they all express that the amount and speed of actions are unsatisfactory – they want to accomplish even more, and faster.

One would have thought that a company such as Vattenfall would make use, through some Green HRM practices, of the green enthusiasm displayed by some of their employees. Green HRM emphasises how employees can be spurred on to become greener beyond the organisation for which they work (Renwick 2018). In this literature, it is not only of interest how an already environmentally engaged employee, or activist, enters the workplace to change the employer. What is also of interest is that the employer is assumed to be able to foster more environmentally friendly behaviours by adopting Green HRM principles. It was notable, however, that this did not happen at Vattenfall in any formal way via HR. Instead, a much looser incorporation of 'the citizen' emerged (cf. Nyberg, Spicer and Wrigth 2013), horizontally within Vattenfall, which was underpinned by a general regulation of the citizen, by extension supportive of Vattenfall's wind business. The circle of deliberation created by an external consultant and moderator in the community hall, is but one practical example of how citizens can be trained in democratic consensus processes at the same time as a corporation facilitates its business. Additionally, employees can stimulate 'ecological citizenship', through their wish to identify as green both internally and externally to the corporation (cf. Crane, Matten and Moon 2008a:151), but without any notable top-down influence.

In comparison with Vattenfall at the time for our study, companies have, at least since the beginning of the twenty-first century, started to shift their CSR activities to be more inclusive of the environment (Kao 2010), emphasising the employee as a stakeholder of both the corporation and the biosphere (Siegel 2001). This encompasses a more deterritorialised conceptualisation of ecological citizenship in relation to the corporation with an emphasis on horizontal relations (Crane, Matten and Moon 2008a). These are relations between citizens, or in our case, employees, that 'are not allocated a fixed membership of a given community, but continually constitute their community of obligation through their material impacts' (Crane, Matten and Moon 2008a:158). To avoid simplification, and in contrast to studies that commonly homogenise employees as an internal stakeholder group, studies that merge HRM and CSR have furthermore been attentive to divergent values among employees (Hejjas, Miller and Scarles 2018). The merger between HRM and CSR thus affords a more long-term perspective on employer branding, that is, attracting and keeping current and future employees with an interest in sustainability and the green environment (Kryger Aggerholm, Esmann Andersen and Thomsen 2010). Perhaps such systematic management of a green personal political agenda is largely underdeveloped at Vattenfall due to the difficulties in balancing between those who care and the rest. With its approximately 30,000 employees (at the time of the study, and in 2020 down to about 20,000) who work with various energy sources and tasks, this encompasses a range of people from those who are directly or indirectly compliant with environmentally polluting operations, to those present in our study who wish to work unequivocally with decarbonisation.

Tellingly, many of Vattenfall's greening processes are initiated bottom-up, by engaged employees aided by an abstractly defined top-down trust in independent and skilled professionals, sometimes referred to by our research participants as 'the Swedish style of management'. In general, it has also been suggested that organisations are becoming 'flatter' due to employees being more knowledgeable in comparison with their managers (Hejjas, Miller and Scarles 2018). As we have described in detail elsewhere (Skoglund and Böhm 2016), the employees can even take it upon themselves to improve the smallest of things in the office, such as common recycling and energy saving practices, as well as querying the delivery route for the weekly fruit basket in the lunch room, or walking up the stairs instead of using the electrified lift (for both environmental and bodily health reasons). Due to their general knowledge of sustainability, they take on more extensive and ambitious environmental initiatives, reaching beyond formal work responsibilities and instructions by their superiors.

Perplexing in our findings about Vattenfall is that some emphasised the increasing need for green enthusiastic employees as this is a crucial factor for getting renewable projects implemented, and for the corporation to perform well. Others, however, emphasised the lack of top-down managerial interest in the potent green enthusiasm on the office floor. If the former is a strategic interest, the latter experience of neglect is not a proof of strategic disinterest, that is, an intentional top-down creation of slack and facilitation of self-regulation to neo-normatively manage and harness an increasingly complex workforce with diverse passions (Fleming 2009, Fleming and Sturdy 2009). From our experience over the years, it rather reflects a lack of time, and very few outspoken tools for taking soft empowering measures with a focus on the employees as 'resources'. This is rather to happen collegially, and at Vattenfall, there are only two persons who occasionally work with employer branding, and their focus is university students. The other human resources managers we occasionally met, and who are located closer to the wind power development unit, mainly spent time on logistics and formal employment rules and regulations, not soft forms of HRM (e.g. see Townley 1998, Barratt 2001).

The lack of time, and consequently, the neglect of green passions and capacities in the workforce, from managers to assistants, also reflects the dilemma many companies face when green ambitions are suggested to be strategically harnessed via soft forms of HRM. Human resource managers, who often need to spend a lot of time on logistical flows of personnel, from recruitments to retirements, are disconnected from other management units, such as the unit for environmental management. From a sustainable management perspective, Epstein (2008:92) therefore elaborates on how human resource managers should work more closely with managers from other areas of expertise to accomplish more sustainable strategies by sharing knowledge. Knowledge movements across organisational units are considered key, which should help management to align everything in connection with 'green' processes and strategies, which are dispersed in the organisation.

While Green HRM has shown some interest in workplace environmentalism (Renwick 2018), it has been more common for environmental activism to seep into organisations via unions (Hampton 2015) and 'labour activism' (Marens 2013). This 'green-red' alliance between green and labour movements has not always been easy to organise (Räthzel and Uzzell 2011), due to unions often identifying environmentalists as being overtly anti-capitalistic and thereby a general threat to job security (Dewey 1998). A growth of green unionism since the 1990s (Silverman 2006) has nevertheless enforced the idea that the workforce should be put at the centre of climate politics. From a Marxist perspective, the argument is that true transformative change can only happen through engagement by the broad masses, that is, the working class (Hampton 2015). This sort of worker-driven environmental activism, brought either to the international political scene or into business, is consequently something very different to the managerial attempts to instrumentally direct it, as in Green HRM, environmental management and CSR. The reintroduction of the class perspective via labour environmentalism is potentially important, given that a lot of green politics still seems to be mostly enacted by young, highly educated and fairly well-off people (Dolezal 2010). Having said that, this class perspective has been widely criticised for being 'old-school', as it is focussed on macro-political structures, rather than the political realities of the everyday (Scott-Cato and Hillier 2010). What is observable in the case of Vattenfall is how the 'green-red' alliance can no longer identify the employee activist as anti-capitalistic. What it needs to consider is rather the threat of extinction of certain polluting jobs, and efforts of lifelong learning that secures a move into new areas.

In relation to class and hierarchical divisions between employee-workers and employee-managers at Vattenfall, we observed horizontalism explicitly in climate activism and environmentalism. Green actions were taken across the workforce at Vattenfall, undoubtedly aided by how the corporation is steeped in a history of Swedish democratic and consensual management, as many research participants testified. No matter whether it was our interactions with the director of environment, the director of offshore wind power, project managers or coordinators, they all shared the same political agenda: to decarbonise for a better world. Differences naturally occurred in relation to what their roles permitted them to 'see' and thereby criticise and take on within their own units. Neither Green HRM – as well as similar attempts to infuse green bottom-up movements from the top – nor the literature on union environmentalism can account for the movement or epistemic community generated by employees horizontally across Vattenfall, which is seen as a hierarchical organisation. That is, an epistemic community arose as a loose gathering of knowledgeable employees who acted in various contexts, internally or externally, as professional experts and on behalf of their employer and/or on behalf of their collectively formed personal green political agenda. There is, so to speak, a quite smooth overlap between the activist employee as a worker and as part of a broad ecological citizenry. As is visible in our findings, even those cynical about CSR or those unhappy with the corporation's current environmental management would, in a prefigurative sense, take the green actions into their own hands – sometimes at the expense of profits and top-down sanctioned environmental management approaches.

Even though studies have attempted to move away from an all too pessimistic view of employee influence, cynicism and detachment, in order to take corporate employee activism seriously, these have largely neglected how political issues can travel horizontally and permeate otherwise seemingly hierarchical structures (cf. Kokkinidis 2015). Hence, bottom-up resistance present in corporate organisations has been explained as just that – a movement that unfolds explicitly or implicitly against the organisation viewed as a unit or actor that imposes an unfair hierarchy via its managerial levels (Courpasson, Dany and Clegg 2012). Even in studies of 'infra-politics', subordinate groups have thus been assumed to be the key empirical source of knowledge of alternative movements (Scott 1990, 2005). Instead of talking about 'activism' among employees, critical management perspectives have kept their analyses focussed on 'resistance' (Fleming and Spicer 2007), often to explain frictions and struggles but also possibilities for emancipation (Huault, Perret and Spicer 2014). With 'epistemic community' as the analytical focus, it is possible to grasp more horizontal organising and self-organising driven by knowledgeable Vattenfall employees, whatever their hierarchical position may be, and who express a deep concern for environmental problems as well as political problems, for example that 'actions' are needed and can be taken through everyday professional work. Their 'coming together' can find more explanations if looking into studies of prefigurative politics in social movement organisations (Haug 2013, Sutherland, Land and Böhm 2014, Farias 2017), in comparison with studies of CSR (Hemingway and Maclagan 2004, Hemingway 2005). Instead of focussing on 'resistance' in corporations, our extended notion of 'epistemic community', which includes a perspective of blurred boundaries between the 'outside' and 'inside' of organisations, brings forth an emphasis on horizontal movements of decarbonisation that permeate the world of work.

Crane, Matten and Moon (2014) point to a problem that can arise for businesses engaged in CSR strategies, where certain subgroups of people might develop an alternative take on social and environmental issues, while the rest of the organisation is engaged in business as usual. Such dynamics were evident at Vattenfall. In this book, however, we are less interested in tracing such contradictions, which would imply that employee climate activism could become some omnipotent solution to an organisation's bad reputation. Instead, the way in which we wish to trace climate activism as boundaryless, and sometimes enacted from within a corporation, aims at understanding processes that are parallel or, depending on the situation, intertwined with CSR activities (Girschik 2020). Part of our experience of employee activism at Vattenfall was that it developed out of a reaction against how 'the social' or 'the environmental' was occasionally used managerially as a means for CSR or for creating shared value. Even though many of the employees were trying to create shared value according to their own ideas of what that would be, they did not believe that it was unproblematic or an easy task within the corporate context in which they positioned their epistemic struggle. On the contrary, they reflected repeatedly on their own complex relation to their host organisation or employer. It did not prevent the employees to take action, and they accordingly pursued their environmental activism in their own, self-organised way. In self-regulative manners they became part of what we conceptualise as an epistemic community whose explicit aim has been to decarbonise not only Vattenfall but also global society at large. This internal countermovement, in our case, maintained at all levels of the large corporation but by a minority of 'tempered radicals', differs from how a majority of employees sometimes manage to align their activism with the goals of their employer. This latter case is more common when the employee activism is part of the business founding, for example when activists start companies, or when activists are recruited early on, to secure a greener world via new forms of business methods and models, as we will exemplify next in four cases of climate activism via small and medium-sized businesses.

6 | Climate Activism via Small and Medium-Sized Enterprises

Not all businesses that operate within the renewable energy sector are spawned by climate activism, but many are. In this chapter, we will encounter business start-ups founded on a mission to respond to human-induced climate change and the call for action. We will follow the details of how they engage in actions and build a collective movement, mainly consisting of customers and employees. Combined with fears about climate change or other environmental issues, activism is taken to business with attempts to speed up the energy transition, which we outlined in Chapter 1 on boundaryless activism under the heading 'activist entrepreneurs'. Spurred on by the possibility to take individual responsibility via entrepreneurship, novel business opportunities and business models, the activist–business–state conglomeration is glued together by start-ups in the renewable energy sector. Here, company founders, employees, investors, consultants and state authorities embrace the possibility to give 'power to the people', politically as well as technically. These start-ups are often small, and even though some of them become big, this chapter speaks about a bottom-up formation of 'enterprising activism'. In contrast, the notion of 'corporate activism' tends to denote top-down management strategies of established large corporations, for example in their encounters with external activism (Grefe and Linsky 1995).

6.1 Small R. Energy

We are an environmentally led company; there's no doubt about that, that's why I run a business, that's what I try and instil into the team and make sure that's what comes over in waves to our customers, really. Yeah, we do it because we're passionate about it and therefore, you know, that's a core part of our recruitment for our team, that's a part of how we run the day-to-day business; as it's an environmentally led business, we're there to be making the difference. (2017, Bob, pseudonym, Small R. Energy)

Renewable energy encompasses the possibility not only to invest your time, effort and money in innovative technology but also to make a moral investment in yourself as a professional. It consequently attracts people such as Bob who wish to make a difference environmentally by way of running a small business. In Bob's case, he grew up in the middle of nowhere on a farm in South West England, where he and his brother roamed around the outdoors, building dens, climbing trees and fixing stuff in the tractor garage. His farmer-parents taught them about agriculture and natural processes and instilled a sense of ecological pride in them; they were not only interested in farm yields but they also cared about biodiversity and how many butterflies and birds were on their farm. Bob loved welding, fixing, building 'stuff', so he embarked on an engineering degree:

A lot of people on that degree scheme were really sort of passionate about going into road building and so on, but I wasn't really. I was passionate about doing environmentally beneficial work, but there weren't so many opportunities to do ecology work. (2017, Bob, Small R. Energy)

After some volunteering work, he ended up working for the Environment Agency, looking after and protecting the land. He was involved in building and maintaining flood defence systems and securing waterways – but the Agency is a very big, bureaucratic organisation. Despite loving his job, he always had lurking thoughts about setting up his own business, to be able to steer his own efforts according to his own decisions. Bob consequently resigned from his secure and steady job to start his own outfit, Small R. Energy. Initially, he went into sustainable building design, as the UK government at the time had announced an ambitious zero-carbon building programme. Bob saw big opportunities in designing and building zero-carbon or at least low-carbon homes. He successfully built a few houses for clients but then realised there were bigger opportunities in installing renewables, such as wind turbines, solar arrays and biomass boilers. The government had back-pedalled on their original zero-carbon homes commitments, so the sustainability drive was no longer there in the construction industry. Bob reconsidered his business strategy and changed direction; his green ambition went where the money and opportunities were, first to wind and solar installations and later to renewable heat.

To create a stable foundation for the company and establish a team that can help him to make a difference environmentally, Bob purposefully looks to employ people with a similar passion to his. He is clearly in business to help transition the world to a renewable energy future and wants people around him who share this goal. Nevertheless, running a business and using commercial methods to reach green goals requires more than green passion. Sometimes he experiences some ambiguity in recruiting for a cultural fit:

It's not easy to get the right mix of values in the right place; so, the business is sort of split; we have to have a front end, you know, designers, project managers and I think it's easier to recruit them with the right values. And then we've got the back end of the customer facing part of the businesses, people who do the installation work, they have quite a broad range of skills. So, we get a mix in there. [...]people who can do plumbing works, people who can do, you know, various sort of building installation work; their core skill is, you know, getting the job done, getting the job done to the right quality and in essence being able to do a range of building work. So, they're not necessarily environmentally focused. (2017, Bob, Small R. Energy)

This kind of pragmatism is repeated by others too and is common in the renewable energy sector. Yes, as the owner of a renewable energy company, Bob might be in business for environmental reasons, but this does not prevent him from working with people who do not necessarily share all of his values explicitly. As exemplified previously, enterprising activism and employee activism can thus be understood as existing in pockets along the entire value chain of companies, rather than being consistently pursued. According to Bob, these pockets of activism have arisen particularly in South West England, where there are many who work with renewables, across production, distribution and consumption. Bob, who knows many people in these renewable energy start-ups personally, explains that '[t]hey started their business because they're passionate about it [...] I've met them and I've rarely met someone that I could see was in it for the wrong reason' (2017, Bob, Small R. Energy).

Bob is surrounded by like-minded business founders that purposefully use their working time to make an environmental difference. He also mentions that some of his corporate peers and his employees previously engaged in more conventional forms of civil society activism. Now that these environmental activists have grown a bit older, often with a family to support, he suggests that they have perhaps mellowed a bit, as they are inevitably more dependent on an income. They are exposed to certain choices defined by the dominant market system, at the same time as the renewable energy industry is a perfect attractor:

Certainly, two or three of the business owners I know are very keen surfers and have come from that background [...] And I've certainly employed Greenpeace activists. I can remember when one employee was saying during the interview, 'I'll have to let you know that I've got a criminal record' and I said 'okay, it's fine, you know, it depends what the criminal record is for, doesn't it?', and she said it was for [...] basically she got arrested because she chained herself to a particular stack of a power station somewhere [...] And I said 'I suppose, yeah, well, yeah, fair enough', that's a tick in the box, rather than a cross in the box. (2017, Bob, Small R. Energy)

Bob has no problem employing passionate people who have taken environmental actions to the extent where they have committed a criminal offence and sees it as positive. He even clarifies that it would not have been a big problem for him if the street-type environmental activism was still part of that employee's life. 'Because actually, you know, I'm all for not sitting back really and just letting things happen; you've gotta be actively pursuing what you're passionate about.'

Bob himself does not sit back either. Occasionally, he takes to the streets: 'if there's a demonstration about something that I'm particularly passionate about, then we'll go and support it' – as, for example, when he joined an Extinction Rebellion protest in London. Furthermore, when the UK government announced that they would radically cut down the feed-in tariffs for renewable energy providers, and a few months later decided to cut a whole range of benefits for the renewable energy sector, Bob got involved with the Centre for Renewable Experts [pseudonym], a renewable energy industry association. They joined forces to lobby and campaign against these cuts and together met up with Members of Parliament. Thanks to the trade association, they crafted a combined voice 'rather than lots of desperate voices', Bob adds. In his personal life, however, Bob portrays himself as less of an aggressive activist who takes counteractions. He likes a quieter life, but 'if there's a beach clean going on, yeah, my wife and kids, we are all doing beach cleanings and will be out doing that this Saturday and Sunday actually'. For him, it is equally the small, incremental things that make a difference, and since every small effort helps, in his view, the passion of people to take action should be supported. He expresses that it makes him 'feel' as if he should be supportive and help channel their will to take action in the right direction.

As Small R. Energy is a customer-facing company, Bob seems to be keen to display his environmental passions credentials on the corporate website for all to see. He even took his family on a prolonged overseas trip, from which he reported in a blog on his company's website. The blog includes ambiguous confessions and personal struggles on ethics in relation to travelling, and particularly flying. One thing Bob made sure of was that the family calculated their carbon emissions, aided by WWF, which resulted in 'a shock'. Nevertheless, the shock was soon to be remedied by new, more positive, calculations. Bob found that Small R. Energy saved hundreds of tonnes in carbon emissions per year. In addition, they decided to plant trees to make up for their carbon footprint, to totally avoid single-use plastics and to clean up parts of the beaches that they visited. In the blog, he also adds that you can take your local action with you when you travel globally and thereby continue to do your bit wherever you are.

Bob's travel blog, available for all his customers to see on Small R. Energy's website, goes on to report on some of the 'Environmental Observations' he is making while travelling. He writes about waste in island communities, and particularly plastic waste in the ocean, and he refers positively to David Attenborough, the presenter of the Blue Planet TV series. He certainly makes sure that his children follow his advice in practice. He also reports on the energy transition, which he finds has reached various stages in the chain of countries they visit. Notable is how little renewable resources, such as sun, wind and waves, are exploited, even though the circumstances seem to be just perfect. He is so annoyed about the fact that some of the island communities they visit run on diesel generators that he decides to engage in more research on alternative energy solutions, such as small-scale waste facilities combined with electricity generation. Bob's childhood knowledge about agriculture and biodiversity has thus been extended to professional work with renewables and ideas to implement new solutions via business across the globe.

6.2 Ecotricity

Perhaps one of the most well-known and mediatised green chief executives in the UK is Dale Vince, who founded Ecotricity in 1995. He was already an environmental activist in the 1980s, using his own wind turbine to power the trailer he lived in. The hippie life and at times violent green activist lifestyle, combined with the newly emerging off-grid technologies, inspired him to visit the first wind turbine built in Cornwall in the early 1990s. In an interview for an ethical food and lifestyle magazine, he clarifies that he was confronted with a fundamental choice: 'I could spend another ten years living off-grid and make a personal difference, or I could drop back in, try and build a big windmill and change things a bit' (Omnom 2018). Rather than continuing to face down the police in environmental protests, he needed to educate himself about renewable technologies and business to animate a larger movement. He essentially knew nothing, had no resources to invest and was left with an amateurish sense of commercial methods. On the one hand, it was good timing, as the industry was so new when he decided to start; he clearly had a first-mover advantage. On the other hand, however, it was incredibly hard to find information on how to go about things, because everything was new and his will to take action was hard to put into business practice. Being used to the insecurities of New Age travelling and moving in any direction without the certainty of where it would lead, he did, according to the mediatised story, have few fears and little to lose. He had no dependents, no house and no other valuables. Thus, he simply went for it; building a wind business became a new endeavour, an entrepreneurial journey and green exploration.

Dale Vince has, according to popular media, kept to his original intent of being mission-led – someone who puts the environment first and the business second, suggesting that he does not 'focus like a businessperson would; I focus like an environmentalist would. [...] Sometimes I describe Ecotricity as a hybrid: we're mission-led like an NGO, but we use the best business tools available to get stuff done. NGOs don't tend to do that – not enough, anyway' (Omnom 2018). Despite this hybrid strategy, Ecotricity are supported by a number of NGOs, including Friends of the Earth, the RSPB and the Vegan Society, a charity organisation initiated in 1944 (Dale Vince is mediatised as a committed vegan). The collaboration with these organisations is not explicitly described on Ecotricity's website, but they are suggested to consist of people who share the company's values. Looking further into the official partnership offered with Ecotricity, Friends of the Earth promote their collaboration with business by calling on people to 'switch' away from 'filthy fossil fuels' (Friends of the Earth 2018). The world of business is thus bridged to NGOs to make moral calls for citizens' actions more legitimate.

Ecotricity are, in comparison with Small R. Energy, a much larger player, producing electricity from twenty-five wind parks (with over seventy wind turbines per park), that cover a quarter of the demand of their 200,000 customers (2022 figures). In green, black and white colours on their website, Ecotricity state that they are 'Britain's greenest energy company' (Ecotricity 2022) – a statement that has been questioned by another company, the electric car manufacturer Tesla, which sent a complaint to the UK's Advertising Standards Authority (ASA). As it turns out, ASA dismissed the complaint, agreeing with Ecotricity that the information given was true. Hence, throughout the website, Ecotricity continue to present themselves as a true national environmental champion, joyfully waving the Union Jack, on which green stripes replace the red. Dale Vince has even published a manifesto on his approach to the green revolution, available on the Ecotricity website to buy. Furthermore, the urgency of switching to renewables is made clear by the 'climate clock' that appears at the bottom of the website, showing how much time the world has left to limit global warming to 1.5 degrees Celcius (Ecotricity, 2022).

According to Ecotricity, the company channels profits from selling electricity to investments in new green energy solutions, under the slogan 'turning bills into mills' (Ecotricity 2022). It is nevertheless difficult to find details on the amounts reinvested. The promotion of this business model strategically targets a customer who wishes to cut carbon emissions at the lowest cost, by only buying green electricity (wind, sun and sea) or frack-free green gas (from organic material), which is possible if you live in the UK (Ecotricity 2022). Ecotricity have not remained in the energy industry only but have worked hard to expand the green agenda to other areas via the Ecotricity Group. One example is Ecotalk, a network for digital communication and mainly a mobile phone service that runs on their own 100 percent green electricity. This service also seeks to attract a customer who wishes to reduce personal emissions generated from each text that is sent, and each byte that is used. Collaborating with the RSPB, the mobile service uses a similar investment model to Ecotricity's energy service. Ecotalk reinvests in nature by buying land to create 'vital new habitats for bees and other wildlife' (Ecotalk 2018). For a while, there was an additional third component of the Ecotricity Group called Electric Highway. Inaugurated in 2011, it was one of the few national providers of approximately 300 electric vehicle charging points in the UK (Ecotricity 2022), which also explains why a formal complaint about Ecotricity's green ambitions was made by Tesla. Media attention was even turned towards a fight between the two respective company founders, Elon Musk and Dale Vince, playing on their status as contemporary green business leaders, with both of their respective industries undergoing major reorganisations (The Sunday Times 2015).

Returning to Dale Vince, then, he does like his money too. He is well known for his aesthetic interest in fast cars and has a considerable car collection of his own, which may seem a bit odd considering his green identity politics and veganism and passions to promote it further, even among football enthusiasts (Coyne 2018). In 2010, he bought Forest Green Rovers FC, his local football club, then in the fifth-tier Conference National in England, with the ambition to get them promoted to the second-tier Championship. Here, his green actions are furthered, expressed in an attempt to re-invent others, as he turned Forest Green Rovers into the first ever vegan football club, which raised an eyebrow or two (Hosie 2017). From veganism to renewable energy, Dale is explicit with his political agenda and also happily intervenes in national energy politics. He openly attacks the government and energy companies for their support of nuclear energy and fracking, which he thinks belong to the twentieth century. What he really wants to see is sensible renewable energy policy, and he supports it by direct funding of the Labour Party. In 2015, Ecotricity donated a quarter of a million pounds to their election campaign to stop the coalition government undermining the 'green economy' (Vallely 2016). Labelled as 'defiant independent', Dale Vince sees Ecotricity as a challenger that will disrupt and mix up the energy market during the twenty-first century, outspokenly saying that he will keep disrupting the status quo to push the 'green revolution' (Vallely 2016). Later on, he announced that he would leave Ecotricity (2022), selling it on to someone who shares his mission-led enthusiasm and who can muster the investment needed to take the company to the next level. With plans to enter politics, he might shake up another domain with his green agenda (The New European, 2022).

6.3 Good Energy

Similarly to Ecotricity, Good Energy works closely with NGOs to legitimise their operations as truly green. They stress that part of their electricity is produced by 'a community of over 1,700 independent generators'. Their homepage also features a section called 'The fight for our futures', stating that Good Energy has been on a '20+ year mission to tackle the climate crisis' (Good Energy 2022). Hence, the company presents itself as a climate activist that invites customers to join their mission to save the world. A political change and transformation, from high-carbon to low-carbon, from unsustainable to sustainable, and from global to UK-based, can, with the help of Good Energy, be accomplished in a single 'switch'. The political transformation is thus materialised by a technical solution that requires simply clicking a button on a website and filling in a postcode and a few personal details, whereby a green energy tariff is calculated based on the number of bedrooms in your house.

Juliet Davenport, the former Oxford student, founder and former CEO of Good Energy, has been advising the British Academy's Principles of Purposeful Business project (The British Academy 2019). While she has recently left the company to focus on her other, multiple appointments in the renewable energy industry, she founded Good Energy because '[b]usinesses can be a tremendous force for good, especially if they focus their attention on solving global problems' (Good Energy 2019). In addition to an interest in academic knowledge production, Good Energy builds on people's knowledge and awareness of climate change and their broader interest in nature, and they also support the dissemination of knowledge about environmental problems, and particularly science on climate change. One of their many stories, written by various employees or 'Good Energy authors', describes how science has been conveyed in less abstract ways with the help of art (Good Energy 2018). One example is the joint work of poet Nicola Davies and climate science professor Ed Hawkins from the National Centre for Atmospheric Science (NCAS). Together they 'explain big issues in a very hard-hitting way that resonates with the masses', as one Good Energy author testifies. The rhetoric used is worth noting, as 'facts' are just to be presented, inviting the audience to draw conclusions themselves; 'they aren't told what to think' (Suter 2018). Other art projects presented on the website lead to more direct messages of hands-on actions that Good Energy supports: it is not enough to be aware and reflect; you need to scrutinise whether 'your eco-actions speak louder than words' (McKee 2018). Here, the Good Energy author alludes to the common separation between talk and action, pointing to the possibilities to move from understanding and awareness to action, that is, to walk the talk. Clearly, a division between thought and action needs to be addressed, since this is identified as a prevalent hindrance to the 'switch' that Good Energy desires. Climate action here requires the correct consumption moves. To complement their worry about a smooth alignment between thought, talk and action, the company also investigates the willingness of their customers to adjust to various environmental problems. On their website, one can find information and tips about broader environmental issues beyond climate change, accompanied by a picture of a cheese followed by an appeal to support the local economy – a topic to which we will return in the following chapters on insider activism in governmental authorities and prosumer activism via citizen groups.

6.4 Community Interest Companies

In addition to the previously discussed, fairly established albeit still relatively small- to medium-sized renewable energy utilities that work with electricity installation, generation and distribution, there are smaller consultancies within the renewable energy sector that deploy activist practices. One example is the community interest company Localism for Renewables [pseudonym], which offers citizens help with company start-up, finance, project development and asset management. A community interest company operates as a normal commercial business, but the profits are reinvested in new local energy projects. This means that a community interest company has to make money and trade, instead of being sustained by grants. Since the clients of Localism for Renewables are often short of monetary resources, their business model is divided into two separate income streams. They either work on a straight consultancy basis, getting paid for their services, or they invest development capital at risk. When the project is realised, they charge a service fee, which is a percentage of the invested capital, but their rate is substantially lower than the development profit a commercial developer would charge. A big commercial developer often aims to sell the project on to a utility company or a venture capital fund, which David from Localism for Renewables especially wishes to put a stop to:

So, for me it's been a long-term kind of aspiration to do this, but I think other people working in the sector particularly from the volunteers' side are coming from a similar perspective, that they see the challenges in climate change, they see flaws in our energy economy, no one else is doing it, so they better get off their arses and do something! (2017, David, pseudonym, Localism for Renewables)

David, who has a commercial renewable energy background, started Localism for Renewables together with some like-minded friends.

He left university after a four-year degree in anthropology, convinced that the nature of our economy needed to change substantially. He was strongly against the idea of a centralised economy run on fossil fuels. From a leftist perspective, he criticises how large amounts of work and power are concentrated in a small number of companies or individuals, bringing with it very negative social and environmental side effects that may be irreparable. To be able to make a difference in his professional life, he nevertheless realised that a degree in environmental technology would be more useful for hands-on work with a transformation, perhaps of both the energy system and the economic system. He thus went back to university to complement his previously attained anthropological knowledge and insights, a change of educational path that first led to a position within Ernst and Young's renewable energy finance team. Here, David obtained in-depth practical knowledge of finance in renewables, which he has been able to implement in a counter-move against big business via Localism for Renewables.

David and his colleagues, three full-time employees and five external consultants, are adamant about enforcing alternative commercial methods that can strengthen localism. They could all have made much more money working for a medium-sized or big developer, but they have chosen to work for a cause. They do not believe it is enough to decarbonise, but a monetary redistribution of the profits from renewables needs to be carried out. This, perhaps more social than environmental mission, motivates the close collaborations with their clients, who are typically people living in small villages and towns, and who wish to become prosumers in collectives formed around local affinities and friendships. These people, David emphasises, have no clue about commercial methods for renewables and often end up in exhausting conflicts with big developers. In effect, this means that decarbonisation is slowed down:

So, from a low carbon perspective, not enough capacity was getting built, but more so for me, the wind and solar farms that were getting built weren't changing the energy economy, they were changing the technology, and reducing emissions, but they weren't decentralising [...] so they're decentralising [electricity] generation but they weren't decentralising ownership and economic benefit, and that was a huge missed opportunity. Like if localities could own their own generation and obtain the economic benefit of their own generation then energy could become a positive multiplier in their economy rather than a drain on their economy, and the key thing that they needed to change for that to happen was that localities needed to get in at the beginning and develop their own project. (2017, David, Localism for Renewables)

David perfectly exemplifies how activism goes into business due to the expertise necessary in commercial methods to be able to both play the capitalist game as well as disrupt business as usual. Localism for Renewables provides high-risk investment and knowledge on how to plan and develop renewable energy projects to make local people more competitive in the renewable energy project market. Being commercially articulate is a must in negotiations for monetary resources in the private sector. Local gatherings of people in villages and towns are often not considered legitimate legal applicants for loans, which is why commercially schooled activists who wish to help them, set up businesses like David's:

That's why we set up Localism for Renewables, to provide that knowledge, and we raised some money to fund the risk stage of the project. In theory once you've got planning and grid and everything else in place, it's relatively easy to raise the capital to build it. So the challenge in building a solar farm isn't the five million pounds it takes to build it, it's the one or two hundred thousand pounds it takes to get through that development process, because that money is lost if you don't succeed, and that is the bit of money that the communities didn't have. (2017, David, Localism for Renewables)

Even though Localism for Renewables is occasionally paid by the local citizens when they have succeeded in raising some grant funding for 'community energy', many of the projects they engage in are pure risk and end up pro bono, although David stresses that his organisation 'are not volunteers'. They rather see it from the angle that they work with volunteers and therefore need to be mindful of the huge amount of time and effort these local volunteers invest, without any assurance of payment or a successful investment. Often, the local citizens put in years of their retirement, but it results in nothing, or it results in a successful project and viable business, but one that is too small and not profitable, thus requiring the locals to work on a voluntary basis to keep the business going. They would need to be working on a megawatt scale before covering their own core costs. The projects are, therefore, very seldom commercially competitive and end up being a lot of hard voluntary work rewarded with environmental and social gain:

I don't think these pensioners really want to get paid, they want to set the thing up, get it going, then keep an eye on it. And they want to employ someone local to run it part time or full time, they're not looking for a second career. But it isn't reasonable that they put their whole retirement into making these things happen, and it's not just the pensioners. In all the organisations we're working with, there might be a couple of people, pensioners, who have the time to do it, but there's also younger people getting involved. (2017, David, Localism for Renewables)

The reason for their voluntary engagement, David suggests, is the same as the reason he set up a business. The locals can see that decarbonisation is too slow and that eventually, their resources are threatened with exploitation by external actors if they do not act themselves. The bridging between business and society is thus very self-organised, motivated by how people 'see the flaw in our energy economy' (2017, David, Localism for Renewables). The bridging is yet again exemplified by David as being aided by the materiality of renewable energy: 'It has got people involved in local politics, local action, that wouldn't have gotten involved before because they can see there's something material they can do'. Hence, Love Seaside Town and the Decarbonised Living Project, who have been their clients, as well as people who generally get involved in the community energy cooperatives that are set up, 'get active', he suggests, because they see that 'they can make a difference to their area, they can see as a way of generating a level of income for their area which is far in excess of what the local councils have to spend, and then they get involved in other things, and then the energy co-op doesn't just do energy' (2017, David, Localism for Renewables), it spills over into more social aspects.

As a community interest company, Localism for Renewables nevertheless needs to ensure that some projects do result in a payback since their salaries depend on it. One way forward is to find the right constellation for each local project while at the same time talking to the political establishment and engaging in professional lobbying, just like any big developer of renewables. This includes writing reports to explain that there is an untapped potential for local renewable energy projects, arguing that working on that front could help the politicians to achieve their policy objectives with carbon reduction and fuel poverty reduction. With a declining market for new installations, due to the required grid connections that are technically constrained,

Localism for Renewables has had to expand their consultancy to a recovery mode of existing investments, to give power back to the people:

> Our main activity now is working to buy operational solar farms back into community ownership. So, for the last two years we've helped to manage over twenty million pounds worth of solar projects that have been bought from commercial developers back into local energy. With each of those we've helped to set up a local energy enterprise to engage in negotiation, helped them negotiate the terms of the purchase from the commercial owner, and then help the communities raise the money to fund the purchase. (2017, David, Localism for Renewables)

This move is possible due to quite a few of the solar farms built by commercial developers being sold on a two to three years' basis. Starting with a small developer that obtains the planning permission and the grid connection, a solar farm is often sold on to a construction contractor, who then will sell it on to someone else. At this point in the life of the project, the solar farm is packaged into a 200-megawatt portfolio and eventually sold to a pension fund. Each time a deal is made, profit is nevertheless taken out of the projects, and the return for the next owner goes down. However, it can still be commercially worthwhile to buy a project second-hand and turn it into a locally driven enterprise. The key is the scale, and that the project can fund the operations needed. Hence, the projects bought back into the control of local citizens are of a size in the order of five or ten megawatts. The benefit that Localism for Renewables sees is that they know there is a viable business, and their challenge is to turn it into an enterprise that really supports the local people:

> We typically have three tiers of funding, so that the senior debt funder that provides the majority of the capital, maybe 60–70 percent will be from a normal bank on commercial terms. Then we raise as much as we can from the community share or bond offer, which is lots of people investing around 200 pounds to a few thousand pounds each, then there is a gap in the middle which is filled by a social investment fund. So, they're charging in some cases quite high rates, but they're willing to lend to this sort of projects because of the social outcomes they are achieving. (2017, David, Localism for Renewables)

As an example of developers who have not offered to sell their solar farms to local citizens, David mentions Good Energy. Even though they set up before there was any real interest in local renewable energy generation and consumption, people wonder why they are not willing to sell their farms to them. They have thus spurred some conflicts with certain localities, where people are starting to realise the potential of alternative business models and that the distribution of profits could be more democratic and horizontal. This realisation has also inspired Localism for Renewables to be more forceful in their attempt to give power back to the people. The envisioned 'coming together' is worth quoting at length:

We've got the solar farm in North Barnsby [pseudonym] which is the biggest community solar farm in the country, but there's not yet a [local] organisation around it. So, we're just trying to work out how we do that. Maybe with that one we'll be a bit more radical and try and set up an infrastructure that is more overtly active than what we've done elsewhere. [...] And can we use that to engage people in climate change and energy and local economic development? Use it as a focus to pull together organisations that are already working in the area, in say fuel poverty, and try and lever up their impact? And perhaps try and channel some of the kind of current discontent that's going in a negative direction, try and challenge that, channel that into a more positive direction? It'll be an experiment to see if that's possible. (2017, David, Localism for Renewables)

6.5 Epistemic Community and Enterprising Activism

Activist entrepreneurship and its outgrowth of bottom-up enterprising activism in the UK could be dismissively analysed as an 'environmentalism of the rich' (Dauvergne 2016). Affluent and knowledgeable people, indeed, take action by combining business and activism in crafty ways. While there are plenty of examples of corporate greenwash, our research participants maintain that they, and others with them, are well-meaning companies whose business models are completely geared towards climate action and broader environmental agendas. These businesses tend to be relatively small-scale and actively promote incremental as well as more radical climate action and reconfigurations of the capitalist system. Not by merging some sort of add-on CSR activity with a corporate core, but by starting from scratch and building activism into the core of the business, it is possible to prioritise differently and steer how the green mission and climate action should result in business success. An attempt is made to sustain a causal chain of commitment to climate action over time, from the activism of the business founder to the employees and customers.

The main themes on climate activism pursued via business found in the examples provided in this chapter revolve around the committed passion of the founders and employees, the sense of community and familialism nurtured in customer relations, and the close collaboration with both NGOs and local governmental authorities. Already in the 1990s, Mirvis (1994) showed how environmental activism within business works across boundaries by way of partnerships with non-profits, and how customers are actively educated about the positive aspects of business-driven environmentalism. Going against brand activism and CSR, used as a rhetorical response to external critique (Cederström and Marinetto 2013), the climate activism we encountered was based on knowledge about nature and the environment, merged with either an awareness or previous experience of activism where it normally is understood to be enacted (in civil society). These aspects then spurred a movement of activist entrepreneurship, providing a purpose to start a business and build a collectivity based on employee and customer relations. Climate activism that goes into business can of course be seen as part of a differentiation strategy and a way to become competitive in the market, but according to our experiences in the field, it did not come across as necessarily planned, but rather something that emerged out of passion and interest. The activists who became business founders were not able to foretell the market reactions since they were very early entrants. They just wanted to speed up the solutions to the environmental problems being faced.

The activist–business–state conglomeration is in a very direct way spawned by what many would see as a conventional activist. The mediatised picture portrays an underdog hero who re-invents her or himself as an entrepreneur, or so-called alternative ecopreneur, guided by a conviction of her or himself as a political subject, purposefully armed to take on the uncertainties of starting and sustaining a business. What seems to matter most is that mavericks such as Dale Vince and Juliet Davenport created their companies, Ecotricity and Good Energy, out of a conviction and passion for making a difference in the world. Other UK energy start-ups, such as Ovo and Octopus, led by people with a background in energy finance, trading and marketing, have grown much faster and now have a much larger market share. Yet it seems that Ecotricity and Good Energy do not necessarily want to be the biggest companies. Instead, they are on a mission to change the way grassroots political actions can be taken, and business can be done. Most importantly, in relation to an epistemic community, both extend their will to enforce a transformation beyond climate actions. Dale Vince, for example, has turned Ecotricity into a group of companies that engage in very diverse green actions and missions, and Juliet Davenport has been advising the British Academy's Principles of Purposeful Business project. Grounded in knowledge production about both politics and business and tapping into demands for an urgent energy transition and more general system transformation, their respective business operations thus expand the epistemic community beyond the initial core operations within renewables. The epistemic community does not start and stop with the various technologies promoted and materialised but expands, effectively aided by ambitions that spill over.

Bob's Small R. Energy is tellingly on a mission to spread knowledge and infuse action, albeit on a much smaller scale than Ecotricity and Good Energy. He employs ex-Greenpeace activists and enjoys Extinction Rebellion protests himself; he writes on his company's online blog about the ethical dilemmas of family leisure time and travel. He actively speaks about how to build a community of like-minded people to effect change. His blog entries are confessions that resonate with a wider epistemic community, admitting that climate activism is full of contradictions and never straightforward. Yet the moment of confession also sends a signal of humbleness, saying that 'we are in this together', with ambitions of building a co-producing loyal family full of imagination, passion and values, where ethical leadership seeks to decarbonise through the inseparability of the personal and professional of the company founder (cf. Mirvis 1994). Bob thus displays a generosity towards others, in the wish to enlighten and re-invent them, as we discussed previously as a historical remnant of *Gemeinschaft* (Tönnies 1957/2002).

The notion of the 'community firm' comes to mind (Kanter 1977, Solomon 1993). Ecotricity, Good Energy and Small R. Energy are all mission- and purpose-led. They wish to see their employees, customers, suppliers, investors and other stakeholders as part of the same 'community' or 'family'. The majority politics internal to these organisations are brought out to effect change externally, similarly to how social movements mobilise, using affect and sympathy, and also confession and self-critique, to spawn social change. Mirvis (1994), nevertheless, wonders whether customers really do believe in environmentalism pursued in the form of a business, pointing to the problematic organisational hierarchies and management present in top-down sustainability agendas – a form of criticism that has often been repeated since then. The conceptual separation between *Gemeinschaft*, with its true generosity and authenticity between thought and action, and *Gesellschaft*, with its machinic and instrumental actions (Asplund 1991), is sustained in the contemporary critique of activist entrepreneurs (Montgomery 2019). Over time, when for example Ecotricity's Dale Vince is no longer considered an activist who goes into business, but a businessman who does activism, the authenticity and possibility for horizontal affinity may be lost.

It is also along this axis of critique of business that a difference between activism and social, ecological and sustainable entrepreneurship is similarly made. These alternative forms of entrepreneurship, which can take place in both profit-driven businesses and non-profit-driven NGOs or collectives, often take action in the same vein as activist entrepreneurs. As we outlined in Chapter 1, it may not even be possible to separate them (Bacq and Janssen 2011), but the ways in which social change via entrepreneurship conflates with activism have multiplied (Dey and Mason 2018). Nonetheless, one way in which distinctions between these similar phenomena have been made is to acknowledge how the founders of the organisations for 'doing good' categorise themselves. Whether a founder of an organisation self-identifies as an activist or prefers to identify as a commercially driven entrepreneur determines what the classification will be. Some may, of course, wish to see themselves as capable of both at once or may prefer to use the category that works best rhetorically depending on the specific situation. What we found that differentiated those who spoke of themselves more in line with alternative entrepreneurship, than enterprising activism, was the wish to expand the community of the company, from an inclusion of the employees only, to an inclusion of the customers or so-called switchers. For the activist alternative entrepreneurs, the attempted inclusion was not with the company *per se*, but with the knowledge movement to which their values responded, and the engagement in climate actions as a need for further co-production of knowledge. The horizontal affinities were in all examples nurtured to be boundaryless, with an expanding epistemic community as a possible result. This will spread ideas and the wish to get others on board to accomplish change is conventionally connected to activism but is with renewable energy taken into business. Whether companies will succeed in building a bigger community around climate change and energy solutions, in the light of the criticism and suspicion they often meet, is, however, a different question. What we can conclude is nevertheless that climate change has opened up for a strong turn to the activist business entrepreneur. Beyond the neoliberal call for everyone to become an entrepreneur and work with social change and community formation (Calás, Smircich and Bourne 2009, Daskalaki, Hjorth and Mair 2015) is the call for an activist with a bent for business.

In contrast to established forms of alternative entrepreneurship, as well as disruptive activist entrepreneuring (Dey and Mason 2018), our research participants took on very open-ended endeavours, from the beginning uncertain about what to do and how to accomplish some sort of outcome that would generate a greener world. Theoretical assumptions of existing causal chains, from knowledge to intentional autonomous action, or from imagination to self-invention, were naturally not clearly expressed in conversations. Enterprising activism in the field is messy and haphazard. In retrospect, it was sometimes portrayed as hyper-strategic, a calculated way of bringing actions up to speed in a directed process of materialisation, but at most times enterprising activism definitely came across as an out-of-control endeavour.

If we acknowledge, for example, the temporal aspect of enterprising activism in more detail, Dale Vince seems to practise declining feral citizenship (Garside 2013). In the beginning, he refers to himself in various media as grappling with the unknown; all the information he needs to find is nowhere to be found, and all the knowledge he needs to get a grip on and put into practice is largely missing. As for many start-ups, the first phase mainly consists of information processing and knowledge production, fruitfully setting things you know, and do not know, in complex motion. However, for Dale Vince, the knowledge production becomes even more ingrained in the actual start-up, being tightly connected to a processual way of testing what works in the here and now. At this stage, the mediatised activism relates more to life lived on an uncertain prefigurative path, where Dale Vince seems interested in identity work, pursued along an unfixed axis that moves along with the intensity of life (Fawcett 2009, Adsit-Morris 2017).

If conventional experiences of activism have been connected to the enjoyment of a stable identity formation within a set countermovement based on specific struggles and anger (Jasper 2011), these experiences are now replaced by more abstract knowledge struggles, differently enjoyed. Based on uncertainties about how to go about it, these advanced epistemic struggles range from a revival of the activist entrepreneur to the making of citizen activists through wild encounters with renewables, in a continuously changing policy landscape.

Climate activism develops a boundaryless attribute due to this advancement of epistemic struggles and initial base of no set knowledge or 'hard' political structures. If no one knows how to take actions, but many are convinced they are needed, lots of interactions and coming together will follow. The less that is known, and the more uncertain the path is, the more of a challenge and emotional ride people experience. This could be observed, for example, with the hybrid organisations that arose, with an increased movement of people in their necessarily feral attempts to co-produce knowledge, without really knowing how or even getting the equation to add up. If no one really knows, then it may also be easier to accept negotiations, get along and just try. Hence, making things explicitly goal-oriented, strategic and foreseeable is not the point, as contemporary public education programmes grounded in *Bildung* also propose (Reichenbach 2002). It is an encounter with the unknown that nevertheless is prone to create smooth adjustments to existing differences in productivity and culture, at the same time as activist entrepreneurs that take startsups to the level of enterprising activism are susceptible to the dominant market system.

As mentioned by our research participants, when incumbents take over smaller, activist companies, for example L'Oréal's takeover of The Body Shop in 2006, or Unilever's purchase of Pukka Herbs in 2017, then there is always the risk that the social or environmental purpose of that smaller business will soon be lost amid the financial expectations of a large multinational firm (Purkayastha and Fernando 2007). Business growth in itself is, of course, riddled with compromises that have led to many of the early eco-business pioneers going under or being taken over by larger companies (Holt 2011). Our research participants, however, seek to protect themselves from this, with a whole array of new legal forms for commercial organisations that should secure a 'coming together' with remnants from old-school community building (*Gemeinschaft*). A collective movement to spread a will to take action is also addressed by Ecotricity and Good Energy, but perhaps most in the case of Bob's Small R. Energy and David's Localism for Renewables.

Both Bob and David can furthermore be described as being part of a 'close community' that consists of people who know each other personally but also as professionals interested in renewables (Guy and Shove 2000). They are both working closely with smaller groups of volunteers that seek to make use of the benefits of renewables for local people who live in a specific geographical location. They seldom seem to make much or any money with these community-oriented endeavours. Therefore, we are back to the book's main concept of 'epistemic community', which suggests that it is not enough to look at a community, preconceived as a unit or a specific juridical form of organisation. We need to engage more deeply with the relationship between *Gesellschaft* and *Gemeinschaft* to understand the boundary-less spread of climate activism across the domains of business and society. In this chapter, we have explored enterprising activism that could quite easily be dismissed as an 'environmentalism of the rich' (Dauvergne 2016) or a kind of top-down CEO activism that hopes to benefit financially from the energy and desire of the global climate (and environmentally conscious) movement of people who wish to make a positive change. Yet our examples show that this would be a crass caricature of what is actually going on in many, often small-scale, businesses where the owners and employees have made conscious and purposeful decisions to use their companies as platforms to bring about positive social and environmental change. In some cases, they have been active in many different organisations in their careers, acquiring knowledge and experience that they actively bring with them from one place to the next. For them, it is not the type of organisation that is important, but how they can continue to pursue and develop their 'actions'.

This is especially evident in the case of David. The experiences he gained in a big consultancy firm have been redeployed in a smaller and less profit-driven organisation. He expands his work on social relations to other people and disseminates knowledge on commercial methods for renewable energy actions, which expands the epistemic community. Localism for Renewables is also part of a growing gift economy, as they invest both time and money, sometimes at high risk, to work closely with local citizen groups, often without much or indeed any financial return. Subsidies, renewable energy schemes, or innovative and challenging grant competitions launched by local governmental authorities enhance the connections in the activist-business-state conglomeration, leading to the epistemic community unfolding across preconceived boundaries between business and society, as we will illustrate in the following chapter on how public servants in governmental authorities act as 'insider activists' at work.

7 | Climate Activism in Governmental Authorities

The dominant view that activism is configured by actions taken by civil society, often located geographically in public space or hosted within a NGO or community, means that other locations and forms of activism and community formation have been understudied. One of the least known forms of activism is so-called insider activism, that is, activism pursued by public servants who are employees within state agencies and local governmental authorities. It is perhaps also the least legitimate type of activism since public servants are commonly supposed to act as extensions of formal political decisions and not pursue their personal politics at work. Nevertheless, this is not always the case, and especially not in times of environmental and climate emergencies, as we outlined in Chapter 2 with a focus on the activist–business–state conglomeration. In relation to existing theories that have made the boundaryless attribute of activism more apparent, we realised during our interviews with council workers in South West England that the local government bodies were seemingly full of environmental activists who wanted to use their professional positions to effect positive change. In this chapter, we will thus narrow in on how activism has been brought into state agencies, and how state agencies have gone into activism. We will follow the details of how insider activists engage in climate actions 'from within' and build a collective movement as an extension of deliberative democratic programmes. Personal political goals are conflated with formal political agendas, and the activist–business–state conglomeration is massaged together by boundary spanning public servants, who empower others to take action and co-produce knowledge. The epistemic community expands as insider activists take their individual responsibility to give 'power to the people' and thereby bring renewable energy policy to action.

7.1 Clean Government

The Stern Review (2006) and the Climate Change Act (2008) were landmark UK climate policy events, spearheaded by New Labour, influencing a range of treasury policies on planning, housing and transport, paving the way for green politics via state authorities. At that time, it was quite uncertain what specific policies people would end up with, as a former employee and public servant at the Clean Government [pseudonym] explained to us. The reason for this was the Stern Review, which functioned as 'a gateway for doing a different type of policies' (2017, Arnold, Local Energy Group (LEG) pseudonyms). Arnold recalls having been called into work to start with new tasks on energy efficiency. At that time, he did not yet think of himself as particularly pro-environment; his wife is the real 'greeny' in the family, he explains, as she has always worked with the environment, urban regeneration and community engagement. Yet in the last years of the New Labour government (2008–2010), Arnold started to expand his horizons, increasingly working for the Clean Government with innovative approaches to environmental issues within the framework of quite loosely defined policies.

Informed about the correlation between carbon emissions, leaking houses and fuel poverty, Arnold started a programme on the basis of the triple bottom line, a unification of social, environmental and economic aspects that underpin the agenda on sustainability. It quickly gained traction, and the reason for this, according to him, was that the triple bottom line approach favoured hands-on solutions that managed to balance human needs and environmental concerns. All political parties in the Clean Government were supportive of the programme, and every single one supported 'a manifesto, a commitment to continuing' the programme (2017, Arnold, LEG). For the first time, this traction resulted in several departments sharing a budget for energy poverty reduction and energy efficiency, which they had never done before. Hence, the economics and regeneration department, the housing department, the environmental department and the sustainability department came together in the belief that investments in energy efficiency would both improve the job market and reduce existing fuel poverty:

My interest in getting involved in this was probably the impact in its greatest sense, but what I could bring to the party at the beginning was my understanding of economics and articulating cases in economic language. (2017, Arnold, LEG)

After only eighteen months, however, Arnold was 'fed up with commuting to Clean Government' and started to work as a consultant. Just a year later, he nevertheless returned to the Clean Government for a new role, with a broader remit, to advise the government leader on the energy strategy for the whole region. The government leader had decided to make energy a personal mission of his own but needed someone who had previous hands-on experience with successfully implementing programmes in the region. In addition, a very brilliant and active environmental minister came to power, who 'led from the front [and] was really passionate' (2017, Arnold, LEG). She had even been voted the third most influential environmental person in the world, but perhaps her anti-nuclear agenda forced her to step down so that the government leader could continue the planning of new nuclear power plant investments. In effect, her opposition had made some difference, and she was moving to other missions. The triple bottom line agenda, however, was greatly downplayed, and Arnold had to turn his rhetoric to a new political agenda of the government: 'smart living'. According to the Clean Government (2018), '[t]he energy world is changing', which requires '[m]ore focus [...] given to local energy use over centrally generated electricity'. In practice, this meant that Arnold worked more with new energy infrastructure networks and different ways of using energy. Efforts were put into research and development of local user solutions, instead of a focus on mass-produced electricity and heat generation on the delivery side.

At the time of our meeting with Arnold, he was no longer employed by the Clean Government but was working at a university in South West England. He volunteers as chairman of the board of an organisation called Local Energy Group, which collaborates closely with the local county council, supporting the start of what they call an 'energy revolution' (LEG 2018). Due to his former interest in party politics, Labour and New Labour agendas, Arnold has thus decided to continue his political green engagement as a hobby that spans academia, the cooperative world and state authorities. LEG makes this possible, in that the organisation merges business methods and new public management to work for the citizens.

7.2 Local Energy Group

On the surface, LEG looks like a grassroots initiative with 1,500 members, functioning as an umbrella organisation under which several sister organisations are hosted, such as LEG Renewables, with considerable assets worth millions of pounds. The legal form that hosts all these sister organisations is considered a 'Society' under the label 'Local Energy Group Limited'. It was set up as a community benefit society in 2013, kick-started via a so-called manifesto commitment by the city council and led from the front by a local Labour administration:

Well, a politician wanted to do something, basically help people with fuel bills and the like, what it appears to me [...], but there were quite a lot of authorities who were talking a lot about collective switching. [But] collective switching never delivered, and still isn't, despite quite a lot of money thrown into marketing campaigns. The energy suppliers are like 'unless you've got 100,000 people, I'm not interested'. (2017, Susan, pseudonym, LEG)

Built horizontally from what would conventionally be seen as two polarised ends, bottom-up individual engagement and top-down politics, the organisation unfolded rapidly. Local politics is very different from national politics, we are told, with local politicians wanting to do things in their closest surroundings, addressing what their closest neighbours talk about. The council thus 'signed up as a cooperative council' and wished to create an energy transition 'by the people, for the people', which is why it made sense for them to pay for some of the LEG staff (2017, Susan, LEG).

The first thing LEG decided to do, without having a clue about how to do it, was to set up a switching service. That is, they wished to help local residents switch towards green energy tariffs and make use of the newly deregulated UK domestic energy market. However, not even the consultants they turned to knew how to do it properly, which is why it failed. They simply could not organise mass switches, which would have enabled price savings. This made LEG realise that they needed to pursue another type of marketing and reach out to people via house visits. Therefore, by increasing their number of staff, these visits provided them with more knowledge of how the end users, or residents, were living and what their needs were. They found that the debt issue was paramount, that is, people simply did not have any cash to do anything with environmental benefits in mind; they were consumed with thoughts about getting the bills paid. The main purpose at the beginning was thus to function as 'a marketing tool [...] for energy companies' that were obliged, by central government, to reduce residents' energy bills and, at the same time, work towards decarbonisation. If these companies sent out a letter to customers, however, 'it kind of just [went] straight in the bin' (2017, Martin, pseudonym, LEG).

LEG is kind of a middle man, a trusted voice if you like, between community and energy supply. So on one side we will help an energy supplier deliver its obligation and it has to by law, on the other side we will make that offer attractive and worthwhile for a resident. [...] But I guess the essence of what LEG does in that space, is that [it is] a trusted voice, that we can get the people on board. [...] it's a bit of a beauty parade to be honest. As a local authority and a community energy organisation, we have to go to market and say 'here we are, we can reach people for you, what can you offer?' (2017, Martin, LEG).

The reason for working closely with business is not only financial but also a way to 'provoke the commercial sector to do it [community benefit] differently' (2017, Susan, LEG). It is 'a way of getting the energy companies to pay for the work that needs doing and a lot of that work is stuff that even the kind of middle income households would struggle to afford' (2017, Martin, LEG) – for example, external wall insulation and other investments amounting to between 7,000 and 8,000 pounds. Staff at Local Energy Group have, nevertheless, been critically asked if they are 'sleeping with the enemy' (2017, Martin, LEG), so the bridging on the ground between state, business and citizen is tricky.

In addition to board members that act as volunteers, who care 'about nothing but energy and sustainability matters, and [who] are part of many organisations beyond LEG' (2017, Arnold, LEG), the core LEG group of paid employees, 'the low carbon team', consists of fifteen people on council employment contracts. Some of them have strong political convictions, as one of the most active employees exemplifies by referring to how she was affected as a child by how her parents shouted at the television whenever Margaret Thatcher appeared (2017, Susan, LEG). The group relies on a mix of educational backgrounds and previous environmental practices, from green documentary filmmaking to work with environmental theatre, festivals and circuses. They also have experience working with charities and smaller businesses. By merging their left or centre-left political agenda with environmental engagement, they are seated in the council offices. Over time, they become more or less immersed in the bureaucracy, as we experienced during a visit:

I was surprised entering the council office today to meet LEG. They don't look as if they belonged to a state institution at all. They don't dress in the same way and they are younger than the average. The way they talk is more in line with prefiguration, they seem to want something to happen, enthusiastically, now. There is a passionate immediacy about them. They do not fit the bureaucracy, but they are politically driven. (Reporting back to co-researcher about the visit, Fieldnotes 2017)

Instead of providing direct financial support, the 'cooperative council' supports LEG and its work in an indirect way, by giving them 'air time', housing them and giving them city council employment contracts (2017, Susan, LEG). The salaries, however, are increasingly paid by other, external sources, and the overall aim is for LEG not to be at all financially dependent on the council. One of the reasons for being self-sufficient financially, we were told, is that there might have been more criticism of the group if salaries for them had a visible budget post. If thousands of pounds went into what in effect could be seen as a voluntary organised 'community' hosted by the city council, the outputs and close collaboration would be more closely scrutinised. Hence, due to the initial council support, LEG was told early on that they would have to make considerable progress and become self-funded as soon as possible.

LEG can undoubtedly be seen as a type of governmental insourcing of environmentalism and climate action via paid voluntarism. Yet it also exemplifies how political agendas are implemented in new ways, with greater flexibility with regard to how work is organised, actions are taken and social changes are enacted. These younger people, who appear to be more devoted to environmental problems, succeed in receiving funds from various sources in competition with others, largely due to their commitment and passion but also due to the legitimacy brought by the council. This is a success shared with the council, which has not been slow to be pictured together with LEG, as 'we delivered more than they'd anticipated' (2017, Susan, LEG). LEG are, however, equally willing to utilise the platform of the council, not only to reach out via the council's vast network of contacts, but also to become themselves a more natural part of a platform that legitimises their actions:

Good relations locally with your city council, to make sure you've got democratic involvement [...] and credibility as well, because regardless of what people might say about councils on the whole, my experience here is if you put a city council logo on a letter, through a door, and we often do that; that's one of the benefits about partnership with the city council; people trust it much more than without it. The two things together were a powerful proposition. People like the community nature, the charitable nature of us, but they like the stability and the credibility and the trustworthiness of the council too. (2017, Arnold, LEG)

By comparison, many other community groups, charities or non-profits live a more hand-to-mouth existence. If councils or local governments wish to, they can thus help these alternative organisations survive difficult times. Even though LEG has an explicit aim and contractual obligation not to rely on the resources of the council and has to offer one place on their board to a council member, they need continuous implicit support to sustain their existence. Perhaps surprisingly to some of the LEG team members, when the Conservatives took over, LEG survived the political shift, with LEG employees keeping their council contracts. Extensive lobbying preceded this political decision, as LEG met with the new leader of the council before the election:

[LEG] is a very, you know, clearly defined Labour administration initiative. We were concerned and uncertain in advance of the last elections, when we were pretty certain the Conservatives were going to come in. We were pretty uncertain as to what the impact would be, so I met the leader of the council, Percy [pseudonym], in advance of the election, to start to build some of those bridges in advance, in case there was a Conservative win. And I found him then, and have found him since then, to be nothing but supportive. (2017, Arnold, LEG)

LEG was, accordingly, still seen as delivering on, and aligning enough with, the Renewable County's political goals. It was flying under the radar as politically neutral, where LEG's environmentalism did not disturb the party politics of either political side. With an annual budget of between one and one and a half million pounds, LEG was able to continue to get things done in the here and now without draining the council's resources. Importantly for the continued support, LEG's reason for existence was based on more than green issues, as they addressed the social problem of fuel poverty and energy efficiency. This made it possible to speak about their aid in terms of freeing up larger amounts of disposable income to be spent locally in the region, which supported an economic and social welfare agenda. In comparison with other councils, however, this focus on monetary issues and circulations differed. For LEG, it was not about setting up energy companies to gain traction from national subsidies, since these would fluctuate and give rise to destructive uncertainties and a lack of long-term thinking. Rather, they wished to avoid peculiar investment schemes, where one company after the other would 'squeeze every penny out of projects' and take over the investment (2017, Susan, LEG):

The Solarsettlers [pseudonym], a five or six megawatt [solar development], [...] had been burned a few years earlier, so as some developers had come in, promised the local community loads of different things and got them all on board and then reneged completely on the deal, sold it off to someone else and the community never saw any benefit. (2017, Arnold, LEG)

Instead of being detached from the local surroundings where the land is used, LEG suggests work with renewables needs to be community considerate, financially sustainable as well as mission-focussed. In LEG's view, this means a priority on how people's purchasing, consumption and production of electricity and heat can be transformed. From within the council, LEG is thus working on its vision to 'create a fair, affordable low-carbon energy system with local people at its heart' (2017, Arnold, LEG). A sister company, LEG Renewables, was formed to develop more commercial efforts. Operating as a separate legal entity gave them the opportunity to craft a clear message for community share offers. It was 'a clean business with a simple funding strategy', where 'shareholders will get their money, their dividends, whatever they've paid, 50 quid or 100 grand' (2017, Susan, LEG). Interestingly, however, some of the supposedly local investors were citizens living in other parts of the UK, or even in other countries. The reason for this was that solar at that time was a good investment, as LEG Renewables promised a 6 percent return. Thus, for those who believed in LEG, the investment seemed to be attractive. Some locals even re-mortgaged their houses, as they viewed it as a 'pretty predictable' investment and 'good offer', while most invested less but did so because it was 'a heart driven decision' (2017, Susan, LEG).

Following the vision of an energy system with local people at its core, one of the initiatives was a set energy tariff for local people, which would be offered in collaboration with a national green energy start-up company, but after at least six months investigating the possibilities to introduce standard and variable tariffs, they ended up saying that 'financially it did not stack up' (2017, Martin, LEG). According to Martin, the business model did not offer a 'game changer' that would either lower prices or 'generate a significant income for the local community'. In comparison, LEG concluded that 'energy efficiency is the biggest bang for your bucks'; fuel poverty was a more sensible service to spend resources and time on (2017, Arnold, LEG):

We had more than the aim of making money and we couldn't reconcile local supply in terms of the current options for it, with the need to lower bills for domestic customers, and we felt less that we could offer something that was different to what was on the market already. (2017, Martin, LEG)

In efforts to diversify their operations, LEG turned to solar share offers, with panels placed on twenty local schools in addition to the local sports centre, which has the biggest solar roof in the county. It all started with the schools, mainly because the chairman of LEG was a school governor. LEG quickly spotted the potential of merging the local benefit argument with the trends in renewable energy technology, by inviting local citizens to invest for the benefit of the schools. They also decided to work closely with other non-profits in the area, since they suspected that 'a private company coming in at that point would have started out from a point of mistrust, particularly given the site [for renewables] further out' (2017, Arnold, LEG). That is, according to him, another development in the area had more or less utilised the local citizens, which is why LEG decided to offer an alternative. While LEG does all the planning work and sets everything up, share capital is mainly brought in from people living in the area. The schools get free electricity, the shareholders make six percent, and in the long run, LEG would also benefit on the returns.

Nevertheless, even though some success has been achieved by projects accomplished by LEG, the high demands on them to operate like a business within the council became more and more apparent and pressing over time. They had to juggle a lot of competing demands. At the same time as they had to convince the general public to take on renewable energy, they also had to convince the council of their right to exist. The difficult task was to make these two fronts meet, by securing their own economic situation within the council, becoming increasingly business- oriented and self-sufficient, at the same time as keeping the trust of the local citizens. One worrying sign appeared when the council started to cut LEG's funding, step by step. The volunteer director then chose to stand down, burdened by the increased responsibility for the overall life situation of the employees. One external factor that contributed was the reduction of the feed-in tariffs, which added to the financial difficulties as well as a deadening of the personal engagement:

I can feel my enthusiasm having waned slightly, I don't know that it affected my role, but I can feel it having waned slightly. We benefit from having a team in the council, chief executive and really talented team, who are just ploughing on regardless, because that is their job, it's their passion and they get paid to do it. (2017, Arnold, LEG)

Many of LEG's employees chose to work for the council precisely because it has a wider social purpose: 'I'm not just doing this because it is a job', Martin explains (2017, LEG). There is something 'geeky' in him, he adds, that loves new technology for households as well as 'something deeper', which is the 'idea of being really self-sustained', 'totally self-sufficient' on energy, food and water. Previously, Martin had worked with things that he did not really believe in, but now, he emphasises that, if he were to go to British Gas and work for their Eco-team, he would perhaps get paid twice as much, but 'it wouldn't sit properly and wouldn't be comfortable and [he] wouldn't like it'. His explicit moral position is worth repeating in detail:

Because, despite the outcome being the same for an individual, so a house gets insulated and their bills get lower, what I'm actually doing is generating an income for private shareholders et cetera, and I have no idea if that is doing good or not. And you know, morally I like the fact that although the outcome might be the same, what I'm doing is, and any surplus that is created or whatever, actually just goes back; it goes back, keeps doing the same thing. (2017, Martin, LEG)

Importantly, though, the 'low carbon group' within the council does not want to come across as 'preaching' (2017, Martin, LEG), but as providing practical paths for empowerment and behavioural change. According to his colleagues, the personal devotion is of importance in the everyday work. Susan (2017, LEG), for example, expresses gratefulness for being able to do 'good' via professional work instead of 'chaining myself to railings, or whatever', which otherwise would have been a viable option. Being personally devoted and reading 'a million papers about it', Susan also tries to write her own communicative pieces to counter the view that renewables are seen as 'an industrial thing':

Because at the end of the day, neighbourhood planning is supposedly about, or what we were sold, was that it was about local communities creating sustainable economic development for their areas, and what nobody talked about, was the fact that people were writing these plans and there was no way of generating the income to pay for any of the aspirations, and whereas if you add community energy, suddenly you've got a community income line going into this self-sufficiency that is ready made to deliver benefit. (2017, Susan, LEG).

7.3 Green Council

With a change in the policy landscape and pressure to decarbonise, councils, which have also had to live with severe budget cuts within the era of austerity since 2010, have had to reconsider how they act politically and economically in relation to more local production and consumption of renewable energy. While some choose to speak about new business models, others speak about redistribution models. In the 2010s, a number of UK councils set up their own energy companies, using a variety of business or redistribution models, some of them for-profit, others non-profit. Examples included Robin Hood Energy in Nottingham, White Rose Energy in Leeds and Bristol Energy Ltd. in Bristol. While now defunct, due to the energy crisis that started during the COVID pandemic, all these initiatives promised social and environmental benefits to customers and citizens, including tackling fuel poverty. Some of them even had the explicit purpose of generating funds for their cash-strapped council owners. With the overall aim of securing fairer and simpler offers, backed by good customer service, these energy providing services were either overseen or run directly from within the councils.

Yet councils have been dealing with energy matters for much longer. When the UK government launched the Renewables Obligation, the Green Council [pseudonym] set up an eco-endorsement contract with British Gas as partners. This resulted in a hundred million pounds worth of eco-funding and fifty million pounds of green deal finance for the Green Council, and with the Green County Programme [pseudonym], ambitious targets were set that eventually led to a shift, from seventy-five megawatts of installed renewables capacity in 2010, to an approximately tenfold increase, resulting in 750 megawatts in 2017. The programme also attracted locals who wished to compete with the established supply chain by setting up their own supply companies as well as test various new 'alternative' business models and novel technologies.

The Green Council has, in parallel, been very proactive, with nine megawatts of its own installed renewables capacity, creating more competition between council-owned and commercial entities. The county farms, for example, have a twenty million pound investment fund for the facilitation of wind power, set up to meet the change in feed-in tariffs:

I was speaking to a colleague yesterday. If a local authority, or anyone for that matter, was looking at replacing a boiler, you don't look at what the payback and return on investment's going to be on the boiler. Because of the environment we found ourselves in a few years ago, now when you talk about an investment in wind or solar or wave, or whatever it is, it's 'what's the return on investment?' Obviously, there needs to be that to attract the investment, but we're having discussions where I've had people who are looking to Green Council to co-invest with them into generating assets. When I take it to my colleagues in finance, they're saying, well, it's only a 7 percent return. That's not sufficient. (2017, Ralph, pseudonym, Green Council)

To cross this investment chasm, some local authorities have installed solar power and then gone to the local citizens to receive funding via bond offers that can be satisfied with a lower return on their investment. This brings about an energy transition under the current austerity measures and reduced budgets, where an invest-to-save model results in reduced energy bills, and an invest-to-redistribute model can result in economic support to other social causes, such as fuel poverty. For example, before its collapse Robin Hood Energy was fully owned by Nottingham City Council, and its main purpose was to provide low-cost energy to households and address fuel poverty in the city, at least according to the official information provided at that time:

It's totally unacceptable that any family today should have to choose between food and fuel, [...] why we're working to put things right, one household at a time, [...] doing everything we can to bring the cost of energy down. Unlike big, privately owned energy companies, our approach is simple: no frills, no paid directors and no private shareholders. We're not here to make a profit. We're here to make fuel poverty a thing of the past. (Robin Hood Energy 2018)

There are obviously redistribution models other than the creation of a local authority-owned company which can generate and redistribute assets. The Green Council has, for example, invested about a million pounds into a loan fund for community energy. Thus far, they have facilitated community ownership that amounts to seven megawatts of installed capacity. Another alternative is joint ventures between councils and existing energy companies as well as collaborations with universities and academic entrepreneurs who can unlock new technologies, such as marine, geothermal and wave power. The question is how direct the local authority investment should be in Green County:

We've had an outlying business case drawn up for a full licence supply company. I'd say there's a decision to be made because if I went up to the Council Offices today, and spoke to any of the new members and said, in Green Council's business plan there's reference to an energy company – what does that mean to you? What do you want from that? The majority would say, just cheaper bills. (2017, Ralph, Green Council)

The calculations to decide on the best way forward are complex. Green Council would have to invest between one and a half and two and a half million pounds to get an energy company licence. The question then is whether that is sufficient in a competitive market, where they will need to cover the operational costs required to service a customer base. The county in question is not that highly populated, and not everyone living there will switch to the local authority company either. Therefore, to create a viable energy company, the business plan would have to embrace the wider UK market, creating new complications and competitive demands.

In the 2010s, the UK's open energy market was slowly starting to become less monopolised. Many new start-ups had entered the market, including Robin Hood Energy, and 6.4 million electricity consumers switched suppliers in 2019 alone (Brown 2020). According to the investigation, many switched for the first time, and the total number of switchers was the highest in that decade, leaving the 'Big Six'[1] with a market share much lower than in previous years, down to 70 percent (Ofgem 2020). The global energy crisis, sparked by the COVID pandemic and the Ukraine war, has changed this picture, as many smaller energy companies had to exit the market. As there is now a renewed focus on national energy security, people might be more prone to understanding that local investments into new technologies are needed, in proximity to where they live. One of the Green Council representative also explains that it is very important that people understand their benefits if a geo-thermal plant or a marine array off the coast needs to be developed.

The councils additionally seek to influence the redistribution or business models to be picked up by the prosumer activists, as we will detail in Chapter 8, the reason being that prosuming should not be an activity that constantly needs governmental support and subsidies, but one that survives on its own merits and operations. We are told that one of the sports clubs in the area, where football, rugby and cricket are played, was extraordinarily successful when it came to receiving grants. In total, they received three-quarters of a million pounds for the instalment of heat pumps and other green energy solutions. In addition, the plan was to install solar panels on the roof of their stadium. Yet in the decision meeting, the assessment panel just sighed, saying that the club was too dependent on subsidies: 'they're just after grant, after grant' (2017, Ralph, Green Council). The panel thought they should turn to their own members instead. With over a thousand people registered with the club, they could have used this as a channel to promote a community share investment. That in turn would have paid for the technology installation, reduced the energy bills for the club and added to the running of the heat pumps and final export to the grid. Ralph was half-defending the UK government's decision, in the early 2010s, to reduce subsidies and feed-in tariffs, which had been so important in kick-starting the renewable energy industry in the UK. He suggested that renewable technologies need to pay for themselves

---

[1] The 'Big Six' is a common term in the UK, pointing to the six big players in the energy industry. However, quite a few changes have occurred in the constellation of these corporations, for example when SSE, one of the Big Six, sold their consumer operation to OVO, one of the newcomers. OVO are now part of the Big Six, having only been a medium-sized energy supplier previously (Shrestha 2020).

now, and that people and organisations should come up with innovative financial and business models to make it work.

Another redistribution model facilitated by the Green Council is also based on loans, to be repaid rather quickly. One organisation partaking in this loan programme provides outdoor and educational experiences to disadvantaged youth, partly powered by their own wind turbine. The renewable project was first set up, supported and influenced by various actors, developed by the local energy power cooperative Citizen Power [pseudonym], and then funded by a big international energy corporation and supported by a Green Council loan fund. In addition, the projects that follow this business model to reduce their own electricity bills, via an investment attached to a financial solution, need professional help to administer their investment. This help can be provided by a Community Development Finance Institution (CDFI) or Industrial and Provident Society (IPS). All in all, this is complex to orchestrate and not for the faint-hearted. It requires expert knowledge, devotion, time and other organisational resources. As a result, our Green Council informant confirms that, unfortunately, many citizen energy groups have faltered or just focus on administering existing renewable assets, rather than starting anything new. Over time, citizen groups have been directed towards more crowdfunding platforms, offering new opportunities and perhaps more simple funding models.

Public servants not only facilitate organisations to understand the possibilities of renewable technologies, but also have to act in response to resistance to renewables. The Green Council representative tells us how he felt particularly sorry for one citizen group that had met heavy resistance, with people demonstrating against them and shouting aggressively at them. The anti-campaigners even attacked one person's car, vandalised it and threw eggs at it. The reason for the public acting out of strong negative emotions was that some people in the area did not approve of a wind turbine being erected, which, strangely enough, would not have been visible from the village anyway. Therefore, when the community organisation applied for the funding, the council representative really wanted to support them: 'In fact, they were one of the reasons we set up the fund. We said, if anyone needs to do this, it's them' (2017, Ralph, Green Council).

However, public servants have to consider all sides of the argument and take broader knowledge of environmental aspects into consideration. Although they want to support green energy projects, they cannot be seen to be partial, and their decisions should instead

be based on expertise. They might have to counter renewable investments on behalf of a local population, and sometimes there are good
reasons for opposition against wind and solar – for example when
'greenfield' sites with a lot of quality agricultural land are chosen
instead of brownfield sites, which are contaminated due to historical
industrial operations. As one of the reasons for their opposition, many
anti-renewables activists cite that they do not want their landscape
to become industrialised. Hence, there are anti-renewable movements
that can sometimes spring out of 'landscape identity', where the history and the potential location of developments in relation to villages
and recreational areas determine the type of struggle (2017, Susan,
LEG):

[Y]ou look at what's happened in Wales; where there's been this massive
movement around anti-wind. But that's not from the farmers, because the
farmers are like 'well, this is a working landscape' and they look at the fields
and they see the local economy in these fields; they don't see a natural landscape, because it isn't a natural landscape. (2017, Susan, LEG)

7.4 Epistemic Community and Insider Activism

The local authorities and governments illustrated here, show how
fairly young public servants, who are flexible career movers, take their
work with renewables beyond formal work practices to build a collective movement via innovative organisational forms in attempts to
secure a bigger impact. Over the years, they have been self-employed
or worked for various employers, NGOs, consultancies and local
citizen groups. The network of professionals previously pointed out
as fundamental in the formation of an epistemic community, which
targets increasingly complex governmental problems (Haas 1992), is
thus more dispersed than anticipated. Insider activism often infuses the
other forms of activism, including activist entrepreneurship/enterpris-
ing activism, corporate activism, employee activism, investor activism
and prosumer activism. At the same time, in our cases they consist of
the same close-knit community of experts who move from one organisation to another (Harrigan, Achananuparp and Lim 2012).

Even though the struggles are different depending on location, they
take their expertise and environmental knowledge with them to accomplish change from within various organisations, as exemplified by
Arnold. Once a public servant, he became a consultant, then worked at

a university and became engaged in the Local Energy Group, a grass-roots initiative consisting of 1,500 members who are supportive of an 'energy revolution' (LEG 2018). His mobilisation of himself and his knowledge shows not only how the activist–business–state conglomeration can be knitted together in a variety of ways, but also how it facilitates a citizen to become an activist. The effect is another sort of 'mainstreaming' of activism (cf. Jamison 2001, Hensby, Sibthorpe and Drvier 2011), which makes it more approachable for politicians too, and not only for public servants who wish to speed up a green transformation from within. As already noted, there are many formal policies that envision a renewable energy transition by harnessing the energy to take action among citizens (Walker et al. 2007, Walker, Cass, et al. 2010, Walker, Devine-Wright, et al. 2010).

Instead of being ridiculed or looked down on, insider activists thus receive recognition for their applicable expertise and commitment to realise policies, which in turn results in practical authority and respect. At the same time, they often enter public authorities under insecure work contracts. They are a precarious workforce who rely on short-term contracts, preliminary positions and specific projects that often end within a few years, when they are forced to move on. Due to this constraint of green work practices, and thus a limitation of actions that our research participants were able to accomplish professionally, they often switched into voluntary work mode and hands-on everyday actions. Although the projects had a clear end, the process of sustainability and energy transition continued with their personal political environmental agenda. Their precarity thus contributes to the boundaryless attribute of climate activism and mobilises the epistemic community.

In their book on 'green insider activism' within state agencies and governmental bodies, Hysing and Olsson (2018) point to the immense amount of networking going on in the area of environmental problem-solving. If there is a prolific policy area that is cutting across domains, it is the green one, they assert. This cross-cutting, including boundary spanning, also involves businesses of various types. While quite a few of our research participants from within the councils seemed to have an inclination towards being anti-big-business, they nevertheless worked actively with businesses of various sizes and certainly applied many business principles and methods. The aim was not always the creation of a close collaboration, but sometimes an explicit or implicit exchange of practical knowledge on how to go about things. Similarly to how activist entrepreneurs must attempt to take action based on non-existent knowledge in their experimental creation of new knowledge, insider activists constantly search for ways forward to realise policies. We have thus found that 'green' public servants who wish to change both their own institution from within, as well as wider society, act under the assumption that it is necessary to involve and include local citizens and businesses to generate realistic paths for action. The triple bottom line unfolds since the public servants have to align pro-environmental values with positive social outcomes and economic necessities.

The everyday practices of Arnold, Susan, Martin and Ralph can therefore not be satisfactorily explained as results of neoliberal decentralisation and decarbonisation only, but instead display a will to go beyond deliberative democracy. They do not only want to deliberate with local residents, perhaps asking for their opinion on some policy. Instead, these council workers seek to invent new ways in which local citizens can become engaged in the energy transition merged with social and economic causes, positively contributing to a transition towards a more sustainable society. Efforts were made to force business down from their perceived dominant positions, sometimes by creating alternative enterprising organisations as vessels – for example social cooperatives acting as autonomous associations and jointly owned businesses (Short, Moss and Lumpkin 2009:164).

What previously could have been identified as conventional civil society activism has smoothly moved into the political warmth of the council to enforce relations between citizens and local government decision-making. The actions take more horizontal routes, enabling citizens to become engaged, first in their own life situation, then with business, as well as with environmental issues. In this way, 'public space' is transformed, both with regard to where it is physically allowed to take shape, inside or outside a council office, at home or on a site for renewables; and with regard to how it can be legitimately expressed and implemented, from fuel poverty to investments of pensions. If deliberative democracy seeks to make an energy transition smoother by preventing opposition to policy implementation, climate activism 'enables an epistemic community to provide information that excludes or enhances different alternatives' (Zito 2001:588). Rather than becoming relevant and valuable to an optimisation of existing policymaking, insider climate activism opens up possibilities for social innovations and creates paths for it to happen, often in locally formed togetherness. These activists experimentally create new bonds within the activist–business–state conglomeration and make novel climate actions realisable by new, quite intricate, formations of collectives. In comparison with the organisation of collectives that Tönnies exemplified in 1887, multiple legal constellations and combinations are now available. Notably, somewhere under the surface of these instrumental combinations for community relations rests a remnant of the earlier separation between *Gemeinschaft* and *Gesellschaft* (Tönnies 1957/2002).

In comparison with the conventional view that public servants should be neutral and apolitical mediators who bring policy to action, a sort of middle man that implements politics (Hysing and Olsson 2018), all of our interviewees were seemingly legitimately displaying their green insider activism at work within governmental authorities. Similarly to employee activists in larger corporations, a personal green agenda may marry very well with the strategic political agenda of the employer. Importantly, though, there are of course limits to insider activism as another type of employee activism, where loyalty and employment contracts can create tensions and novel epistemic struggles can arise (Icaza and Vázquez 2013). In the case of insider activism, these epistemic struggles are driven by the high complexity of environmental problems, which can lead to a quite desperate search for new paths on how to put the loosely defined and constantly changing policies into action. In other words, the public servants are more or less forced to stretch their formal responsibility, which 'presents challenges to the democratic system; raising important questions about the power of non-elected officials and how it affects democratic legitimacy' (Hysing and Olsson 2018:4).

Looking at the examples of insider activism presented in this chapter, it is nevertheless difficult to ascertain what an accepted limit of the voluntary actions was, and which actions needed to be more covert than overt to pass the judgement of both elected politicians and citizens. Hence, as pointed out in previous works about institutional change and institutional activists (Abers and Keck 2009), 'public officials can act as "activists" within governments and public organisations' by merging politically and officially sanctioned authoritative measures with a more personally driven political agenda and even secret subversive actions (Hysing and Olsson 2018:5). This means that environmentalism and climate activism are quite unproblematic for politicians, who need to facilitate decarbonisation as well as tackle energy poverty. Similarly to other contexts, there is a convergence between new-right and new-left political positions on how local citizens should be prioritised against an increasingly centralised state (Oldfield and Stokke 2007). As UK local councils have been starved of monetary resources in favour of centralised budgets in London since about 2010, when austerity took hold in the UK, they have been prone to finding other ways of working closely with people to generate funds to reclaim some independence. In this way, climate activism has become an economic saviour.

There was another interesting aspect of the horizontal cross-party politics on display among our council interviewees. Many expressed an explicit critique of the 'Big Six' energy companies, repeating their dominant position as oligopolies, largely in control of the UK's energy market. This critique, also apparent among politicians in several of the councils under study, went smoothly hand in hand with the anti-capitalist agenda expressed by some of the public servants we interviewed. Business models were transformed into new redistribution models and 'marketised' to citizens via insourced environmental movements that were given council employee contracts. A more intense entanglement of party politics, personal politics and stimulation of corporate and prosumer activism is probably hard to find. If the epistemic community in the beginning was mobilised by natural scientific knowledge about atmospheric changes and simulations, it is here expanded by knowledge on business enterprising, strategic legal planning, marketing and, most importantly, how sustainability can be actively brought to people's backyards.

In addition to Hysing and Olson's (2018) insights, we thus find an even greater variety of political goals and personal aims behind the actions taken. Based on social missions and decarbonisation, the public officials tied together people who worked across sectors – a flexibility supported by various enterprising schemes and models, from community funds to loans and crowdfunding. A council loan fund was even set up specially to meet citizens' resistance to citizen-owned renewable energy. Hence, the public officials we met worked more outwards than inwards in their efforts to infuse change and were not typical 'policy entrepreneurs' or 'institutional activists', who try to change political agendas from within (Kern and Bulkeley 2009, Abers 2019). They did alternatively express a certain dissatisfaction with the lack of focus on climate change by pointing to an imbalance between various polarised citizen groups, a disinterest in decarbonisation on the one hand, and a keen interest in social and economic value creation on the other.

The dissatisfaction resulted in public servants desiring more direct, visible and impactful engagement in environmental problems in the public sphere. Their reasoning was not aligned with the most common already existing neoliberal agenda on how to make 'economic motives and measures' infiltrate increasingly 'new spheres of activity' (Dowling 2010:489). Instead, their targets were fuel poverty, which is an immense social problem in the UK (Healy 2017), and climate change, bringing together an alliance of so-called red-green politics (Benton 2017). This is local council politics with a purpose, indeed using market dynamics, to deliver key social and environmental policy outcomes. What drives the insider activists we engaged with is an idealised synergy between the social, economic and environmental in their implementation of the triple bottom line. Secured by them, albeit on a small scale, they effectively become a relay for sustainability governance (Adger and Jordan 2009), but without being deadened by consensus processes or quests to adapt to complexities. Rather, such thwarting of what they conceived to be true politics can be seen as the reason for their enthusiasm. The slowness generated by consensus processes, and the lack of action resulting from formal political focus and policies in favour of mere adaptation, enlivened their prospects and opportunities to take individual actions, in the particular cases illustrated here by professional work with collective actions pursued from within formal political bodies.

The insider activists are reacting not only to the slowness of their employers but also to the slowness of citizens. They are operating in a field characterised by a relative lack of green thinking among the local citizens, and it became clear that these activists saw part of their mission as helping to fix that lack and to alter and re-invent others. They have had quite a bit of success, at least considering the relatively high demand for the renewables programmes offered by the three councils. The redistribution or business models owned or facilitated by councils are thus a way of securing a position for the state in the growth of citizens' efforts to create green businesses together. The state is brought back in by how it is made into an active business partner in the energy transition (cf. Mazzucato 2015b). Robin Hood Energy neatly exemplifies how a merger of social and environmental justice unfolds with market assessments and disruptions, aided by public servants, who are not necessarily insider activists. The innovative forces previously identified to exist in business and civil society are thus incorporated within the political body of a local authority, where 'insider activism' can be recognised by searching for actions at the edges, where tensions are created. The councils are becoming buzzing zones of insider activism, opening up business opportunities for citizens increasingly envisioned as potential activists themselves, sharing investment risks, facilitating the entry to market and supporting creativity on the ground for small-scale energy transition efforts (cf. Conklin Frederking 2010).

We were not able to observe the whole apparatus of the three councils under study to follow their complete work on green enterprising endeavours, sometimes against capitalism. What was notable was how insider activism spread in a somewhat strange mix of public service provisioning, business enterprising, anti-capitalist resisting and doing good. Whereas these aspects could feed discordance, we observed their harmony and symbiotic relationship stretching to offers of 'getting along' and gathering, directed towards citizens as well as business representatives who equally enjoyed an empowerment of local groups. The insider activists secure the 'throughput', that is, the level of capability to implement policies in participatory governance programmes (Abers and Keck 2009:292). Similarly to the findings of Abers and Keck, we found that insider activists collaborate with external actors to enable them to better meet resistance to transformations. Hence, state responsibility is not fully transferred to private actors, but 'public space' is mobilised in efforts to 'defend the public interest' (Abers and Keck 2009:293). Diversity on how to implement the policies is furthermore actively included in the three councils, which shows that they do not treat citizen participation as exogenous. Insider activism is even supported across the conventional political positions, where it is democracy itself that would be conceived by some idealists as 'deepened' (e.g. see Abers and Keck 2009). The state is not only deliberating business enterprising, financialisation, consumption and individuals who seek to invest in themselves and others monetarily or morally. The state is also embracing the right to assemble by affirming the freedom of association, that is, by nurturing collective movements and community relations. Democracy is smoothly delivered as if generated by the people for the people (Rancière 2005/2014), via enticing technologies and promises of social, environmental and economic value creation. As we will illustrate further, and also discuss from more critical perspectives in the following chapter on prosumer activism, the inevitable ungovernability of thought, actions and excess, including the human capacity for generosity, gift-giving and coming together, is alluring for a horizontal transition of the energy system, to be pursued by Do-It-Yourself solutions, prefiguratively, in the here and now.

8 | Climate Activism via Citizen Groups

Although insider activism, as presented in the previous chapter, was configured around a political awareness of how climate actions could be organised to bring about an 'energy revolution', it has mainly been up to affluent people to deliver on this political opening by taking climate actions via renewable energy technology. Renewables, such as wind and solar, have enabled quite a radical so-called decentralisation of electricity generation. Whereas in the modernisation of the past states provided electricity and heat almost exclusively generated by large hydro, nuclear and fossils power stations, the twenty-first century has seen a shift in policy and technology. Energy production and distribution has gone through an outsourcing process: from the state, then to private corporations and lastly to citizen groups and individuals (Walker et al. 2007). People are offered the opportunity to invest in, and possess, their own electricity and heat generation in this centrally enabled decentralisation.

In practice it is not quite as easy as that; one needs financial resources, suitable space, expertise and enabling legislative frameworks in place to join the micro-generation revolution. Nevertheless, millions of citizen-users worldwide, or so-called prosumers, have installed solar panels on their roofs or have invested their cash into citizen-owned renewable energy projects. If an individual alone does not have a rooftop or enough financial resources, there is an abundance of new organisational paths to choose from, so as to gather and join forces with neighbours, friends and family. The will to connect with others, in tandem with a will to possess renewable technology and take climate action, is dependent on new ways of relating to each other, for example by launching local currencies to redistribute profits from wind turbines or solar farms outside of towns. This chapter is about these relational processes among citizens who share their diverse knowledge backgrounds, mobilise their professional experience and get together to realise a transition of the energy system as prosumer activists.

8.1 Love Seaside Town

Decarbonisation is essential, you know. I mean; that's my big picture, essential for our survival as a species. I mean in that way we're [Love Seaside Town, pseudonym] just a tiny little dot on the map, but I think, you know, there has to be action on all dots on the map, worldwide, for kind of proper transitions to a low carbon way of living. (2017, Liam, pseudonym, Love Seaside Town)

When we met with representatives from the renewable energy volunteers Love Seaside Town, the group had already been in existence for six years; it was initiated in 2010 in the kitchen of one of the lead local enthusiasts with the ambition to enable an entire seaside town and its inhabitants to be more energy self-sufficient. When asked, the then director of the group of volunteers recalled a question posed during the first meeting of the group: '[I]n order to be effective, we need to be an organisation; does anybody know how to set up an organisation?' (2017, Liam, Love Seaside Town). The legal entity suggested by one of the members with experience from previous citizen group initiatives is similar to a 'community benefit cooperative'. It is a legal entity that allows operations founded on broader grounds than a sole interest in energy, stretching to a holistic view of an environment prosperous for humans to live in, including cultural ambitions and energy poverty alleviation. This reflects the composition of Love Seaside Town, mainly consisting of two categories of people: those with relational and social priorities and those with green priorities. Perhaps less strategic than it seems, they slowly found each other and realised that it was possible and fruitful to merge the two. Somewhat in parallel with the councils and insider activism, they started to merge the social and the green to create fruitful synergies:

If you are sort of able to use renewable energy as a means of improving the wealth and welfare of the town, and so just looking at things, like if you could establish renewable energy of scale. If you are doing that as a community enterprise, then where you would normally have shared all the profits, you'd actually got money that you could plough back into the community. (2017, Guy, pseudonym, Love Seaside Town)

The plan was to set up local renewable energy projects for local citizens to invest in, and by spending their money on these investments the locals would get a lower energy bill as well as sharing the returns as shareholders. Instead of wasting their money on goods and services provided by big national companies, the local initiative aimed to keep the resources in the town, according to a redistributive model, thus supporting the local economy. Before starting their renewable energy initiative, some of the members of Love Seaside Town, many of whom were middle-aged to older retired people, had been involved in an anti-globalism campaign to stop three large supermarkets being built in their town. The supermarkets were considered to be culturally polluting organisations, which would destroy local shops and the character of the entire town, as they argued had happened in 'many, many, many towns' (2017, Liam, Love Seaside Town). Their anti-supermarket campaign was largely successful, which gave them the impetus and collective energy to continue their pro-local engagement. One thing they wished to do was to transform the previous anti-globalism movement into something less oppositional and based on resistance, to become more firmly based on a pro-movement: positive and affirming. The best thing, they felt, would be to work with renewable energy schemes, since this would be positive for both the environment and the local economy. Their anti-big business resistance – which is a bit of a surprising stance, given that some of them used to work for big oil and gas companies – was thereby transformed into a pro-local enterprising initiative:

Based on the fact that the way the energy companies operate, the big ones, is kind of smoke and mirrors, because it's very difficult to actually tell what their generation costs are. Because they're, as you know, both generators and suppliers, [...] and you have a centralised energy system, you have massive costs associated with balancing and maintaining supply. So, our analysis, and it is probably an extremely naïve analysis, was that if you could address any of those kinds of factors, you would be able to extract money back out in the local economy. (2017, Liam, Love Seaside Town)

To ensure that the money stayed local, the renewable energy prosumers created their own currency, called Beem [pseudonym], which could be used in seventy shops in the local area. The currency, with a special locally designed note, was partly connected to an energy scheme, meaning that one would be able to receive the local currency by insulating one's house or installing solar panels. Love Seaside Town ran a tender to find an insulation partner that would not only give the insulation to the household for free but also pay Love Seaside Town forty pounds per household, since they would get referral fees. The local prosumer group would then split the forty pounds, with twenty pounds going to the 'community funds' in the town, and twenty pounds going to the householder in the Beem currency. With this redistributive model and some marketing, 100 households were insulated in two months. Further on, Love Seaside Town made the subsidies for cavity wall and loft insulation more easily available, creating new incentives for people to sign up for this energy- and carbon-saving scheme.

Connected to Love Seaside Town's initiative is the UK government's Carbon Emissions Reduction Target, which meant that big energy companies had to comply by providing insulation and other carbon-reducing measures to households free of charge. The big companies were desperate to sign people up to the scheme to secure compliance with the government's obligations. Yet when company representatives knocked on people's doors in Seaside Town to try to encourage them to use the subsidised offer, the result was poor. However, when members of Love Seaside Town approached the inhabitants, the willingness to take part in the insulation programme increased considerably. People trusted their neighbours more than the company representatives, and the novelty of the local currency was alluring. It attracted many to engage. Even though this helped spread the word about the benefits of localism, there was no plan to leave the central monetary system completely. The main idea was rather to engage people in climate actions and to build a bridge locally between the government and the energy industry in a way that served the local interests of the town, rather than commercial business. It also meant that Love Seaside Town encouraged the taking up and active pursuit of information. That is, they tried to reach beyond scientific facts to foster new relations with others and establish in-depth understanding of the links between the green environment and economic issues in general:

People loved the novelty of the local currency. So their motivation to get free insulation wasn't that it would save them £300 a year, it was that they'd get a £20 Beem note. People aren't rational, but that's what it takes! It takes people to realise that people aren't rational. The government has begun to realise that, they've begun to realise that people won't take things up just because it's economically rational; that there is a role for local energy organisations to be the interface between the energy industry and a community, and that people find it … there's a greater element of trust with a local energy organisation than there is with an outside utility. (2017, David, LEG)

Love Seaside Town accomplished other achievements with hard work, guided by passion, localism and a good dose of scepticism towards big businesses. They have installed solar PV to power around 1,200 homes and renewable heat for about 250 homes. Love Seaside Town has, in addition, facilitated various wind power developments, receiving community funds that amount to seventy thousand pounds, as a percentage of the profit generated from the wind power business. Technically, however, the local initiative encountered many obstacles. This meant that those who took the lead and infused a collective movement had to become technical experts, on top of handling the regional support mechanisms and subsidies. As one of the consultants working with various prosumer solutions clarified:

I don't understand how these tiny organisations do it, [...] with their, you know, solar development or wind developments, whatever it might be, I do not understand how they do it. Although they mostly work with volunteers, they must have significant consultancy costs, in order to advise on a lot of the technical aspects. (2017, Arnold, LEG)

In fact, many prosumers were activated and seduced into becoming technical experts themselves, sometimes building on their existing knowledge bases established in their previous careers, which included the oil and gas industry. However, often it took hard work for pensioners to get their heads around complex technical and regulatory issues, leaving them quite exhausted and confused, yet more collectively involved and rewarded. The struggles with knowledge were not about fixed positions of ideas or opinions but were driven by the will to find some sort of direction in an uncertain technical and political landscape. As they explained, their mutual co-production and mobilisation of knowledge was experienced as an adventure, which created strong bonds and friendships.

Having been granted funds for a feasibility study of a three- to four-megawatt solar installation, Love Seaside Town's plan of creating community ownership was nevertheless challenged. One obstacle was the quickly reduced return on investment in renewables due to changing incentive schemes brought in by the new coalition government at Westminster, and additional problems were surfacing, such as the lack of stable and functioning grid connection points. The cables and wires were not scaled up sufficiently for the vast amount of solar power that would be generated in the summer months. Love Seaside Town, therefore, decided to look into energy storage, which was to be achieved together with some bigger energy companies in the region, combined with funding possibilities from Ofgem, the government regulator. One solution they found was the process of electrolysing water, feeding the hydrogen into the gas distribution grid whenever the electrical grid would not accept the high generation of electricity. After having set up a company for the transformation of electricity into hydrogen generation and submitting a bid together with established companies for electricity and gas distribution, Love Seaside Town nevertheless lost the competitive funding process:

[I]t seemed reasonable and so there were people sort of very keen on it, but it didn't come through, so that sort of capacity to build large-scale solar was sort of taken away. So that was the problem. The next thing we were looking at was a large-scale wind farm, and that, there was a very valuable opposition to. [...] [G]enerally, there's a sort of feeling that the turbines are good things, but if you see them everywhere you look, then people get fed up. (2017, Guy, Love Seaside Town)

The local citizens who tried to facilitate prosumerism had to deal not only with governmental authorities, but also with financial and technical challenges and solutions. As with any corporate developer, they had to face civic resistance, but in their case from some of their closest neighbours and old friends. The pensioners who were active in Love Seaside Town, and who had fairly recently moved to the area, explained to us that those who had lived in the town for a long time met them with suspicion, and this may have been a reason, they suggested, why so many initiatives by Love Seaside Town were actively blocked. Part of the resentment, we were told, was because the incomers represented 'well off, middle class, and educated' people. Their affluence was assumed to be a threat to those who already lived in the area and who, according to our interviewees, were against any type of change, not just those proposed by Love Seaside Town. In comparison with renewable developments made by large industrial actors, such struggles between people who are essentially neighbours require even more passion, engagement and conviction – to overcome the resistance to the energy transition. The prosumerism experience is thus coupled with an emotional ride, a stronger 'we' against a reluctant 'them', togetherness and exhaustion, uncertainties about how to take climate actions, but eventually finding comfort in each other to meet these challenges and the negative stress incurred:

[O]ne particular person, from the town council, turned around to me and said, 'oh, you know, we're not living in a communist state, you can't make people do things', and you think, when you get things like that said to you, I mean, there's no room for discussion, is there? (2017, Liam, Love Seaside Town)

Another strategy was to work even more closely with a bigger developer a few miles outside the town centre. The idea was to share the ownership with the developer and thereby secure community ownership and income. The developer, however, only offered up a very small share in the investment, and since it was the last reasonable site for development, Love Seaside Town dropped their support and the project was later turned down based on planning issues. Nevertheless, the local lead initiator approached the developer again and said, 'look, we could still get something out of this, if you do actually make it a local project rather than a commercial one' (2017, Guy, Love Seaside Town). At this time, however, the government changed the rules yet again, which meant that the town and parish councils had a veto over all developments:

So, we tried speaking to the half-dozen town and parish councils around the wind farm, including Seaside Town, who would all oppose the commercial developer. And when we came on to what we want to do, to get a community-owned one, some didn't understand it. Some of them I think wilfully didn't understand it. So, they just opposed it. (2017, Guy, Love Seaside Town)

The argument over the bigger investment continued for a while, especially based on uncertainties about the financial and economic aspects. The question was whether the investment would eventually have a payback. Due to the uncertain economic details, Love Seaside Town could only tell the councils that 'yeah, if you come in we can see and make it work' (2017, Guy, Love Seaside Town). This economic uncertainty unsurprisingly meant that the councils kept to their original decision, and in the end, not even a commercial development disconnected from citizen engagement went ahead. This led the local prosumers to conclude that it was a bad business case anyway and would probably not have been such a good opportunity for scaling up and establishing local ownership for electricity generation. In this particular case, the scale meant a wind farm of four to five turbines of a total size of ten megawatts, which would cover approximately 7,000 households, depending on the annual wind, technology and exact usage per household per year.

The prosumers did not give up, but with whetted appetite they soon embarked on another project, wishing to make their town into a so-called smart hub, or centre for smart electricity, supported by EU funds. They thus tried to build a consortium, which included a university, smaller consultancies and organisations, as well as a big business, a Japanese multinational technology corporation founded in the nineteenth century, with approximately 170,000 employees – all devoted to crafting a realistic bid for an EU grant:

But it wasn't successful, and at that point we felt that we had sort of used up our sources of grant funding, which was intended to get us in a state of owning or being involved in major projects, which would have provided an income stream [that] could keep us going [...] as a group, in terms of what we wanted to do. And retain the sort of skilled people that we had, some of whom were on a paid basis, some of it were volunteers, [which] meant we had to change what we were doing. We had a couple of successes, we did build a 100-kilowatt solar ray, which produces its electricity to a sewage treatment works. [...] It is just a power purchase agreement and all the electricity generated goes into that [...] by direct wire by bypassing the grid connection. (2017, Guy, Love Seaside Town)

The solar power for the sewage works started due to an expressed interest from the regional water and sewage company. They were interested in improving their operations by investing in renewables, and they wished to do it together with a local group of citizens. Via a non-profit organisation, Centre for Renewable Experts [pseudonym], which functions as an association for the renewable energy industry in the region, to which Love Seaside Town belong, the water supplier chose to work closely with Love Seaside Town. The planning took a long time, due to processes of consent with people in the area and numerous legal requirements. In comparison, the actual building was quick and smooth.

The skills required during the work with the solar planning and installation were manifold, and Love Seaside Town received help from the Centre for Renewable Experts and retained control of the legal and business side, enforced by a twelve-person-strong board. They worked very well together, developed a collective confidence and thought that if they could not accomplish this, no one else could. They tried to work harder on building a political consensus with the local council and the county. One particularly important person in the process was the charismatic chairman of the board of Love Seaside Town, who 'was very good at articulating and developing the vision and ambition of what the group could do' (2017, Guy, Love Seaside Town). Even though he had a known track record of getting things done, it was harder than expected to develop a close relationship between the prosumer activists and the seniors in the council. In comparison with how the insider activists in the Green Council facilitated for citizen groups (see Chapter 7), Love Seaside Town experienced a strong lack of interest among council representatives.

At Love Seaside Town, one operations manager was paid an almost full-time wage, complemented by a part-time operations assistant. Except for the directors, most of the others worked voluntarily. The Energy Shop, for example, open between 11 a.m. and 3 p.m. six days a week for five years, was entirely staffed by volunteers. Establishing a physical presence via a 'shop' in town, where people could enter just to be informed about energy-related matters and possibilities to go green, allowed Love Seaside Town to promote domestic solar power, resulting in 1,100 members in a town of 6,500 people, and a turnover of fifty thousand pounds per year. The Energy Shop was nevertheless not as busy as was hoped for, especially not on Saturdays, when only one or two locals would typically drop by for advice. However, depending on the additional information they provided about offers on the website and signs outside the shop, the number of face-to-face meetings occasionally increased. Love Seaside Town also received a 'fact finder fee' of 2 or 3 percent per installation cost from certain solar panel providers.

All the effort put in by Love Seaside Town did pay off in some respects. The town has an extremely high penetration rate of domestic solar, with 10 percent coverage of all private homes, in addition to a school and a holiday home. They were keen, however, to keep the work organised through volunteer engagement and not personal gain. The image they sought to portray was not that they were selling something, but that they were giving impartial advice. Added to the investment advice was thus another volunteer mission, to reduce people's fuel debts, which they sometimes managed, although over time they had to realise the limits of the help this could provide. The challenge Love Seaside Town faced was that those who had fuel problems had multiple problems, such as disability in the family, substance abuse problems, imprisoned family members and generally inadequate incomes that affected especially their children in depressing ways. Only one of them was professionally equipped to deal with this assortment of underprivileged conditions. The set of skills needed to solve their situation was unattainable within the group, and Love Seaside Town only had the human resources and grants to work on specific energy solution actions, such as better insulation and new investments:

For a lot of time we were there, we were able to sort of understand and interpret all the various schemes that the coalition government was promoting, in terms of energy and climate change. So, we had installation schemes for houses, [and] the green deal, when it came in we tried to get to grips with that. We had solar panel installers, a couple on our team, so that we could direct them [locals] to someone we thought was reputable. All of those sort of things, you know; switching electricity suppliers, even something as simple as that; we had old couples come in who couldn't use computers and we would sit and do it for them. (2017, Guy, Love Seaside Town)

Another redistributive business model was tried thereafter, based on a programme set up to install solar panels on people's roofs, where Love Seaside Town would get the feed-in tariff and the roof owner would get free electricity. Out of thirty people who applied to join the programme, only four remained. The problem was spotted during the lease contract design, when the mortgage lenders of a majority of the interested people requested that Love Seaside Town should become a member of a particular industry society. Becoming a supplier, with their own generating station, was not possible due to the way the electricity market was set up. In addition, the policy environment increasingly became very averse to what Love Seaside Town was trying to accomplish, and the charismatic and experienced director, who earlier had played such an important networking role, gradually became worn out and eventually left the prosumer group. The ambition to establish a self-sustaining organisation, earning its own income, was disappearing when the local market for solar power became saturated, and Love Seaside Town decided to scale back to survive.

By the time we visited them in 2017, we felt they had peaked as an organisation in support of local prosuming. By then they had a new chairman, who confessed to us that 'to be honest, I haven't got the kind of ambition or the vision, or the energy to, you know, to sort of take it in any big direction' (2017, Liam, Love Seaside Town). The new chairman is mainly managing the community funds, given to arts projects, social projects and educational projects. Hence, Love Seaside Town have accumulated a reasonable amount of money by administering the community funds donated by three larger commercial renewable energy projects, amounting to approximately seventy thousand pounds per year. They were, in addition, partners in a project called 'the Sunshine tariff', which tried to get people to think about shifting their electricity consumption away from peak periods, typically from early evening to daytime. To accomplish this, Love Seaside Town partnered with a supplier, a distributor and the energy industry association that acted as project manager, and then offered the locals a commercial tariff. This was set flexibly to five pence between 10 a.m. and 4 p.m. from April to September, and eighteen pence for the rest of the time. The latter is higher than the commercial tariff, with the aim to steer the demand effectively. Fewer locals than expected were, however, interested, saying that they could not be bothered to go through the hurdle of switching, especially not if they had just done so. In total, only sixty households enrolled, of which forty-six are followed up regularly as part of a research study, and the rest function as a control group. The funds brought in by the Sunshine tariff are added to the other community funds and distributed to local initiatives. This means that Love Seaside Town have very few costs, although they retain some bank savings in case of a future change in renewable energy policies. They still hope to establish themselves as a self-sustaining renewable energy community, but so far it has not quite happened for them.

8.2 Decarbonised Living Project

After a bit of a bumpy car ride on muddy and winding roads with custom-made road signs pointing to estates of various sizes, we reached the Decarbonised Living Project in Farmers Village [pseudonyms, also see the Prologue]. A home-made road sign told us to slow down as we approached a little wooden roundhouse used to

Figure 8.1 Slow snail, home-made road sign, Farmers Village. Photo: Annika Skoglund

host children's forest school activities (see Figure 8.1). Next to it was the old farm where our meeting was to take place. It had been renovated to host bigger occasions, such as weddings, corporate events and anniversaries.

We were guided around the property before being offered tea, coffee and eventually raw milk on the second floor of the stone barn – the dinner and dance venue. The milk could only be given away since the local farmer, who is part of the renewables voluntary group, did not yet have a licence to sell it. The group spoke proudly about the nutritious and tasty raw milk which had not yet been served, since the farmer was running a bit late. The milk discussion effectively brought us to what the meeting was supposed to be all about: their coming together, connectedness to nature, gift-giving and generosity. The group of volunteers spoke warmly about their collective effort, emphasising its uniqueness several times, especially in relation to how successful they were in the state-subsidised Decarbonised Living Challenge, a competition that attracted local citizen groups, what in daily terminology is talked about as 'communities', to take policy to action:

So it is, I think, nearly unique in a community, and was pretty complex from a legal point of view. I think this is why we are unique, yeah, the fact that we've got a revenue stream, we are able to go well beyond what a lot of the transition groups have become, which is just talk shops. We're able to action initiatives on the ground, I think that's been key to probably the reason why you're here talking to us today. (2017, Focus group, Farmers Village)

Their engagement in renewables all started with a meeting where a handful of initiators decided to set up a local food market once a month, to promote local produce. One thing led to the next, as they kept inviting people to meetings. It was during the first decade of the new millennium, when renewables were becoming more and more a trendy remedy, so when the government set up the Low Carbon Community Challenge in late 2009, our research participants attracted a wider audience. Twenty-four villages/towns were to be granted half a million pounds each, and Farmers Village was offered the chance to team up with Community Energy Network [pseudonym] to apply for the creation of a small off-grid test site, consisting of various renewable energy sources and technologies to be installed in different types of buildings, from Victorian to modern houses, schools and community halls, as well as barns. All were to be equipped with technologies ranging from ground source heat pumps to water solar panels and a small wind turbine, complemented by insulation schemes. At first their bid was not accepted, but quite soon an opening appeared:

The people at Community Energy Network had a call from the Department of Energy and Climate Change, to say that one of the people that they'd awarded it to realised that they couldn't do it by March the 31st, [and were thus wondering] whether we would still be able to do it by March the 31st. To which we replied 'yes'. So, then it was a very rushed job, which was not a good feature. [...] It was an incredibly rushed thing, which of course wasn't very helpful. (2017, Focus group, Farmers Village)

The Decarbonised Living Project had to speed up their voluntary work and get all the planning permissions accepted, solar panels installed and a wind turbine purchased as quickly as possible, before the budget year came to an end. The funds would otherwise be sent elsewhere. Another reason for the rush was the upcoming political election in 2010: the outgoing government wanted climate actions via renewables to happen before then. Due to the rush, things were installed before people even knew about them, which created some resistance, especially against the wind turbine, 'even though it was a titchy little thing' of twenty kilowatts (2017, Focus group, Farmers Village). The rush meant that the resistance movement had a very short time span to assemble properly. Others never thought the Decarbonised Living Project would make it, that is, that they would succeed in getting the test site and all the solar panels funded. When their fellow villagers and sceptic audience later realised their success, they came to ask for some of their own, perhaps knowing that the successful bid meant that the prosumer activists would take all the feed-in tariffs and heat incentives and use them for further installations. At that time, a solar panel of 2,000 watts cost them eleven and a half thousand pounds, while the later technical development of the panels reduced the prices remarkably, to around four thousand pounds:

The model that we adopted was to actually give these solar panels to people, so that they took ownership and they wrote a contract with us, […] and our liability was to keep them maintained, in return for all the feed-in tariffs coming back to us. (2017, Focus group, Farmers Village)

The scheme was complex from a legal point of view, and the Decarbonised Living Project had to be extra creative and seek professional advice to make a strategic and practical choice among legal structures. They thus formed an Industrial and Providence Society in addition to an Industrial Society Cooperative. Why two separate organisations were needed in the end was still unclear to us as well as to the representatives of the Decarbonised Living Project. It related to the type of investment and redistribution plan they created, which allowed free electricity to be given to the owner of the panels, with the feed-in tariffs going to the Decarbonised Living Project, which would reinvest the funds for the benefit of the local citizens.

From having been offered raw milk and listening to how the volunteers had come together to create new friendships, our conversation slowly turned into a proud presentation of organisational legal structures and technical-economic specificities. Entangled in the affinities and togetherness that we were invited to experience were quite instrumental arrangements, but also tensions in meetings with other people, the local counter-movement and NIMBYism. Inevitably, the conversation in the repurposed barn turned to alternative business models and redistribution schemes, and details about how the test site was set up with possibilities to compare technology efficiency. Since they each got a different technology to try, these comparisons strengthened their togetherness, based on 'techy' discussions about functions and outputs. What was more than disappointing, they echoed, was the lack of formal political interest shown by the local authorities that first promoted the competition, or so-called community challenge. There was in the end no interest whatsoever in the knowledge they had been offered to co-produce, where some of the installed technologies definitely had a more positive effect than others. Despite these internal differences among the group of volunteers, with some enjoying their machinery more than others, this did not seem to affect their togetherness in, for us, an observable way – perhaps because they moved quickly from the specificities about the installed renewable technologies to common learnings about business and redistribution models.

We were told that solar PV installations were easier to install on the roofs of people's houses and communal buildings as there were normally no objections from the wider community. Solar was popular as the power generated was fed into the national grid, which generated income through the feed-in tariff. In the case of communal buildings, such as schools, a company would be created, and the feed-in tariff would cover the operating costs of the solar installation, the administration costs of the company and the cost of finance. Importantly, any surplus goes into the local redistribution purpose that was set up at the start when the organisational structure was designed, so there is a double benefit here. The first aim is to generate as much affordable renewable power for families and schools as possible. The second purpose, however, is to maximise the income of the prosumer company to generate surplus profits, which are then distributed to local citizen projects, such as fuel poverty work, insulation schemes or non-energy-related charity projects. These redistribution models are thus built to take control of revenue streams in a two-way grid system, and as one of the consultants working for a non-profit organisation with the aim to facilitate for prosumers explained:

Well, they [the prosumer groups] can see the flaw in our energy economy, and the slow progress we are making towards carbon reduction, and the issues of fuel poverty, and the cost of energy for their area, and they can see there is a way of doing something about that. That's their driver. (2017, David, Localism for Renewables)

Even though the general redistributive business model sounds straightforward, there are considerable technical barriers that disturb or delay the implementation of the models. If electricity generation is to be built up locally, by the people who live there, then they first need to acquire the rights to connect to the grid. This can be costly and cumbersome, or simply impossible due to constantly changing regulations. While the New Labour government established pro-environmental renewable energy policies in the 2000s, including a relatively generous feed-in tariff, many of them were scaled back or abandoned after the coalition government, consisting of the Conservatives and Liberal Democrats, came into power in 2010.

Many prosumer groups were encouraged to take action under Labour, but when the regulatory and funding scene changed dramatically in subsequent years, their business and redistribution models were invalidated. This meant that prosumer groups such as the Decarbonised Living Project were more or less on their last legs, and it was notable that we encountered them when they were exhausted and had 'run out of steam'. For many years they had been eagerly trying out various business and funding models, experimenting with different technologies and renewable schemes, which would have cost them a lot of time, energy and spirit. In the end they were getting tired of trying, and many people dropped out. The Decarbonised Living Project nevertheless still expressed a hope that alternative solutions could be found to make local ownership of renewables worthwhile. While there exist various experiments to become more economically and energy self-sufficient, most investments presented to us were dependent on the changing policy landscape, with subsidy models and the assumption that a connection to the national grid could be made.

The entanglement of private finance and state subsidies in the realm of renewables meant that actions taken by the Decarbonised Living Project developed into more of an everyday job as a non-profit consultancy, there to limit the barriers of entry for prosumerism, for example by setting up networks for innovation projects together with already existing local citizen groups or larger businesses, or by investigating the best pricing schemes in relation to consumption behaviours. Hence, their expertise is mobilised at the intersection of business opportunities, policy demands and technical options, for example when investigating whether or not one can connect a community-owned solar farm to a constrained grid. Yet even with additional help from professional renewable energy consultants (see Chapter 6), available at a relatively low cost for laypeople acting as prosumer activists, it has proven very difficult to process the vision of an alternative electricity generation system into a material reality. Even so, during this process, the community relations prosper and the members of the prosumer groups enjoy their new friendships and connections, often as newcomers in a small town or village. It is a 'transformation' that keeps them going, as one of the professional consultants testified:

They've trialled various business models, some that have worked quite well, but others small scale. But they've not been able to get the whole thing off the ground at the scale that they wanted to, and they were very clear from the outset that they want it to be a transformation thing. They're not interested in owning a few solar panels on school roofs, they want to generate energy at the scale of the town's consumption, otherwise it's not worthwhile. It has to be material. And that wasn't possible, not because of, it wasn't their fault, they were too late to the game. The sites had gone. (2017, David, Localism for Renewables)

Another professional consultancy that seeks to support knowledge transfer across various organisations in the area is Prosuming More [pseudonym]. Their mission is specifically to help local volunteers to understand the renewable energy industry better, pointing out realistic paths forward and suggesting ways one can adapt commercial business models to redistributive community models. They have an acclaimed good understanding of the whole industry and what perspectives the commercial developers have in their specific geographic area. This stretches all the way to the actual negotiation of contracts between the locals and the commercial actors. The key issue is how local initiatives are to prosper beyond a high number of enthusiastic members and local supporters, by creating large-scale community-owned generation. The timing for this has proven crucial since there are limited areas for development around the villages.

The conversation we had with the Decarbonised Living Project confirmed the manifold problems faced by prosumer activism, one of which has been competition over suitable sites (see Figure 8.2). In this particular geographical area of England, there has also been growing tension. Some villages were early movers in prosumerism, while others saw the opportunities too late. Furthermore, the council supported prosumerism in principle, but by the time citizens became mobilised, most of the suitable sites had gone to commercial developers. What the nascent prosumers lacked was the capacity to sign up land to have

Figure 8.2 The failing wind power turbine of the Decarbonised Living Project at Farmers Village. Large-scale commercial solar panels fill up the fields in the distance. Photo: Annika Skoglund

control of their own projects, since this required high-risk investment. Hence, prosumer activism has to compete with commercial developments set up by professionals who normally have more experience, more resources and are better organised to move quickly to accomplish an actual implementation of renewables. One might think that it does not matter who is accomplishing the decarbonisation, as long as it happens, but this is not how the prosumers reason. They strive to accomplish a decentralisation to disrupt the ruling energy economy:

Most of them [prosumer activists] went down the path of a conflict between an outside developer and a local community, and that meant not enough were getting planning permission quick enough. So, from a low carbon perspective, not enough capacity was getting built. For me, the wind and solar farms that were getting built weren't changing the energy economy, they were changing the technology, and reducing emissions, but they weren't decentralising ... so they're decentralising generation but they weren't decentralising ownership and economic benefit, and that was a huge missed opportunity. (2017, David, Localism for Renewables)

Consequently, in prosumer activism, there is often a will to merge the drive towards decarbonisation with a larger ambition of decentralisation and redistribution of economic opportunities, resources and profits. Renewable technologies taken up by locals can counter the 'drain' that normally happens in specific locations when large-scale developers enter, as one of the consultants we talked to described. That is, renewables, as a natural resource, are connected differently than nuclear, hydro and fossils to humans. Renewables are similar to an agricultural field, insofar as they can be directly observed, sensed and harnessed locally, as the farmer in the Decarbonised Living Project implied.

However, it was not only local citizens, but also some people based in the renewable energy industry, who realised that the benefits were unequally distributed, something which fed resistance and thwarted the energy transition. Hence, to infuse a more rapid decarbonisation of the economy, more commercial players have also started to attract local citizen groups with prosumer incentives. Not only did the local volunteers try to find solutions to decentralise the energy system, but also some parts of the industry, too, saw this as a market opportunity, where innovations on many levels were needed to accomplish a more just, two-way grid system, if not a totally local one:

They [the local prosumers] just wanted to own the technology and it was almost about – and this is just purely my opinion – is it about saying we've installed this capacity, or is it about saying we've made this difference? The difference can come in a number of ways. For a lot of the groups, it's almost idealistic in what some want to achieve. Because of that there's an issue of opposing ideologies, almost, between some of the groups. (2017, Ralph, Green Council).

Most of the prosumer activists in the Decarbonised Living Project are retired or fairly senior people. As pensioners, not only do they have more time, but also they expressed their wish to build new friendships and be included in the already existing togetherness. Some had moved to this particular area of England quite recently and saw an outlet for their professionalism and individual need for human relations in the creation of prosumer possibilities. The energy transition and renewable technology offer them a way to be useful in their retirement, to be included in existing citizen groups who could then benefit from their professional expertise. One pensioner described to us how he became a distant member of the citizen group even before he retired and decided to move to the village. He exemplified perhaps a stereotype of those who have time, energy and money to invest: a pensioner who wishes to live well in a more rural landscape towards the end of life, having friends around and something useful to do, which contributes both locally and on a planetary scale. As the members of the Decarbonised Living Project say in chorus, they want to give something back at the end of their lives, for the sake of future generations (2017, Focus group, Farmers Village). Perhaps they wish to leave life behind in the best way possible with the means at hand, that is, with what is left of their time and money.

Another common story that cropped up during our conversation at the dinner venue of the repurposed barn was a sort of U-turn that some had made when they had retired: they had previously worked for big fossil fuel companies, including Shell and BP, either in offices or on oil rigs, but then felt the need to switch to working with renewables and doing something good. Their narrative took a redemptive twist, with clarifying reflections about their past occupation and present learnings. Some confessed to us that they had eventually realised that what their former employer had been doing for decades, with them on board, was more than wrong; it was devastating. Hence, wishing to redeem themselves for having contributed to anthropogenic climate change, as if facing the final judgement, they came across as highly motivated and energised, wanting to accomplish something before it was too late.

This motivation was quickly turned into technical and commercial perspectives which they brought with them from the big corporations. As one of the interviewees clarified, changing the production side of the energy system is hard and perhaps not the real driver. What he now realised was that it was the demand side that needed to go through a transformation. With prosumerism, nevertheless, he could address both the production and consumption sides, influencing the demand for both the investment in production and the consumption of certain energy types. The key new thing for him and his new energy transition friends, which is perhaps something that comes later in life, is the contrast between big business and local initiatives, where their solution to climate change targets improvements on the demand side.

8.3 Epistemic Community and Prosumer Activism

Love Seaside Town and the Decarbonised Living Project exemplify how various types of renewable energy action can be pursued via prosuming as a form and force of coming together. Prosuming encompasses a mix of community relations and activism described in Chapter 3: community as collective renewable energy actions taken locally, human relations fostered within business exchange to create a sense of belonging and extended professionalism, as well as individual attempts to take things into one's own hands, co-produce knowledge and prefigure another world in the here and now. Activism goes into business, and vice versa, when the local volunteers become both activist entrepreneurs and very hands-on investor activists. The citizen groups become choosing consumers both in the first and last steps of the value chain, from the first investment in a certain technology through to the production and final consumption. At the same time as local benefit is clearly generated, the resulting income is also connected to individual prosumers. These act as suppliers of voluntary labour and as peer-to-peer communicators of governmental regulations and business opportunities.

The two groups overall testify to how the UK political agenda on climate adaptation, consensual deliberation and a top-down creation of market pull, has been slowly revised by a call for climate actions and a collective movement. It is in effect a 'harnessing of community energies' (Walker et al. 2007), which in the UK has resulted in a bottom-up market push. The main policies and subsidies did not seem to spur but definitely directed the climate actions, mobilising citizens to become climate activists by tapping into an existing conception of so-called community-based localism. This means that the citizen groups talk about their neighbourhood collectivity in terms of a community, as do policymakers and businesses. Importantly, however, this talk has long been embedded in the expertise that is mobilised. Hence, thinking about the governing of populations though 'community' (Rose 1996), aided by the concept of 'epistemic community', lets us see community (conventionally understood) as part of a wider knowledge movement that adds to the boundaryless attribute of climate activism. Consequently, Love Seaside Town and the Decarbonised Living Project lubricate the activist–business–state conglomeration by means of their free labour, collective treasure of broad professional knowledge and imaginations of what community relations based on renewables could be. Their retrospective reflections on life, actions and will to communicate, gathering and getting along, target a specific geographical location to create a direct sense of belonging for their last years.

Love Seaside Town, on the one hand, decided to invest a lot of time and energy into communicative goals to enlighten their neighbours about options of switching to green energy suppliers or making solar panel investments. The Decarbonised Living Project in Farmers Village, on the other hand, started by setting up something similar to a test site for locals to try out, compare and discuss various green technologies. The former initiative addressed fuel poverty and redistributed the profits with the help of a local currency and community funds, while the latter unfolded more conventionally, with legal entities apt for holding community assets, accumulating profits and pursuing further investments in renewables locally. This resulted in what can also be termed 'ecopreneurship' (Dixon and Clifford 2007), with an emphasis on the accomplishment of entrepreneurial self-sufficiency and mobilisation of (local) markets for a specific cause (Dubuisson-Quellier 2013). It meant that the two groups of volunteers collaborated differently with the local authorities and had different approaches to how fellow citizens could be convinced to participate. The particular collectivity that was nurtured was based not on kinship or culture but on economic investments and relations of knowledge exchange. What prosumer activism does do well is thus to align *Gemeinschaft* with *Gesellschaft* in a variety of innovative ways, a variety that nevertheless shared a mutual aim of decarbonisation by radically engendering a decentralised energy system that would bring production and consumption together in a home or specific location.

In this fecund hands-on entanglement of individual actions via community business and governmental decarbonisation, we were able to observe tensions and a peculiar mix between self-resentment, passion, autonomism, localism and 1960s cultural radicalism. Similarly to the 1960s popularisation of community relations, prosumerism continues on an axis of critique against remote and detached bureaucracy as well as globalism and corporate power. This axis is complemented by an aversion to human-induced problems, especially big polluting businesses and climate change. Even though this aversion to 'big ills' was mentioned by our research participants, these ills were quickly turned around to become something more constructive, reframed as challenges to be met. This rhetorical reframing, from big ills to grand challenges, is equally visible in numerous subsidised competitions set up by the UK government to accomplish decarbonisation. When the notion of grand challenges meets the notion of entrepreneurial opportunities, prosumer activism seemingly prospers. It is a natural step to take, mirrored in how our research participants easily made green political changes their business, literally speaking.

The two groups of prosumer activists managed to merge climate change and sustainability with business methods to infuse an already existing local sense of belonging. This resulted in the creation of one problem space instead of two, a problem space that unified big concerns about the future with small concerns in the present. Within this problem space, people could then start to balance their lives in relation to close and far away affinities: human relations and relations to the environment, the ecosystem or nature. The links created between climate change and local life thereby opened up new possibilities for how to address mutual obligations, which led to these becoming more forcefully and heterogeneously acted upon. All in all, what we thus witnessed is an odd mixture of identity politics coupled with localism, a pinch of anti-big business sentiment as well as a new kind of materialism that has not always been the bedrock of grassroots movements.

Perhaps this inevitably means that prosumer activism is an extension of self-regulation through 'community' (Rose 1996), and especially so when the call for entrepreneurship and business creation has been complemented by sustainable development and resilience (Summerville, Adkins and Kendall 2008, Zebrowski and Sage 2017). Prosumer activism rejuvenates the historical fascination with community building and collective experiences in the UK, especially in villages, where 'human intellectual, political and moral authorities, in certain places and contexts' can be 'acted upon' (Rose 1996:329). Arguments against globalisation and the experience of bureaucratic distances of *Gesellschaft* raise possibilities to delineate more local territories (*Gemeinschaft*) that can be governed in accordance with issues closer to home and closer to the hearts of the citizens themselves. The voluntary 'grassroots' action taken could be seen as successfully stimulated via a 'nudging' of existing behaviours, rather than an overt top-down regulation of new behaviours (Ockwell, Lorraine and O'Neill 2009). The two citizen groups were activated and empowered in relation to their community (*Gemeinschaft*), conceived as a potentially prosperous cosy unit to belong to, an extended family that provided not only security but also an outlet for professional leftovers and gift-giving – a generous giving of one's surplus time and money, caring friendship and rich professional experience. Through the merger of technical and social innovation, renewable energy implementation and alternative ways of organising community-based localism, the volunteers attempted to maximise a do-it-yourself approach to pre-figure a different world in the here and now (Epstein 1991, Maeckel-bergh 2011). The aim of the prosumer activists was to put into place what they deemed 'good' and proper economic behaviours: redistribu-tive business models, local currencies or localised circulation of mon-etary means, as well as limited profit-seeking. At the same time, they strengthened the 'relation of allegiance and responsibility to those one care[s] about the most and to whom one's destiny [is] linked' (Rose 1996:330).

In contrast to earlier discussions about community as a way to activate, mobilise and direct citizens, the prosumer activists did not attempt to uncouple themselves from a national territory (Rose 1996), but instead attempted to couple themselves to a global territory. Still, they did nonetheless manage to relate to their 'community' as a 'func-tion of their own particular levels of enterprise, skill, inventiveness and flexibility' (Rose 1996:339). Similarly to how close encounters with nature and its wonders have been assumed to transform individu-als and cause them to reconsider how they live (cf. Dowling 2010), the local citizens were enticed to get closer to green technologies, with invitations to re-evaluate their micro-moral relations and chosen affinities. The two groups studied also took individual responsibility for communicating as professionally as they could with their fellow citizens, spreading knowledge about the need for technical fixes and a disruption of established businesses. There was, so to speak, no need for any other deliberation, as any support or opposition was taken up by the prosumers themselves.

The social contract was thus complemented by how prosumer activ-ism legitimately bridged the previous instituted boundary between the public and the private (cf. Ockwell, Lorraine and O'Neill 2009) and even succeeded in circumventing critique against the 'scienticisation of politics', that is, the assumption that political and social issues are bet-ter resolved through top-down, science-based expertise (Bäckstrand 2003:24). In comparison with previous studies of top-down and bottom-up processes, it would therefore be more accurate to describe how horizontal allegiances emerged when Love Seaside Town and the Decarbonised Living Project smoothly aligned political decisions based on knowledge about climate change and citizens' understanding of the need for individual and collective climate actions. The prosumer scheme in Seaside Town took on a more inclusive outlook when it reached out to people via a local information point on the main road, the Energy Shop, in comparison with Farmers Village, where prosuming was first limited to information meetings organised by a more exclusionary group of close friends who were keen early adopters of new technologies (cf. Felicetti 2017).

Prosumer activism can, however, only buy the volunteers, of whom many were local newcomers, limited acceptance. As was clear, they were countered on several occasions and their actions fed local resentment. As much as prosumer activists enjoy the sharing of their time, capacities and money, their generosity is not recognised as such by everyone. Hence, it is not the most efficient way of getting citizens to agree and gather their forces, equally, around a mutual cause. This may also be why local movements have rather turned to governmental authorities to institute change, instead of solely relying on communicative groundwork in the closest neighbourhood. That is, localism has in other transition movements become increasingly intertwined in bureaucratic processes (cf. Pink 2008), and the two cases presented in this chapter show a similar tendency in how the prosumers and volunteers, of whom many were newly retired pensioners, exercised refined strategies in encounters with governmental authorities, consultants and businesses. Similarly to Felicetti's (2017) case studies of transition town movements, one of our cases even showed a high dependence on one individual for fruitful relation-building with local authorities. As illustrated in the previous chapter on climate activism as insider activism within governmental authorities, however, the need for such core individuals may not always be so crucial, depending on how the councils themselves decide to take green activists and supporters of prosuming on board.

Those critical of capitalism would, with a focus on prosumerism, argue that prosumer activism is nothing but an appropriation by capital (Comor 2011), as introduced in Chapter 3 under the heading 'Community and Capitalism'. That is, green prosumerism can be seen as growing into a possibly lucrative politics via innocent calls for sustainable development and global democratisation, albeit controlled by 'big data' solutions in the hands of international institutions, large corporations or entrepreneurial states. This suggests that prosumer activism would be left helpless in the hands of a techno-political movement that reproduces existing socio-economic relations predetermined by income generation and accumulation, and consequently, a movement that even extends and refines these capitalistic elements into more individual and collective endeavours for the affluent only. Climate activism could hence, yet again, be dismissed as an environmentalism of the rich (Dauvergne 2016), this time enacted not by big corporations and their brands but by their former employees and other professionals who have lived well within the capitalist system.

Certainly, the most advanced Marxist critiques realise that production is no longer simply carried out in the factory, instead focussing their critical attention on how production and consumption often go hand in hand (Ritzer 2015). Repeating Toffler's (1980) original definition of the prosumer, stating that production and consumption have always been intertwined but have been differently utilised during the developmental stages of capitalism, Ritzer (2015) pessimistically points to how prosumers can be enticed into investing in more means of production than they, or anyone else for that matter, actually need for their later consumption, that is, generating and accumulating a surplus. Being seduced by this, our research participants may also lock themselves into forms of enterprising that require free labour, increased personal debts and overconsumption. They are, in Ritzer's (2015) critical terminology, oblivious to being exploited and alienated, in tandem with being affected. Prosumer activism consequently can thrive on what Beverungen, Murtola and Schwartz (2013) summarise as a 'socialisation of capital': individually owned or jointly owned means of production that make up a 'communism of capital' (Balibar et al. 2010); the making of a value chain that aligns with human affect, engendered by an activist and community formation rhetoric. Undoubtedly, this rhetoric is more than a semantic shift in capitalist regimes. It mobilises people who have internalised capitalist values and imaginaries, and this drives the capitalist system forward, enabling it to reproduce itself and grow.

However, there is perhaps more to prosumer activism than an intricate alignment between capitalism and the human will to experience belonging when challenges are to be met. Of specific interest to us is the way in which our two groups of prosumer activists attempted to take charge of the entire value chain, from the first step of planning to the later investment in technology, the production and consumption of electricity and the final decision on how to distribute the profits. We thus detected a desire for autonomy (Böhm, Dinerstein and Spicer 2010), which drove these groups to seek decentralised, local solutions that would not benefit shareholders in the far future, but real people in the present, even their neighbours. Of course, this autonomy turned out to be an illusion, as the groups soon found out that they were dealing with a complicated value chain that was in both cases affected by state policies and regulations as well as an uneven distribution of expertise and resources. Yet both groups tried to muddle through using the means they had, which on occasion touched on a space of potential autonomy due to the way a range of actors – local government, big corporations and smaller consultancies – were engaged critically and reflexively. The aim of Love Seaside Town and the Decarbonised Living Project has been to merge quite a mainstream energy transition with a more transformative social agenda (Stirling 2015). They imagined not only an energy system that is decarbonised but also one that creates alternative ways of accomplishing a more environmentally friendly progression together.

Despite these clearly articulated goals and 'doable' renewable energy actions, the collectivity that unfolds is nevertheless diffuse, and so are the effects of the actions taken. If there is anything left from previous deliberation attempts and governing via community, these are by now finely embedded within the activist–business–state conglomeration. The two cases of prosumer activism are, in the light of the boundary-less attribute of activism, characterised by somewhat random actions, as people both create and respond to challenges and opportunities in haphazard ways. They try hard to find clear routes forward, but that is impossible, and they try to create autonomous spaces for themselves, but that is doomed to fail. What they do seem to have accomplished, however, is hybrid communities, 'sometimes learning from each other, sometimes socially feral, but always interdependent' (Fawcett 2009:234). In comparison with ideas about ecological citizenship and deep democracy, they were not feral in the sense of wandering around aimlessly (Garside 2013), but they definitely lacked any idea of how their wandering in the policy, enterprising and environmental landscape would end. They were curious about what the future would hold for them and their new friends, as well as the environment, in the energy transition. Perhaps surprisingly, then, there was neither indifference nor cynicism, but the two groups enjoyed the process of energy transition as such, with its hardships, and without knowing where it would all lead. They were thus following some sort of nomadic ethics, undergirded by a wandering with others that forms nourishing alliances (Fawcett 2009).

Perhaps prosumer activism is the last station for the professional wanderer – the one that we have exemplified in all three previous empirical chapters. Prosumer activism would furthermore hardly exist without help from employee activism, enterprising activism and insider activism. The prosumer becomes the main catalyst for the material evolution of the epistemic community. It is with the prosumer that the activist–business–state conglomeration is brought together in the most intense way, where it develops and thrives on the sharing of knowledge. The dissemination of knowledge and the creation of understanding to infuse the will to take action seemingly grows horizontally, rather than bottom-up or top-down. This horizontal quality is nevertheless hard to accomplish fully on the ground during planning, implementation, management and redistribution due to the affluence of the prosumers. Still, by an active sharing of challenges and opportunities, struggles and failures, the prosumers prefigure a world-to-come, which strengthens a collectivity and close affinities between what is normally separated into different spheres or actors: the state, business and civil society.

9 New Ways of Knowing

The four previous chapters empirically illustrate boundaryless climate activism analysed through an extension of the concept of epistemic community, that is, a knowledge movement formed when people come together and co-produce knowledge within a shared topical realm, in this case climate change, including an awareness of the need for 'action', sooner rather than later. To complement the conventional understanding of epistemic communities as driven by science and validity, or a specified domain of expertise and way of producing knowledge (Haas 1992, 2015, Zito 2018), we have broadened the view on what type of expertise, knowledge production, and thereby members and directions, the 'episteme' can evolve to encompass. When the knowledge base is uncertain and the complexity of issues is taken for granted (Painter 2013), people from all sorts of social and professional backgrounds seem very willing to voluntarily partake in and generously share their expertise with the epistemic community. They are members of various organisations at the same time, from families to NGOs, from businesses to villages, and from local governmental institutions to industry associations or consumer groups. They move flexibly between these to put themselves to work with renewable energy action and, as we will discuss further in this chapter, accomplish a horizontal transition of the energy system.

Our focus is thus on how people who work with renewables in different settings, and are protagonists thereof, become part of the same dispersed movement by choosing to pursue quite mundane everyday actions to decarbonise. Instead of approaching climate activism from a political perspective with a focus on policymaking, from a business perspective with a focus on CSR, a material perspective with a focus on technological paths, or a critical perspective based on the Anthropocene, this chapter will further discuss how people in our four empirical chapters became involved with renewable energy actions in very diverse everyday ways. We summarise the main findings according to four themes, namely, experiment and Do-It-Yourself; share and Do-It-Together; wander and speed up and alter and materialise. These themes are interconnected and bring the various empirical and theoretical threads together to show how climate activism thrives on epistemic community relations and renewable energy actions. The chapter also explains why our empirical insights matter theoretically and practically by going into the details of community formation and *Bildung*. It is not necessarily the case that *Gesellschaft* (society), with its rationality of exchange and mechanistic relations, is completely taking over *Gemeinschaft* (community), with its relationality and life (Asplund 1991), but in fact, these increasingly co-exist and thrive off each other (Bershady 2020). We end by problematising the conventional polarisation between activism and business, community and capitalism, to see their proximity in the light of an epistemic community that provides bridges between community and society/business, rather than business and society.

9.1 Climate Activism in the Energy Transition

9.1.1 *Experiment and Do-It-Yourself*

The people we encountered when tracing climate activism in the field came across as extremely engaged and passionate yet they were desperately searching for ways to reach a more sustainable society. They did not choose to use existing and established decarbonisation tools to 'do their bit' (Paterson and Stripple 2010:341) but engaged more extensively and innovatively by creating possibilities for new decarbonisation solutions (Scoones, Leach and Newell 2015), often in the 'here and now' to prefigure the greener world they envisioned (Boggs 1977). Our research participants all chose to do what they could close to their own backyard, and the challenge was to make the renewable solutions technically and organisationally feasible locally. They showed a strong will to take individual responsibility and act in the here and now, according to their own means, previous experiences and present professional knowledge, wherever they happened to be located, at home or at work – much like the self-organising that is stimulated in social movement organisations devoted to prefiguration (Maeckelbergh 2016, Farias 2017), and particularly so when these experiment with new organisational forms (Yates 2015). In our cases, the experimentation was nevertheless as much an individual endeavour as it was a collective one.

Despite a clear conviction to decarbonise in as direct a way as possible, our impression was that our research participants had no clear idea on which path to take. Even though renewable energy was taken for granted as the solution to meet the climate emergency globally, there was no clear information or secure knowledge base for the actual implementation of renewables locally. At the same time as renewables were conceived as key to actions, no one seemed to hesitate about that fact that there were immense uncertainties when it came to how an actual realisation and implementation should be pursued to accomplish the energy transition. This uncertainty required a review of alternatives, which ended up in contemplation and extensive experimentation to find some sort of path forward, a path that should succeed to encompass the triple bottom line – the environmental, the social and the economic – and thereby secure that the process of realisation was fully compliant with sustainability, from start to end. Sustainability could not wait, and neither could our research participants, who thus took it upon themselves to do their best to accomplish the energy transition based on very limited certainties on how to go about it.

Depending on their backgrounds, current contexts and starting points for their actions, they came across as impatient, and perhaps therefore willing to experiment. Utilising either their profession or their will to learn new things, they functioned not only as relays of expertise and active implementers of quite specific knowledge, but also, most importantly, as combiners of existing knowledge and experimenters with new untested knowledge. They tended to meet the knowledge uncertainties by testing their way forward and sharing their learnings with others, who were equally willing to step into the unknown and become active co-producers of applicable knowledge. At first disorganised, this co-production of knowledge unfolded horizontally and seemed to circulate freely among our research participants, whether they knew each other or not. This was one of the most common characteristics in our cases on climate activism, and it provides an explanation for its boundaryless attribute and how the activist-business-state came together: the will to experiment in various work settings (Vattenfall, a business start-up, a local governmental body, a village group), rather than demonstrating in the streets, which bridged effectively between what is often constructed as separate organisations or domains (civil society/business/state).

The employee activists at Vattenfall, for example, expressed a lack of clear green directions internally, and a strenuous uncertainty about the corporate view on climate change. In the wake of Vattenfall's peculiar history of CEO activism, CSR activities and corporate anthem, they were left to get on with whatever they could do to improve the environmental record of the company and society at large. They openly demanded more top-down managerial green leadership and hierarchically organised regulations on how to behave in an environmentally friendly way on the office floor or out in the field, but since there were no formal attempts to pursue Green HRM internally (Renwick 2018), they had to take things into their own hands and experiment. Senior managers engaged in more extensive environmental actions than they were managerially obliged to, alongside junior employees who were equally engaged but had less managerial room to create an extra official green workload for themselves. In between these employees, the epistemic community grew horizontally across managerial levels and specific work roles.

As illustrated by the media stories about Dale Vince, founder of Ecotricity, he had to experiment more wildly in the creation of his own renewable business. Dale Vince is portrayed as having no limitations when taking climate activism across the assumed boundaries between business and society, similarly to other examples of environmentally progressive businesses (Mirvis 1994). While he might have been a traditional radical street protest kind of guy in the 1970s and 1980s, he quickly saw the opportunity to become a renewable energy entrepreneur in the UK, one who is not afraid of taking up the positive challenge of renewables through his own hard work and bringing it up to scale and speed.

Experimentation and taking things into one's own hands in the here and now was also characteristic of the prosumer activists and the insider activists. They constantly had to find new paths forward but seemed very keen to try untested technologies and intricately configured organisational solutions, often as what they expressed to be a counter to entrenched village or small-town life, as well as ingrained local governmental bureaucracy. Both of these were conceived as slow and therefore thwarting the will to accomplish change in line with sustainability and an energy transition. Experimentation was thus as liberating as it was necessary for our research participants. It responded to both an experienced lack of momentum and a lack of clear paths forward for the implementation of renewables. Hence, the epistemic community shares a fundamental will to experiment within a very broad and opaque topical interest: climate change, sustainability and renewable energy technology.

9.1.2 Share and Do-It-Together

The strong emphasis on individual experimentation in boundaryless climate activism spurred a will to share how to Do-It-Yourself, collectively. The focus on the individual effort needed was thus backed up with a collective stance and shared goal to create a sense of belonging in tandem with sustainable decarbonisation. Sometimes the individual was inextricably linked to the collective from the start, as is common in social movement studies on activism (Simon and Herring 2020). In many cases, however, we were able to see that the uncertainty on how to go about things needed to be balanced by an increased connectivity, which was necessary to make the individual experimentation grounded in something that would actually make a difference on the ground. The experimentation among novices had to be shared with more professional actors to make it sufficiently feasible for implementation.

Overall, renewable energy technology invites intellectual engagement, as an understanding of how the technology works is mandatory if it is to be sufficiently utilised. As pointed out previously, renewables lay forth an abundance of environmental, technical and economic alternatives that need to be contemplated. The dry and 'techy' element of the energy transition forces people together as it requires them to interact quite extensively with each other so as to be able to bring renewables home and make them useful locally, or even a dominant part of a larger central grid system. Without tapping into the popular focus on symbolism or identity formation in studies of activism and community formation, the epistemic community in our chapters thus shares what Wenger (1998) points out to be of importance in 'communities of practice'. The engagement with renewable technology leads to first-hand impressions of what is feasible to do as an individual in relation to the world and to others. It feeds imaginations, which takes them beyond engagement, and facilitates ideas about how new connections and bonds with others can be made presently. The alignment between people and certain ideas grew and intensified in the four chapters, and renewables made our research participants '"larger" by placing [their] actions in larger contexts' (Wenger 1998:196).

The insider activists who worked as public servants played a funda-mental role in this expansion by means of their efforts in linking the individual will to experiment, to the level of a collective experiment. Arnold, who worked at Clean Government with the triple bottom line and 'smart living', exemplifies this very well. He was employed under loose instructions to set up a local energy infrastructure and networks to stimulate citizen engagement and 'energy communities' (cf. Walker et al. 2007). His formal work to bring about an energy transition and more sustainable society thus required that he too experimented. He later started to work for a voluntary group and grassroots initiative, taking the collective efforts to the next step in their so-called 'energy revolution' (LEG 2018) – a notion that the EU equally taps into (Citi-zenergy 2018). In turn, the voluntary group had to experiment together with some local consultancy firms by setting up a number of different juridical organisational forms. These organisations left individual as well as collective experimentation as open as possible but channelled it into one of LEG's sister organisations that had been created to make renewables bureaucratically and economically feasible.

In this whole experimental knowledge process, the research partici-pants in all four chapters thus choose to entangle themselves with each other; voluntary groups; local politicians; large, small and medium-sized businesses; as well as incomprehensible and flighty renewable energy policies, alluring crowdfunding platforms supported by the EU and personal financialisation of sorts. The technical and organisational solutions provide corporate riches as well as individual self-sufficiency at home, in a sort of prolongation of the 'knowledge economy' (Pow-ell and Snellman 2004), at the same time as they were planned for and implemented by a very active sharing of knowledge that went hand in hand with acts of solidarity. It was in effect difficult to distinguish the need to share the experimental mode of knowledge co-production from the human will to come together to experience togetherness and belonging (Christensen and Levinson 2020: Introduction).

The tendency to merge the individual experimentation with a general wish to get along and gather was explicitly found in Chapter 5 on cli-mate activism at Vattenfall, where the research participants as employee activists occasionally connected with each other through an unspeci-fied but taken-for-granted belief that people need to work together to achieve a decarbonisation of society from within business. Here, the struggles were foremost epistemic (cf. Icaza and Vázquez 2013), as the employees fought more against other energy sources rather than specific organisational members or competing Vattenfall units. The activist employees became part of the wider epistemic community at the same time as they furthered the knowledge movement in more specific directions internally (cf. Taro Lennerfors 2013) – both digitally and face to face, in efforts to find new paths forward as well as like-minded close or distant employees within Vattenfall. They shared their reflections about the global importance of their everyday jobs yet expressed emotional exhaustion due to how the rest of the corporation actively contributed to environmental problems and contradicted their efforts. In this case of employee activism, the pursuit of renewables as a 'challenge' is thus complemented by the 'struggle' of finding others and coming together.

The sharing of knowledge due to the uncertainty and epistemic struggles with renewables often morphed into a more general mode of sharing to make renewable energy actions a broader engagement with other people. All our research participants stressed the importance of complementing decarbonisation with educating the public about the need for further actions. For example, Bob, the founder of Small R. Energy, sought to share and establish bonds with, and between, his customers. He founded a small but relatively successful renewable energy company in South West England and came to employ activists who might have gone to prison for their environmental beliefs, because this depth of engagement is what he values and what is partly needed in the kind of business he runs. In addition, he used the company's communication platform and blog to promote environmental actions based on his own family life. The promotion of actions among others seems to be almost as important to him as his own contribution to the material realisation of decarbonisation via business. Dale Vince, the founder of Ecotricity, communicated in an equally activist manner by campaigning against fracking via his company, using it as a corporate springboard for expanding green thinking and speeding up the actions of others. Sharing thus not only is enforced due to the necessary experimental knowledge co-production but serves a more general purpose of speeding up the energy transition and creating momentum.

9.1.3 Wander and Speed Up

Ecotricity and the other smaller activist businesses illustrated in Chapter 6, which focussed on enterprising activism, exemplify more coherence – certainly in comparison with Vattenfall – with regards to their organisation's take on environmental problems and climate change. In the businesses or non-profit organisations presented, there were a number of people who had voted with their feet and set up their own purposeful or mission-driven companies to secure such coherence (Hockerts 2006). The preferred media stories of Ecotricity and Good Energy narratively emphasised their previous successful civil society actions, now geared up to the challenge of taking climate change more seriously by starting a business. The mediatised heroic picture merges the underdog activist hero with the proactive green entrepreneurial hero and strengthens the traditional focus on activism as an individual identity project (cf. Bobel 2007). Activist entrepreneurship perhaps best exemplifies the remnant of this focus on an intentional individual, through how media points to the need for a leader and model enterprising activist for effective decarbonisation to happen. The activist entrepreneurs also take it upon themselves to widen the reach and speed up the results. They wish to see quicker results and expressed that taking renewable energy actions into business was a more promising and swift way forward. Hence, by embracing their feral capacity to wander and explore new paths (cf. Garside 2013), they utilised the fast rhythms and authority of capitalism to augment their previous conventional civic activism (cf. Sloterdijk 2014), but the competitive advantage of speed was inevitably not the only reason for them to walk the talk by going into business. These civil society activists had also mellowed into economic subjects in need of monetary resources personally due to family constellations and increased obligations.

The activist–business–state conglomeration is, in the case of enterprising activism, spawned in a very direct way by activism conventionally understood as located in civil society and dependent on a clearly identifiable activist. Here, the subjective, emotional and affective dimensions of climate activism cannot be neglected in the accentuation of rhythm or 'movement' (cf. Gould 2009, Jasper 2011, Ottum and Reno 2016). The activist entrepreneurs had to plan and prepare their actions, as much as they had to take direct and unplanned action in the moment. In comparison with the employee activists, insider activists and prosumer activists, the activist entrepreneurs strategically turned their past civil society 'struggle' into an enjoyable 'challenge' via business start-ups. Taking activism to business turned their previous hardships into a thrilling enterprise and (ad)venture, and as former activists, they could now legitimately configure themselves as vanguard ecopreneurs who were there to passionately speed up the energy transition.

However, not everyone is tempted to vote with their feet and start a business to pursue their activism with a focus on themselves as individuals; others instead choose to wander more freely and flexibly in between NGOs, state agencies and other non-profit organisations to accomplish smaller acts and micro-politics (Jacobsson and Sörbom 2015) as well as create new organisational forms (Land and King 2014, Sutherland, Land and Böhm 2014, Kokkinidis 2015). Susan, who worked for Local Energy Group, showed that, for her, working closely with business was not only done for financial reasons but was also a way to provoke new organisational forms and involve big corporations differently in local projects to secure the balance of power and limit unpaid labour. She was adamant about altering how capitalism function. Chapter 7 additionally illustrates how several environmental movements had been naturalised to become a unit within the formal political bureaucracy, actively creating space for insider activism. These insider activist employees were not the stereotypical public servants who should be neutral and apolitical middlemen that implement policy (Hysing and Olsson 2018). Instead, they acted more as institutional activists (Abers and Keck 2009) who passionately displayed their climate activism at work, both to change the institution as such and to enact change based on their institutional authority.

Business models, for instance, were transformed into redistribution models, all marketised to citizens, who were to become prosumer activists via the insourced environmental movements with members on council employee contracts. Commercial change in the here and now was thus created by the insider activists who attracted funding for small and medium-sized renewable energy infrastructure, such as solar and wind. Here, party politics, personal politics and citizen business enterprising all became entangled and packaged by a climate activism that accomplishes more than a decarbonisation of the economy and saving of the planet. Local solutions to climate change are only implicitly directed towards faraway vulnerable others and explicitly call for a strengthening of the 'relation of allegiance and responsibility to those one care[s] about the most and to whom one's destiny [is] linked' (Rose 1996:330). Cash-strapped local councils in the UK subsequently found manifold ways to generate income from a variety of sources, leaving ideological thought lines behind. In one sentence, our municipality interviewees might have critiqued the 'Big Six' corporations that control the UK energy market, but they also accepted cash from them to speed up decarbonisation and fight energy poverty in their area out of solidarity. The epistemic community is thus formed in a mix of decentred efforts of deliberative democracy and the entrepreneurial state (Mazzucato 2015a, 2015b), both of which are furthered by the personal politics of inventive insider activists.

In our findings, the council and the decarbonising environmental movements that, with time, became deeply rooted within the council, thrived off each other when it came to successfully reaching out to the general public, and, as Mazzucato (2015b:145) suggests, 'it is clear that no clean technology firm emerged from a pure "market genesis", the State has always been involved'. What looks like civic mobilisation in our case, could thus be conceived as a mobilisation of the state, so as to reach beyond deliberation and achieve results more horizontally, as we observed in the case of the Green Council. In comparison with the activist entrepreneurs, who voted with their feet to enter business, we observed an intensified wandering between local government, universities, voluntary citizen groups and consultancies. In these cases, people seemed to know each other and formed what looked like a 'close community', consisting of people who were professionally interested in renewables (Guy and Shove 2000), complemented by an interest in the need to rejuvenate localism, collectivity and a 'politics' that would actually work.

9.1.4 Alter and Materialise

All four empirical chapters show how renewable energy as a promising solution, including the machinery in its very presence, succeeds in turning the activist struggle into an experimental challenge to be shared. Without being a communicative tool or digital platform, the technology is in a causal way conceived to lead to a transformation of society (*Gesellschaft*). A decentralisation could, for example, lead to a deeper democracy, where the personal and professional, as well as the thinking and the doing, are effectively knitted together via the understanding it takes to engage properly with renewable energy as an advanced technology. To complement the extensive co-production of knowledge that massaged and glued together the activist–business–state conglomeration, artists and poets were, for example, invited by Good Energy to create reflexive wake-up calls for the 'masses' (Suter 2018), and, as clearly shown by Dale Vince in his vegan transformation of a football club, Ecotricity even expanded the decarbonisation actions to a wider environmentalist agenda, similarly to what the employee activists within Vattenfall sought to accomplish. Renewables thus seems to come with a built-in pedagogic re-formation of the human, affirmative of the need to mobilise people to alter themselves and others.

Moreover, the research participants not only took concrete action into their own hands but also spoke about politics and the need for more 'action' (cf. Latour et al. 2018). This communicative agenda, alongside the materially measurable acts of decarbonisation, shows that renewable energy is much more than a physical entity or a natural, endless source of energy. It is a rhetorical resource used to legitimise progression and the advance of technology to modernise ecologically, as much as it is a rhetorical resource for connecting people across the world to political ideas of decarbonisation, the energy transition and sustainability (Toke 2011b). Renewables are not as scientifically distant as a proton accelerator but offer gadgets and devices for individual use, effective for taking the idea of decarbonisation and energy transition to its material reality, infused by an experience of real transformation (cf. Marres 2012). The material aspect of renewables makes the ambition to alter oneself and others authentic; it rhetorically provides more to the action than just talk. In comparison with how the bicycle brings together the material and political in everyday use (Horton 2006), renewable technology is, however, not yet equally available. At the same time, there is for now a much stronger expression of a personal politics built into the materiality of renewables (Eyerman and Jamison 2019) than there is in the bicycle. So far less mainstream than the bicycle, renewable energy technology can aid people to more fundamentally transform their everyday lives at the very same time as they may experience this as an eco-ethical process of becoming (Skoglund and Böhm 2016), instead of just a behavioural change.

This was perhaps most evident in Chapter 8 on prosumer activism, where the conglomeration of activist-business-state was visibly materialised on rooftops and in fields. The prosumer activists were commonly of retirement age, some having recently relocated to the South West of England and forced to alter their lives anyway. They were looking for new friends, getting along and doing something worthwhile and positive in togetherness, whereby prosumerism conveniently became a new political imaginary of 'the community' and its proper relations, dependencies and functions. Toffler (1980) insightfully predicted this, suggesting that prosuming would grow especially in relation to environmental concerns due to the decentralisation of state functions and regionalism, as well as the spread of expertise via specific actors and an increasing will to self-manage according to this expertise. To complement their experimentation and test beds for innovative technology, the prosumer activists organised interest groups, knocked on doors, provided investment opportunities and set up an advisory energy shop – often in the name of creating a stronger social bond among people in a primary attempt to accomplish an enjoyable 'gathering' and, secondarily, with a will to save the planet and recover from globalisation, capitalism and pollution. Prosumerism, as a form of Do-It-Yourself approach to self-sufficiency, is thus not only driven by an environmental and economic agenda, but also coheres with a pre-existing wish to belong, alter oneself and others, and transform through Do-It-Together (e.g. see Pink 2008). A public experience of the self was created alongside collective solidarity (cf. Bennett and Segerberg 2011), as the prosumer activists' historical notion of a village or town 'community' was actively repositioned based on decarbonisation and renewables.

An intensified link between togetherness and action was, however, contradicted by the frictionless offer to 'switch'. Switching was in a material way supposed to spawn a mental alteration regarding the way in which people related to their depletion of finite resources in general. Consumers were offered the chance to switch from a bigger energy utility to a smaller, less 'filthy' one (Friends of the Earth 2018), complemented by how Ecotricity turned 'bills into mills' (Ecotricity 2022), and Vattenfall was urged to close down its coal operations and switch to renewables only (Deutsche Welle 2015). Switching thus requires a negative, an 'anti', to be substituted for something better, and especially so when conventional civic activism promotes it, as exemplified by Friends of the Earth and Greenpeace (cf. Dixon 2014). However, switching, as offered to the masses, creates a frictionless struggle, quickly solved by a small single action, 'switching', hardly felt or delivering on any future sense of belonging or need for a struggle or challenge, experienced as a thrill. The shared switching agenda thus succeeds in mainstreaming the call for alteration, action and materialisation (cf. Jamison 2001, Hensby, Sibthorpe and Drvier 2011). From a market perspective of potential activist segments, switching hones in on those assumed to care the least but who are still to be mobilised for the common good, by those who care more, like their closest neighbours.

Tellingly, the insider activist public servants worked closely with activist entrepreneurs, bigger corporations and prosumer activists to switch as many citizens as possible to a solar tariff. At the same time, the prosumer activists fought hard to establish redistributive business models and even a local currency, to ensure that the switching resulted in something more than a single unchallenging act. They decided how the investment was to be fed back into their local surroundings to have an effect on their closest relations, to facilitate a more substantial alteration of others. Switching was for them too simple and perhaps boring, and not sufficient in the mission to alter others properly. Instead of switching, prosuming and owning the means of production became a way to give real 'power to the people'. It required that people voluntarily and generously invested their time, gave from their previous professional expertise and provided free labour to bring about the energy transition and an economic change, mainly locally. It is in these rich repertoires of gift-giving that Tönnies' (1957) distinction between *Besitz* and *Vermögen*, that is, the belongings of community and the assets of society/business, becomes interesting again. Owning the means of renewable production based on a generous exchange of knowledge brings the mechanical assets of *Gesellschaft* into the realm of belonging and caring of *Gemeinschaft*, which leads us to think that *Gemeinschaft*, as traditionally understood community building, and *Gesellschaft*, as its more contractual and rational counterpart (Tönnies 1957/2002), are fruitfully merged, especially in prosumer climate activism.

9.2 Beyond a Polarisation of Community and Business

One of the most well-known ways to diminish a belief in a sense of belonging and generous gift-giving within a community (*Gemeinschaft*) in efforts to reach contractual and exchange relations (*Gesellschaft*) has been the offering of loans at an interest rate. In our empirical chapters, we were also able to note how each and every person was invited to engage economically, or to become entangled in a movement underpinned by some sort of funding scheme, leading to long-term relations of exchange across the conglomeration of activist-business-state. There was an abundance of financialisation and loans, and citizens were even offered the chance to become activists by lending money to businesses prompted by governments or transnational institutions via eco-ethically alluring crowdfunding platforms

(European Commission 2018b). Another example of this was businesses that secured loans at specific interest rate levels and provided collateral for prosumers who wished to take their self-sufficiency to larger scales. An extension of monetary lending also included how states set up increasing exchange relations with citizens based on feed-in tariffs and other subsidies that required some sort of payback. Usury is thereby reinforced and moderated in all sorts of directions to keep the exchange cycles going via climate activism. Inevitably, boundary-less climate activism is thus part of a more general financialisation of human relations.

Climate activism also becomes empirically indistinguishable from relations of exchange since it advances materially hand in hand with business and contractual relations. These relations are nevertheless redirected to go beyond a maximisation of economic value creation. *Homo economicus* is, after all, a figure that poses a threat to the biosphere and therefore elicits a wish for replacement by a more updated, morally and ecologically correct investor or business-driven activist. Many of the commercial genres of activism discussed in Chapters 1 and 2 are fully and unproblematically merged with the civic activism that is present in climate activism. In comparison with activisms that are anti-capitalistic (Dixon 2014) or anti-hierarchical (Kaufman 2016), pro-environmental activism thereby succeeds in aligning with modern progression and certain corporate profit-seeking goals (cf. Meyerson and Scully 1995). This also explains why climate activism is easier to pursue at work. It is less threatening to businesses in comparison with other types of activist struggles (cf. Creed, Scully and Austin 2002, Briscoe and Gupta 2016).

The facility with which climate activism is pursued, boundaryless in connection with business, could meet a lot of criticism. For example, critical theorists have questioned brand activism (Cederström and Marinetto 2013), an incorporation of citizens to secure business as usual (Nyberg, Spicer and Wright 2013), or an accentuated neo-normative control of employees (Fleming and Sturdy 2009, Fleming 2014). Even though there are many different angles to these and other intellectually driven critiques, there is a general tendency to discursively continue a historical debate clarified by Tönnies' (1957) writings on *Gesellschaft* and *Gemeinschaft*. As derived in detail by Asplund (1991), these two concepts should be understood as a broader thought-figure, which entails that '[t]he economically rational action has an antithesis', in the form of 'an action that is direct, unpremeditated and ambiguous, an action that is not realising a preceding plan and thereby is emptied of meaning, but instead anticipates its implications or seeks its meaning' (Asplund 1991:81, author's own translation). Historically, then, the actions taken in, or perhaps for, *Gemeinschaft* were appreciated due to their direct relational effects and generative processes of seeking, or being 'moved', in togetherness.

In comparison with contemporary studies, Tönnies shows how *Gemeinschaft*-like relations succeed in excluding *Homo economicus*. Business, for him, would not necessarily always be stronger than community. He suggests that humans can be utterly generous and act without expectations of reciprocity, just as non-human animals can. Throughout the critique of capitalist development and modern progression, insistent attempts have nevertheless been made to intellectually erase the generous capacity of humans. According to Asplund (1991), this erasure has taken much more time and effort than is normally acknowledged by critical theorists. The polarisation of community and business, and the separation between generous gift-giving and commercial exchange, has had to be explicitly forced and repeated throughout modernity. This, he maintains, is the reason why many scholars have taken it for granted that *Homo economicus*, and the economic domain in general, have always been masculine and dominant, erroneous and oppressive (Asplund 1991), a way of thinking similarly present in the anti-capitalist environmental movement, which has polarised commercial exchange and generous gift-giving.

9.3 Conclusion

There is undoubtedly a big difference between the past wish to distinguish *Gemeinschaft* from *Gesellschaft*, and the possibility to carve out such distinctions in our findings. Our exposure of how climate activism is experimental, shared, speeded up and materialised reveals how new experiences of community relations across previously constructed boundaries are mobilised. Efforts to speak anew on *Gemeinschaft* and *Gesellschaft*, as in the debate on social enterprising versus capitalism (Shaw and de Bruin 2013), or in the merger of the two in a fecund core of CSR strategy (Porter and Kramer 2011), are in our study more relevant to view in the light of contemporary imaginaries of community.

Is there anything left from Tönnies' description of community as an organism, versus society as a mechanism?

As mentioned in Chapter 3, 'community' has in business studies been historically more theoretically present than 'activism'. Peredo and Chrisman (2006:313) do, for example, in their paper entitled 'Toward a theory on community enterprise', suggest that we can evaluate the level of community within society: 'The more "community oriented" a society is, the more its members will experience their membership as resembling the life of parts of an organism'. Instead of showing the distinction between community and society/business, however, as Tönnies did, the authors turn to a later emphasis on 'embeddedness' and an actor-based network theory, pointing to interpersonal relations being crucial for how behaviours and institutions evolve. Everything takes shape by virtue of how it is part of something bigger, whereby community relations with their gift economies are positioned to exist within modern organisations, such as non-profit and profit-making businesses. Consequently, there is no separate domain of *Gemeinschaft*, but 'community' is inserted to play a role within *Gesellschaft*.

Noticeably, such insertion of community relations into the 'market society' had already been conceptualised by Karl Polanyi (1944/2001) in the 1940s. Hence, community, as understood by Tönnies, has later on not been constituted as anything particularly distinct and possible to separate out from a society taken over by economic behaviours and market relations. Rather, for Polanyi, the market constituted a part of the larger economy, which in turn constituted a part of an even larger society (Stiglitz 2001), hosting such things as communities. Moreover, a further development of this stepwise conflation of society and business has treated the economy as a subsystem of society, which in turn has been linked to the larger network of social relations based on how economic actions are taken by individuals (Olofsson 1999). Theorising community building, as a distinct way of living non-instrumentally, has thus slowly been phased out from sociology during the twentieth century. Instead of seeing community as a basis for certain human subjectivity and relationality, community has come to be treated as a pre-existing local subgroup to host people within society made up of social and economic relations and networks (Appadurai 2013). This leads us back to the subtitle of the Cambridge University Press series this book appears in, and specifically the 'bridging' between business and society that the boundaryless attribute of activism exposes. In the four empirical chapters, it is perhaps not mainly a bridging between the domains of business and society that has been traced, but an active bridging between forgotten community relations and the already unified business/society.

The Vattenfall employees are, for example, looking for belonging and togetherness, as much as the prosumer activists are. They cannot find this belonging solely based on their economic and social relations but rather come together around the episteme on climate change and renewables. The insider activists and activist entrepreneurs are perhaps less inclined to search for forgotten community relations, but they already see themselves as part of a community formation that needs to grow. Based in society/business, they craft contemporary ways to stimulate community relations, mainly for others, and it is here that the link between climate activism and alteration becomes strongest. This is especially the case in climate activist entrepreneurship, where there remains a strong belief in a fruitful link between an intentional individual, someone who takes action, alters the self as well as moves and mobilises others, to alter the world (cf. Curtin et al. 2016). It is no longer only by lifelong learning and self-development that *Bildung* is meant to nurture specifically human qualities, as renewables stimulate extensive co-production of knowledge and lay the basis for novel human–technology relations that rejuvenate the possibilities for community relations. Interaction is stimulated in very open ways (Rönnerman and Salo 2017:458), similarly to how Tönnies (1957/2002, also see Adler 2015) imagined more cooperative organisational forms, *Genossenschaften*. Renewable energy consequently is not only a means for policymakers to govern the climate via community-based localism (Walker et al. 2007), but also a way to reconfigure human relationality *per se*.

10 | *Horizontal Organising*

This book has highlighted novel trends in both studies and practical pursuits of activism and explored the increasingly boundaryless character of climate activism. Facilitated by a broader knowledge movement, or 'field of scientificity' (Foucault 1980:195–197), we have been able to observe how climate activism was enacted from within state agencies by government employees (cf. Hochstetler and Keck 2007, Hysing and Olsson 2018, Abers 2019), from various levels within corporations and organisations (cf. Meyerson and Scully 1995, Spicer, Alvesson and Kärreman 2009, Wickert and Schaefer 2015, Briscoe and Gupta 2016, Girschik 2020), by activists who chose to start their own businesses (Mirvis 1994, Dauvergne 2016), and by anyone in their home, neighbourhood or local surroundings. The European Union rhetorically speaks about 'a revolution' (Citizenergy 2018) in the same way as we had previously heard only radical environmentalists do, and small consultancies seek to deploy alternative monetary redistribution models to fight the worst outgrowth of global capitalism.

Activism, and particularly climate activism, is thus no longer confined to social movements or political ideas about the role of civil society (Lichterman and Eliasoph 2014). It is also not possible to provide insights into activism based on the established canon of research: the long-standing discussion about political subjectivity, agency, justice and equality. Studies of activism that commonly see collectivism and geographical proximity as prerequisites for activism to take place (Simon and Herring 2020) were, for us, of relatively little use for understanding the climate activism and collectivity we encountered in the field. It was not always the case that actions could be linked to a specific individual who would identify as an activist, and those who took renewable energy actions did not always know of each other, were often not part of one single organisation, and did not necessarily live geographically close to each other, although some definitely took advantage of geographical closeness to create a sense of belonging.

The boundaryless attribute of activism made it possible to speak about the agent of climate activism in terms of an activist-business-state conglomeration, configured and glued together by a knowledge movement, a movement that seemed analytically fruitful to view through an expansion of the concept of epistemic community (Haas 1992). Guided by repetitive discussions about knowledge uncertainties in climate change science and policymaking (IPCC 2011b, 2014, Howarth and Painter 2016), stretching to contemporary attempts to address policy design complexities (Zito 2018) and move away from mere adaptation to action (Deichmann and Zhang 2013), we found it necessary to reconsider the formation of epistemic communities to better encompass the dispersed yet forceful mobilisation of knowledge on which climate activism thrives. We thus suggest that an epistemic community should no longer be limited to experts who struggle with policy uncertainties, share a common worldview and believe in causal relationships to steer action (Haas 1992, Zito 2001), but accept that direct actions are continuously taken in quite random responses to uncertainty and the slowness of formal political processes. Such an extension of the epistemic community concept makes it possible to better trace and understand the boundaryless attribute of climate activism, how it is sparked and how it spreads.

In this concluding chapter we will summarise the implications of this extension and how it relates to our findings. As illustrated in the empirical chapters, the climate activism we encountered was dispersed and its collective form and force were diffuse, at the same time as it shared a strong grounding in a certain way of co-producing and implementing knowledge. The epistemic community not only lays the foundations for the same topics – the climate emergency, renewables and the desire to accelerate solutions by speeding up action – but also opens up new ways of knowing through experimentation, sharing, wandering, altering and materialising. Furthermore, all these aspects, we suggest, contribute to horizontal organising. This chapter will detail this claim, starting with a focus on how renewable energy technology facilitates horizontality, to then discuss horizontal organising generated by an outsourcing of deliberation attempts, followed by horizontality that arises with the increasingly popular trend of prefigurative politics. Based on this emphasis on horizontality, we end by specifying four new elements of importance for a more generous conceptualisation of epistemic community: feral proximity, epistemic struggles, radical equality and human relationality.

10.1 Renewable Energy Technology and Horizontal Organising

Renewables, once heavily criticised for their intermittency, technical complexities and market immaturity (e.g. see Moselle, Padilla and Schmalensee 2010), are increasingly taken for granted as a positive solution to how humans can retake control of industrial impacts. The control is to be secured through individualised or collective machinery, complemented by an increased digitalisation of production and consumption via so-called smart solutions. The technology we chose to focus on in this particular study was not the digitalisation, but rather the machinery for electricity generation. Together, however, these are responsible for the practical decentralisation of electricity generation, effectively implemented via ideas of localised ownership of the means of production. The 'smartness' (via digitalisation) has thus succeeded in entering everyday life to infuse 'togetherness' (via renewable technology), combined into an alluring offer of enjoyable hands-on solutions to the problem of climate change, otherwise experienced as overwhelming. The formerly industrial and centralised solutions to electricity generation, installed to provide energy security, have thus been complemented by a decentralisation that simultaneously turns climate adaptation into collective climate action.

Overall, the research participants did not express pessimism but used renewables as a prosthesis for their own incapacity to decarbonise sufficiently in other ways. They were not disempowered by the climate emergency but capacitated by the technology; they were empowered to take action. They came across as accepting the emergency as a very acute problem that demanded the instant co-production of knowledge, sooner rather than later, here and now. Reflection upon the potentially erroneous human and ethical implications of individual actions underwrites the epistemic community through an advancement of *Bildung* and creates a positive but potentially blind devotion to a specific technology and machinery. Thanks to renewables, they were finally authorised to make amends and push an experimental mode of becoming, impatiently gathering and altering themselves and others via the technology. Supported by a shared quest to materialise solutions that had previously been kept on the level of talk as action, renewable technology thus facilitates the communicative aspect of an otherwise complex issue (Incropera 2016) and brings the science into everyday life at home or at work. This was observable in how the technology authorised public servants to finally unite the often clashing elements in the triple bottom line: the environmental, the social and the economic. It galvanised a new shared focus to prefigure around and shaped togetherness across organisations and generations by cutting through political and professional hierarchies.

We suggest this leads to a fecund horizontality, for example in how renewable energy enables a merger between 'power to the people' and 'individual responsibility' on the ground. The hands-on technology has gained an immanent quality of being able to encourage people in an otherwise crippling discourse on climate crisis, emergency or breakdown. In this climate of fear, our affluent research participants expressed that they felt more authentically involved when they were able to do something physical, for example by being part of the instalment of renewable solutions, be it on roofs or in fields. It was perhaps not so much an experience of getting one's hands dirty, even if some did, as it was an experience of relation-building and later visibility of the effort. Rendering wind turbines or solar panels visible, even in your own backyard, was turned into something positive. It became a sign of mission accomplished, the creation of memorabilia for future generations. The technology, as rhetorical resource and device, therefore functions as a solution that creates bonds between an existing people, of responsibilised individuals, and a people to come, giving rise to a stepwise replacement of NIMBYism with PIMBYism (Please In My Back Yard).

Renewables is thus a solution that succeeds in responding to uncertainty and the expectation of a catastrophic future of climate emergency by drawing people into productive relations with a positive outlook. The technology provides a constructive and practically possible path for people to take action in the here and now and thereby finally accomplishes the transition so longed for. This underwrites a less desperate movement and makes climate activism more 'pro' than 'anti' (Dixon 2014), enabled by the technology as such. However, as noted in the empirical chapters, uncertainty was also reintroduced in another form. Only the overarching goal was clear, to decarbonise, while how to do it yourself or together was largely left open to the unknown.

The expected outcomes of the implementations were additionally expressed to be, and experienced as, highly uncertain. To complement the certainty about the Earth's common uncertain future discovered by climate science, renewable energy technology thus introduces other, more mundane uncertainties, surrounded as the technology is with practical complications due to economic and technical challenges, as well as social tensions and NIMBYism expressed by others. The planning and implementation phase of renewables is experienced as ambiguous, a mine field, by employees within larger corporations such as Vattenfall, by citizen groups such as prosumer activists, and by activist entrepreneurs. Their mutual learning is thus centred around and builds on an individual and collective wandering, an encounter with untrodden paths that lead haphazardly here and there, which results in horizontal organising.

Renewable energy lays the ground for a continuous searching mode that repositions 'action'. In comparison with activism configured by radical actions, climate activism finds new bearing within contemporary *Bildung* processes and a continuous mode of lifelong searching to yield 'transformation with unknown outcomes' (Reichenbach 2002:411). Notably, instead of an activism rooted in struggles, anger, eventfulness and radicalness (Jasper 2011), climate activism is rooted in knowledge seeking and sharing, characterised by edgy experimentation as well as smooth adjustments. Renewable energy and the expertise it demands bridges continuously between theory and practice, thought and action, to calibrate in the uncertain knowledge landscape. This furthers horizontal organising at the same time as it keeps uncertainty alive. That is, renewables capacitate humans beyond a state of climate uncertainty and adaptation, only to result in actions that in themselves are situated within another layer of uncertainties.

Renewable energy actions are furthermore cultivated by a specific way of responding to human-induced climate change, hand in hand with a will to address global environmental degradation and social-economic difficulties in general. This could especially be seen in the chapters on insider activism and prosumer activism. In comparison with previous studies that emphasise lack of awareness, concern and action (Norgaard 2011, Poortinga et al. 2011, Capstick and Pidgeon 2014), we found ample examples of how the technology is embraced and affirmed, alongside other environmental problems, showing that it has become easier to respond in the everyday to carbon dioxide pollution, in comparison with other pollutions and environmental problems that are conceived as industrial. By first turning against industrialisation through the introduction of individual production options and consumption choices, renewables are, however, still embedded in a techno-optimistic discourse of economic modernisation (Hajer 1995) and reconfigured industrial progress (Jan, Farhat Durrani and Himayatullah 2021).

The shared episteme among the people we encountered rested on general knowledge about environmental problems, and more specific knowledge about the climate emergency and its solution, based on renewable energy expertise. What makes the gathering within this episteme different to instrumental and formal organisational processes – for example studied as strategic action fields, institutions that arise with collective action, or various forms of advocacy networks, coalitions and constituencies (e.g. see Sabatier 1988, Kraemer, Whiteman and Banerjee 2013, Keck and Sikkink 2014, Mey and Diesendorf 2018) – is how mutually constructed environmental values are merged with a tangible technology and belief that urgent action can be taken in more relaxed and often disorganised ways. Renewable energy technology thereby gives way to direct action, which is why there is no need to wait for an election, nor is there a need to wait for an official consultation to take place. The informality and disorganisation opens up space for further horizontality as actions are taken across established organisations and in parallel with formal political processes. What our empirical chapters testify to is that a broader category of people can take less aggressive action in their everyday settings, resulting in an activism that goes beyond 'alternative' lifestyles and heroic underdog actions (Katzenstein Fainsod 1998, Bobel 2007). One does not have to join Extinction Rebellion protests or a political party or become a paying member of Greenpeace. The activism rather grows around the capacity to morph a problematic situation into a challenge to overcome, and an opportunity to take.

Recognising this shift in language towards business talk and entrepreneurship also explains how the technology is key for bridging between business and activism. In comparison with how ecopreneurs especially have been shown to struggle in their creation of a coherent story and sense of self, with strong tensions between economic and ecological value creation (Phillips 2013), we did not find such a binary to be disturbing for our research participants. Whatever their reasons and personal backgrounds, it was notable how people chose to make sense of their green devotions and succeeded in forming new relationships with others, based on very different self-narratives. Many of the activist entrepreneurs, for example, comfortably self-identified as activists, although others, such as journalists, wished to categorise them as heroic green or social business entrepreneurs, which, in turn, no one seemed to mind. This shows that a simplified polarisation between activism and business methods is empirically untenable, which also has been problematised in entrepreneurship studies (see further Hockerts 2006, Bacq and Janssen 2011, Hjorth and Holt 2016), where examples of activism has influenced theory.

Similarly, environmentalism has historically been positioned in relation to capitalism and anti-capitalism differently (Leach 2015), where the Alternative Technology movement opened up for renewables to enjoy more open and diverse, but also symbiotic, relationships with capitalism (Eyerman and Jamison 1991, Smith 2005, Elliott, 2016). Morphing the languages of business and activism, and repositioning emergency and fear into a practical solution in the here and now, has been shown to create a relaxed and engaged way of coming together to share climate change knowledge in efforts to build enduring, meaningful relations. Horizontal organising thus encompasses all sorts of actors and also suggests that the capitalist speeding up of action is furthered, rather than resisted (cf. Sloterdijk 2014). At the same time, the findings complicate this picture, showing that specific elements of contemporary capitalist excesses are identified and resisted, namely market monopolisation by big businesses and the distance and detachment created by market globalisation. As noted previously:

We may see an unfolding of 'clean technology' promoted by large investors, corporations and entrepreneurial states, and an attempt to install a co-evolving framework for sustainable development by elites. However, if we look carefully enough, then we will also notice it is accompanied by a more unruly, anarchic and messier exploration of everyday sustainabilities involving the kind of practical reasoning evident in grassroots innovations. (Smith and Ely 2015:116)

10.2 Outsourced Deliberation and Horizontal Organising

Climate change is at the same time global, national, regional and local, which brings about tensions between centralised and decentralised thinking (Vasi Bogdan 2011). On the one hand, there is an international UN-led centralisation of knowledge about environmental problems, its politics and business (United Nations 2020), and on the other hand, there is an outsourcing of these very problems to the people (cf. Evans and Reid 2014), now in terms of a lack of 'action', with 'challenges' to meet and 'opportunities' to take. As the empirical chapters detailed, people became intertwined in attempts to govern actions but also took action in 'more unruly, anarchic and messier' ways (Smith and Ely 2015:116). There was no pure translation or mediation to be had between state authorities and civil society, but an uncharted and dispersed knowledge movement grew (cf. Roy 2009). Relations were spontaneously formed across established, instrumental and technocratic hierarchies, which unshackled the bureaucracy from its ideology of deliberation and opened up space for horizontal organising and a more diversely configured conglomeration of passions. Climate activism consequently is not about polarised positions between the elite and grassroots movements but has transformed deliberation into a pluralist space, according to which there is more room for different values and supposedly more healthy confrontation, something Mouffe (1999) called for with her agonism approach.

Climate activism is consequently positioned in the midst of centralising–decentralising tensions, which gives rise to a horizontal movement created by how people's engagements spill over otherwise centrally or decentrally regulated organising. Importantly, though, it is not the process of decision-making that is decentralised, for example by deliberative democratic programmes (Smith 2003, 2009, Bäckstrand 2010). We rather found that it is a decentralisation of the decentralisation effort itself that is accomplished. That is, deliberation is let loose to be accomplished on the ground without interference from any overtly obvious policy remnants of its normative basis, that is, top-down creation of a bottom-up movement. Everyone is made responsible for their neighbours' possible inclusion in decisions and implementations through a self-organised, sound, neighbourly dialogue and empowerment to take action. As pointed out by the prosumer activists, for example, no one besides them was interested in the results of their attempts to deliberate as well as decarbonise.

The prosumers we followed were, without knowing it, becoming their own laissez-faire experts on democratic decentralisation as they placed decision-making on their fellow citizens or local authorities. They facilitated dialogue with their neighbours, conceived either as potential privileged co-investors or as under-privileged victims of energy poverty, who should be helped, materially and mentally. Employee activists, activist businesses, insider activists and prosumer activists were, in addition, all empowering deliberative democracy on the ground as they made sure that the reason-based dialogue led to actions, often aligned with their learnings about self-sufficient energy communities. Ideas about 'community' were thus being revitalised by the knowledge movement that underwrites climate activism, with people called upon as believers in 'community' (Walker et al. 2007). Our research participants were inviting each other to play out a desire to alter their own lives and selves in tandem with the crafting of communities, conventionally understood as human relations hosted in a specific unit. Here, only some of the mutual green ambitions were economically beneficial. Hence, the notion of community, traditionally understood as a 'persistent well of warm-hearted association' that needs revival, has proved

capable of accommodating a necessary diversity in the scale, type and purpose of small scale renewable energy project development, and, along with the under-strategised and hands-off approach to connecting national programs to local action, has provided opportunities for experimentation with different models of project management, ownership and distribution of benefits. Whilst therefore from a normative position we could be critical of the degree to which the meaning of community RE [renewable energy] has been stretched, pragmatically its malleability appears to have been purposeful and productive in supporting many different types and forms of local renewable energy activity. (Walker et al. 2007:78)

In comparison with previous literature on deliberative democracy, we found that a decentralisation of solutions to climate change involves both an outsourcing of decarbonisation as well as an outsourcing of deliberative democracy efforts in themselves. Deliberative democracy is let loose, to be ferally pursued hand in hand with a decentralisation of electricity generation, whereby citizens are given a higher stake in the process of decision-making – particularly by how dialogue, voicing and feedback processes are brought much closer to where the resistance and potential NIMBYism are located, in the 'community'. As we illustrated briefly, the prosumers handled and met resistance themselves, on a Sunday stroll or at the farmers' market. This also happened to the Vattenfall employees when they were out on wind power field sites. Even if Vattenfall occasionally used a moderator who was a professional deliberator, the employees often acted as deliberation amateurs, becoming directly involved in negotiations to freely moderate debates. Empowered to deliberate as they saw fit, our research participants were to craft feedback processes by means of home-made participatory techniques. In comparison with how policy is taken from the top down, to result in action via deliberation, and in comparison with conventional grassroots bottom-up actions, horizontal organising thus emerged through a deregulation of all sorts of expertise, not only technical and economic but political as well.

However, not all aspects of the political, technical and economic were let loose. A formal political recognition of anarchic, messy, everyday sustainabilities has also taken deliberation processes onto new paths, with a tendency to infuse and recognise latent activism within the citizenry. Deliberation partly bypasses the normal procedures of top-down moderation with its weighing of advantages versus disadvantages to deregulate deliberation and re-wild the grassroots. Renewable energy becomes an effective tool for harnessing people's energies by stimulating a very diverse capacity to act in the here and now (Walker et al. 2007), in effect governing not only through 'community' but also through 'activism'. Governments and companies no longer have to consult civil society and various stakeholder groups or communities to the same degree as before, but through the outsourcing and re-wilding of renewable energy actions they can obtain full and more detailed disclosure on unresolved differences in opinion. The messy, anarchic and active participation exposes what is already happening 'here and now', even from within small businesses, big corporations and state institutions. It is not people's imaginations and desires that are in focus. Governing has become more agile, connected not to expectations but to ongoing prefiguration – to what has already been made possible on the ground by the turning of citizens into activists.

Consequently, anyone involved in sustaining progression via renewable energy can in a very direct sense smoothly adjust, depending on what sort of technology and business models citizens-becoming-activists have shown possible in their everyday lives. Even though some strategic planning for renewables is needed, less and less is decided on beforehand. It is rather experimentation, sharing, wandering and altering that seems to secure the 'throughput' and implementation stage (cf. Abers and Keck 2009: 292) with people who are led not by causation but by their will to alter themselves and others by trial and error. Even though the decarbonisation occasionally did not succeed, the implementation was accomplished through experiences of togetherness. Just hanging out together and having fun was a major driver to engage in decarbonisation and the energy transition (cf. Smith and Ely 2015). This self-organised advancement and transparency additionally meant that the inclusion and participation came across as more authentic, less open to criticism for being half-hearted, created by pseudo-dialogue, and just for the sake of democratic and consensual ideals (cf. Fast 2013). It consequently results in a climate activism that spills over onto other things and relationships, where its centrifugal forces create horizontality and find new, previously unknown resources with which the movement will prosper further or become exhausted.

10.3 Horizontality and Prefiguration

A renewed focus on prefigurative politics can give other insights into the outsourcing of deliberative democracy and the horizontality it generates (Yates 2015, Maeckelbergh 2016, Reinecke 2018). As our empirical findings showed, it did not really matter which exact support mechanisms or policy instruments the research participants were involved with. They were sometimes targeted with the same sort of support, but this led to very different actions and ways to transition the energy system. Several of them made things happen in spite of the difficulties and uncertainty they encountered in relation to the technocratic and instrumental political-industrial landscape that still wished to make them democratically participative. Their experiences of complexity and uncertainty seemed to spur a need for direct doable actions on the ground, in the here and now. The bridging across domains was accomplished by how our research participants created the change they wanted to see around them – whether they were placed in a large energy utility, in small- and medium-sized businesses, in governmental agencies or in a village/town. Thus it is also possible to understand the boundaryless attribute of climate activism as a form of pragmatic directness that leads to horizontality (Maeckelbergh 2011).

From the perspective of prefiguration, with its emphasis on 'praxis' and human relationality (Farias 2017), we contend that climate activism could happen in all sorts of contexts, in parallel to, or even immersed in, other more formally organised dialogical spaces of deliberation.

Similarly to calls for deep or true democracy (Heyley 2014), boundaryless climate activism could even come across as a 'radical democracy' due to this embodiment of certain forms of relations between people (Cornish et al. 2016) that are as much a means to decarbonise as they are a goal in themselves. Perhaps the horizontality arising thereby accomplishes an inclusion and transparency that is more in line with the 'depth' and partnerships envisioned by Appadurai (2013:176), at least if the movement creates an outreach that rejects narrow confinements. The prefiguration at play is not only about combatting climate change, although this was a motivation for quite a few of the people we encountered. The activist employees, entrepreneurs, public servants and prosumers were also looking for friendship and solidarity, which their direct engagement with the technology facilitated. Self-development and collectivism were thus glued together via the technology, similarly to how Pink (2008) points towards the intermingling of rhythms and social bonding in her study of 'indirect activism' in the Cittàslow movement. Though first conceived as a dry and techy subject, the perspective of prefiguration thus clarifies how renewables have succeeded in stimulating human relationality.

The research participants took renewables to be a 'positive solution[s] in the here and now', to just do it (Leach and Scoones 2015:127), meaning that they refused to wait for commands from above and had no patience with seemingly powerful actors who wanted them to participate or engage in dialogue in a specific way. Instead, they got together, organised and engaged in a variety of renewable energy actions that constituted a hybrid and open-ended form of organisation without a clear political position (cf. Jamison 2001). This ambiguity has nevertheless been problematised (Scerri 2019), particularly in relation to a depoliticisation or post-political condition (Smith et al. 2017). That is, since prefiguration focusses on human relationality in a present 'becoming' of the world that is wanted (in the future), it may lose sight of the capacity to detach sufficiently from the present world. This means that climate activism seen through prefiguration makes it into a movement pursued from 'within', one that has been argued to open up for greater equality with regard to who can take actions and how they can be taken (Butler 2017).

This sort of coming together, interconnectedness and participation, be it in a specific sensuous place or not, does not necessarily inhibit the ability to imagine a different world. Without having the same empirical basis for our study as Pink (2008), it is interesting to compare how she found the material conditions and the close sensorial environment of importance for how the activism developed. We can concur with her that rather than talking about ready-made communities, it is more relevant to look at what sort of activities and bonding that brings about certain human relationality, collectives and directions of a 'movement'. In the four empirical chapters, these collectives or gatherings were often about people seeking to fill their lives with, for them, meaningful activities based on their previous professional experiences or lay expertise as citizens within a knowledge society and economy.

10.4 Epistemic Community

Haas' (2015) conception of epistemic communities has mainly been applied to trace types of knowledge and formal processes of knowing, while disorganised and mundane dimensions of how knowledge movements function are also of immense importance for a better understanding of climate activism. Based on our findings, we will in this concluding section specify how we wish to broaden the earlier conceptualisation of epistemic communities with emphasis on feral proximity, epistemic struggles, radical equality and human relationality.

10.4.1 Feral Proximity

In the context of our specific study, the concept of epistemic community has been developed to encompass a collectivity, or movement, formed when people experiment, alter, come together and share knowledge about environmental degradation and climate change and, by hands-on everyday direct actions, further this knowledge via work with renewable energy solutions. Just as climate change, via the episteme, is made into a global phenomenon which is uncontrollable and unconfined, the epistemic community itself continuously expands, underpinning the boundaryless attribute of climate activism. This feral character of the problem is mirrored in an increasingly feral mobilisation of solutions, even though humans are told to travel less and be more disposed to local proximities and bounded connectivity. The epistemic community is thus established similarly to 'close communities', with experts who *flâneur* and flexibly wander between organisations (Harrigan, Achananuparp and Lim 2012).

To some extent this continuous knowledge movement is thus shaped by the *flâneuse* or *flâneur* who strolls through modern life (Böhm 2005). These walkers, who are of particular importance in Walter Benjamin's (1997) analytical exploration of nineteenth-century Paris and the modernisation of urban life, develop a particular proximity to a whole range of 'things': fragments, artefacts, waste, images, texts, objects, relics, allegories and so on. In our study, the research participants also nurtured a sort of closeness by wandering, not only between specific organisations but through what seems to be close to their hearts, creating a sort of personal proximity. They were not particularly interested in changing policies or structures directly but were more interested in transparently altering themselves by exploring openings and opportunities for what could be realisable under uncertainty. Just as this uncertainty fed experimentation and sharing, it also fed novel proximities, through acts of connection and reconnection, the sharing and Do-It-Together, which we discussed in Chapter 9. Flexibly wandering between domains therefore generates openness and new proximities, and in some instances the participants occupied and transgressed several domains at once, making a mockery of traditional institutional analysis of organising and change.

Feral proximity can moreover be seen in how material devices function as rhetorical resources. In this case, renewable energy technology allows people to bring their techno-optimistic passions and political imaginations of economic redistribution closer to themselves, each other and daily life and also to bring these into material fruition. Characteristic for the epistemic community is thus a perfect merger of the personal and professional (Kanter 1977), and how this merger drives a knowledge movement based on proximity, rather than detachment and set organisational goals or rules for decision-making. The epistemic community acts without a leader or managerial committee that seeks to steer and rule (Sutherland, Land and Böhm 2014). Although some feral visionaries or 'leaders' exist, for example the founder of Ecotricity, who has been portrayed as a kind of larger-than-life figure, such heroic positions were not fundamental for the human relationality and proximities we experienced in the field.

When looking more closely at a broader set of research participants, the epistemic community does not seem to rely exclusively on moral models for action but can rather be described as being reliant on anti-leadership processes (Sutherland, Land and Böhm 2014). The epistemic community consequently does not wait for higher powers to solve contradictions or make decisions but fosters a feral proximity with governmental bodies and big business, who become exposed to the knowledge movement, its disorganised processes and haphazard outcomes. There are no formal rules and there is no obvious hierarchy, but knowledge is brought closer to the people by the people. The epistemic community grows through everybody's individual capacity to alter and take action. It creates a very diffuse form of activism, exemplifying an alteration process *par excellence*- always on the move- whereby it becomes difficult to pinpoint 'the true activist', one that shows the supposedly correct intentional mode, conscious choices and political agency, or muscles and voice (Butler 2017). People can join by just doing some 'work' (cf. Jamison 2001:141), at the same time as they act as relays of decentralised expertise and hobby engineering. While this feral quality was not as unruly and disruptive as others have suggested (Garside 2013), our findings have nevertheless shown the scattered ways in which renewable energy actions were taken, and the unpredictable paths that followed.

As a movement of the everyday with people trying to reconfigure a terrain intellectually and passionately (cf. Davis Cross 2013), the epistemic community does not necessarily need to express a distrust in governments, nor does it need to be explicitly anti-capitalist, as many ultra-right- or left-wing movements can be. Rather, the horizontal organising generated a proximity that refused both cynical distancing and exhaustion due to nihilism. A dynamic proximity arose that constantly balanced between the supported and unsupported, the unplanned and the planned. The flip side of this proximity was thus precarity, with some of the research participants having to live quite scattered lives, embracing various possibilities for exploration and disruption, whether this was in their own personal lives or in their professions. They gave up jobs, changed careers, established activist platforms in stale bureaucracies, engaged in small-scale incremental changes in large corporations, set up their own small business enterprises and rallied entire villages and small towns around their pro-environmental causes. This feral mode disturbed the normality of orderly democracy and deliberation attempts, and, for that matter, the normality of activism.

10.4.2 Epistemic Struggles

Even though the epistemic community prepares the ground for a boundaryless movement, it is also constituted by epistemic struggles that create thresholds where content and membership are negotiated (Icaza and Vázquez 2013). The people we met were not 'card-carrying' members of environmental organisations or even part of a collective action group. Climate activism is seemingly open for everyone to join, yet it is dependent on an active sharing of specific knowledge claims and negotiation thereof, that is, a mix of scientific knowledge, lay expertise and citizen science (Leach 2015). This means that knowledge struggles are part and parcel of how an epistemic community creates distinctions to which one can belong, where the activism grows through a process of conversation and knowing, rather than 'rational persuasion' (Mouffe 1999). Hence, epistemic communities are not necessarily 'happy families' where everyone agrees, but the struggles foster a will to move on – a feral attitude against passivity.

As exemplified in Chapter 5 on Vattenfall's corporate activism, CEO activism, brand activism and employee activism, these were enacted not through violent struggles, nor through protests and demonstrations on the street, but through epistemic struggles consisting of differing opinions about the feasibility of various types of renewable energy sources and of renewable energy technology in relation to conventional energy technology. In Chapter 8, on climate activism via citizen groups, with a focus on prosumer activism, we showed how the epistemic community was created around the sharing of knowledge and negotiations about the benefits or drawbacks of renewable technologies, stretching to diverse views on commercial methods and redistributive business models. The epistemic community grew stronger as the practical realisation was uncertain and had to develop through knowledge struggles on how to best accomplish voluntarism, a gift economy or profit-sharing. This caused the knowledge movement to be incredibly detailed, bringing 'actions' down to all sorts of mundane doings, which in their diversity still solidified a mutual cause of decarbonisation and energy transition.

It was not always clear in the findings whether the epistemic struggles accomplished a distinct demarcation of an 'outside' that would exclude people and things that did not fit in (Etzioni 2004). Rather, it seemed as though the epistemic community encompassed struggles to host immanent conflicts, for people to handle daily and make into an expected and appreciated part of their lives. When carrying out the empirical research, we seldom encountered combat situations with people openly challenging each other, either physically or verbally, even though such resistance sometimes cropped up in stories people told us. The research participants did not come across as aggressive competitors that saw themselves as fighting a kind of war, opposing some sort of incumbent enemy. Instead, the struggles we observed were agonistic (Mouffe 1999), characterised by respect and carried out with devotion. We observed acceptance of other people's views in efforts to establish new connections and a sense of belonging. Instead of meeting and handling conflicts to establish consensus, people chose to move on, relentlessly exploring other possibilities, often created by themselves despite hindrances that might easily have caused others to capitulate.

This kind of agonistic activism should not be mistaken for something tame, such as adherence to the rules of consensual democratic naivety. It does not close off and exclude alternative views but 'make[s] room for dissent' and gives up on the idea of an ideal order by embracing a multiplicity of voices (Mouffe 1999:15). By affirming immanent knowledge struggles, the epistemic community goes back and forth between clarity and non-clarity, which means that the capacity to critique should be conceived as immanent to the concept of epistemic community itself. It is in part also this conflictual milieu that keeps the members together within *Gemeinschaft*, in contrast to how conflicts serve organising in *Gesellschaft* (Tönnies 1957/2002). That is, in the economic and market-driven sphere of *Gesellschaft*, conflicts are based on how individuals relate to each other as individuals who compete to win or lose, whereas conflicts in community formations are supposed to lead to togetherness and prosperous gatherings.

Furthermore, the epistemic struggles show how an immanent axis for self-critique embeds a *Bildung* process within the epistemic community. The struggles invite reflection and judgement, self-critique and a possibility to alter oneself and others through constructive negotiations. *Bildung* takes into account the collective mobilisation that happens beyond factual, scientific knowledge that was also part of shaping new (affluent) organisational forms and horizontal togetherness in the energy transition. What is clarified when looking at the conflation of renewable energy actions and *Bildung* processes is how the epistemic community encompasses a drive for lifelong personal perfection and a belief in self-formation and one's own capacity to think and act. By turning our attention to *Bildung*, it becomes evident how the epistemic community attempts to create an ideal of intellectual equality, under the pretext that everyone can obtain knowledge about themselves in relation to the world and nature. Furthermore, this should presumably lead to a more reflexive, aware and concerned knowledge position that is necessary as correct grounds for action. In this opening up of the mind, people are supposed to be interested in working on themselves and susceptible to contributing and co-creating a dispersed episteme, defined by openness and endlessness, but perhaps not 'independence' as we know it through *Bildung* (Rönnerman and Salo 2017:458).

An interest in oneself as a transformable subject is still part of the entry exam for the epistemic community, but what decides whether or not one is contributing to one's human relationality is the acting out of an inseparability from the world in which one currently lives. Hence, we suggest that looking more closely at contemporary forms of *Bildung* processes could enrich the mode of thinking involved in climate activism. Although the epistemic community does involve specialised and scientific knowledge about climate change and renewables, it relies more on how people are continuously experimenting and altering themselves in a futural mode, on untrodden paths towards renewable energy expansion and alternative organisational forms. It thrives on feral proximities based in a mutual problem space, brought 'home' with hands-on solutions that demand close co-production of knowledge and sharing – a kind of knowing – rather than a certain stock of knowledge.

10.4.3 Radical Equality

Feral proximity and epistemic struggles lead to inclusions, of oneself and of others. This implies an intensification of the link between knowledge and politics, which is why we propose that climate activism can also be explained by recognising anyone's ability to partake in politics (Rancière 2016). Rancière's perspective is of use for expanding Haas' concept of epistemic community further, to neglected partakers, beyond acclaimed experts with scientific authority. The 'politics' in climate activism is not to be found along the lines of a specific geography or position of authority, but in the co-production of knowledge that mobilises the epistemic community and activist-business-state conglomeration. Rancière (2016) stresses a basic principle of intellectual equality that in effect enforces horizontality by virtue of how it looks beyond class differences and other structural explanations of inequality. Acknowledging that politics is not confined to formal political bodies and policymaking but is a possible pursuit for anyone under the pretext of potential intellectual equality makes it possible to analyse a broader set of political partaking (Skoglund and Böhm 2020). In the case of renewable energy actions, which in this study are undoubtedly taken by affluent and privileged people, this would mean an acknowledgement of their 'politics', by making them into 'equals', instead of granting them power as evil accumulators of resources. The question is, nonetheless, whether it is possible to categorise the 'privileged' as equals in light of the common polarisation between activism and capitalism.

In the context of this study, we encountered an epistemic community that was full of enlightened and affluent people, and perhaps even an 'overdeveloped' activist-business-state conglomeration (Skoglund 2014). The research participants were often academically educated and most of them had a specific socio-economic position that could be described as 'middle class'. Yet perhaps this insight should not over-code our findings if the aim is to follow the trans-valuation of 'politics' in contemporary expressions of activism. While we do not deny that class is a potentially interesting analytical angle to take (Catney et al. 2014), this book has tried to shed new light on activism by exposing how productive horizontal relations are created in the midst of all sorts of other organisational explanations. If one link in the activist-business-state conglomeration is weak, the other links seem to take over in a very self-organised and fecund way, resulting in a generous spilling over that has an impact across social and economic backgrounds, professions and means. Hence, an expanded conception of epistemic communities, which is prepared to include anyone in political partaking, makes it possible to understand how knowledge and a dispersed renewable energy expertise succeeds in mobilising people of different backgrounds and with very unequal resources.

Even though this may not be what Rancière had in mind when laying the foundations for the principle of everyone's ability to partake in politics, such an affordance definitely puts a finger on how 'politics' can be pursued from within a big or small business organisation, a municipality or a citizen group. It strengthens an empirical and analytical possibility to diagnose the merger between deliberative democracy and prefiguration, as well as community and business, in a constructive light of 'radical equality'. Without Rancière's (2016) proposition of equality of partaking politically, it would perhaps be hard to see anything other than 'privilege' and 'class' in our empirical chapters. The thought of radical equality therefore provides an additional way to explain our experiences in the field and another theoretical entrance to understanding the blurred boundaries between civil society and business (Soule 2012, Weber and King 2014, den Hond, de Bakker, and Smith 2015).

In our findings, radical equality does not stretch to post-human assumptions about everyone partaking in an ecological system (Tsing 2015) rather than a political system. The concept of epistemic community we can offer through our findings is thus indebted to a sense of anthropocentric dominance over things and others. The humans we met and followed did not wish for, nor did they experience, a total subjection to ecological systems thinking. They passionately expressed that they would be able to take action through human-created scientific knowledge and technical solutions. In other words, it is not a community of equals with regard to any type of species or life form. It is a community shaped by a connectivity chosen by humans, a shared formation of knowledge or episteme that has been moulded over time, steeped in philosophical and philanthropic historicities, to cohere with, but also deviate from, more contemporary moral trends (Foucault 1980:195–197), prevalent both in efforts of ecological modernisation in the knowledge economy and in post-human vitalisations of biospheric life (Bennett 2010, Haraway 2015, Latour 2018, Morton 2018). Renewables thus open up for technical fixes that manage to bypass a critique of human domination on Earth, to reposition ideals of progress within the realm of 'togetherness', mainly of a human sort.

10.4.4 Human Relationality

Whereas other means exist for studying soft forms of knowledge sharing, albeit mainly with a focus on how these forms affect policymaking, we found them – as well as Haas' (1992) original conceptualisation of epistemic communities – to mainly follow a logic that belongs to *Gesellschaft*, and not *Gemeinschaft*. In contrast to Haas (1992, 2015), we were from the outset uninterested in how certain acclaimed experts seek to strategically reach specific policy objectives authoritatively, which is why we turned to Tönnies' (1957/2002) conceptualisation of *Gemeinschaft* and *Gesellschaft*. We were able to see close-knit human relations on the one hand, and disconnected, instrumental or even marketised actions on the other (Asplund 1991). In comparison with the prevailing academic debate, we focussed less on how *Gemeinschaft* has been increasingly trumped and over-ruled by the growing dominance of *Gesellschaft*, with its reliance on marketised and atomised social relations. That is, we suggest that the existence of human togetherness and belonging has been downplayed when submerged in society conceived as a broader category for all sorts of (contractual) social relations, of which community relations have become but one type. By instead advancing epistemic community and giving it a more people-centred status, our analysis resurrects the type of human relationality that, according to Tönnies, existed within *Gemeinschaft*.

It is, however, easy to fall once again into the polarised debate between *Gesellschaft* and *Gemeinschaft* since it has served a great number of authors, creating a believable but simplified dichotomy visible in repeated contrasts between activism and business. What we wish to emphasise in all of this are the rich interactions between community and society/business, between *Gemeinschaft* and *Gesellschaft*, which, we have argued, are of heightened importance for understanding climate activism (Scoones, Leach and Newell 2015). Perhaps unexpectedly in this political condition, we have found an abundant will to come together and an expansion of community relations and cooperative forms. A dispersed and generous movement under education is growing, which leads us to conclude that it is possible to look beyond theorisations that are stuck in old repetitive polarisations between dirty exchange and pure gift-giving. The research participants were, for example, not only hoping that renewable energy technologies would be able to 'fix' climate change, but they had already experienced meaningful social interactions in what had previously been conceived as a lifeless and atomised form of life. It is not a resilient coping with disasters based on an abstract 'doing good' for the planet, wider society or future generations (*Gesellschaft*). On the contrary, indebted to this advertised mode of life, climate activism manages to push back at *Gesellschaft* through prefiguration focussed on the actual proximities within which one lives (*Gemeinschaft*).

This updated form of community relations and *Gemeinschaft*, which we have explored and illustrated throughout the book, has thus moved beyond the creation of an active passivity among citizens, as well as an easy appropriation of 'a personal politics' (Bennett and Segerberg 2011). In this sense climate activism is a unique merger of technical and political innovation, using specific technologies and prosumer-type localism to mobilise people into prefigurative action in the here and now. It is important to emphasise again that the climate activism we encountered was not organised in one place as a unified collectivity. However, feral proximities that we argue are fundamental to climate activism can nevertheless be sensitive to novel exploitation by a smooth and geopolitically segmented appropriation (Guattari and Negri 1985/2010:49). As Deleuze and Guattari (1988) propose, any smooth, horizontal or feral movement can be re-territorialised by hierarchical machines that feed on the creativity and inventiveness of that movement. The canonical story of power and resistance is in that sense never ending, largely due to humanity's singular capacity for inventiveness, enterprise and politics, where activism thrives on the ability to creatively judge with the help of others – not only how to (dis)connect and (non)adapt, but also how to imagine, take action and live differently to before. It is a collectively shaped prefigurative movement, one before symbolisation and capture.

We may thus envision an accentuation of future environmentalisms that thrive equally on feral proximity, epistemic struggles and radical equality in the bridging between business and human relationality. By thinking beyond a polarisation of community relations and market relations, and of activism and enterprising, we thus hope to have explained how and why climate activism has grown increasingly opaque. Although the study is mainly empirically based in the UK, our development of epistemic community as an analytical framework can be applied across nations and policy contexts, to better understand existing desires to establish self-sufficient energy communities via alternative forms of organising (Zebrowski and Sage 2017). With an analytical focus on how epistemic communities unfold as a fecund hotbed for climate activism, it may also be possible to trace more transnational movements and how people may partake in politics in the everyday, either at home or at work. By tracing the boundaryless attribute of activism, the epistemic struggles it thrives on and the human relationality it furthers, we thus hope to have shown that climate activism prospers beyond the logistical or rhetorical consolidations of the nation state or transnational governmental bodies, including the lucrative energy transition and instrumental sustainability agenda.

Appendix

Table A.1 *Examples of commercial activism*

Types of activism	Description	Examples from the academic debate
Shareholder/Investor activism	Activism by investing in shares to attain influence over value creation (economic, social, green)	(Proffitt and Spicer 2006, Kurtz 2008, Goranova and Verstegen Ryan 2014, Perrault and Clark 2016)
Corporate activism	Corporations that use their clout and resources to further certain political aims	(Sethi 1982, Grefe and Linsky 1995, Davis and White 2015,)
Corporate environmentalism	Corporations that use their clout and resources to engage in green political aims	(Menon and Menon 1997, Hoffman 2001, Banerjee 2002, Bowen 2014)
Enterprising activism/Activist entrepreneurship	The utilisation of commercial means to reach political ends, for example activists schooled in business who seek to accomplish environmental and social changes based on new business models and redistributive monetary flows	(Mirvis 1994, Barinaga 2013, Ahl et al. 2016, Chouinard 2016)
Activist entrepreneuring	Disruptive organising, for example via generosity, collective action and truth-telling (parrhesia), which removes constraints to facilitate human imaginary capacities that breaks with established norms	(Hjorth and Holt 2016, Dey and Mason 2018)

Table A.1 (*cont.*)

Types of activism	Description	Examples from the academic debate
CEO activism	CEOs of companies who use their authority as leaders to further their employer's politics, or to pursue their personal politics via their employer	(Chatterji and Toffel 2015, 2019, Mayer 2017, Hinterecker, Kopel and Ressi 2018, Branicki et al. 2021, Hambrick and Wowak 2021, Rumstadt and Kanbach 2022)
Brand activism	Companies that use external and internal branding and marketing activities to rhetorically work with the personal politics of their customers and employees	(Hartmann, Apoalaza Ibanez and Forcada Sainz 2005, Morsing 2006, Kryger Aggerholm, Esmann Andersen and Thomsen 2010, Cederström and Marinetto 2013, Jeanes 2013, Muhr and Rehn 2014)
Employee activism	Employees who pursue a personal politics at work	(Meyerson and Scully 1995, Creed and Scully 2000, Scully and Segal 2002, Girschik 2020, Skoglund and Böhm 2020)
Insider activism	Public servants inside governmental and other public institutions who pursue their personal politics at work	(Hochstetler and Keck 2007, Olsson and Hysing 2012, Hysing and Olsson 2018, Abers 2019)
Prosumer activism	People who seek to take charge of the commercial process by investing, producing, consuming and selling, based on a Do-It-Yourself approach	(Toffler 1980, Van Der Schoor and Scholtens 2015, Wood 2016)

Table A.1 (*cont.*)

Types of activism	Description	Examples from the academic debate
Consumer activism	Taking a political stand as a choosing consumer, or 'voicing' by voting with your money, either as an individual or as a business (B2B consumer activism)	(Glickman 2009, Hilton 2009, Mukherjee and Banet-Weiser 2012)
Community activism	Citizen groups who collectively campaign and take action for social, environmental and economic change	(Pink 2008, Seyfang and Haxeltine 2012, Van Der Schoor and Scholtens 2015, Lewis 2016, Simon and Herring 2020)
NGO activism	Mostly formal, non-governmental organisations that take actions towards social and environmental change	(Gough and Shackley 2001, Doh and Guay 2006, Yaziji and Doh 2010)
Social movement activism	Informal and formal groups/movements of people that take actions for social and environmental change across different locations	(Soule 2012, Felicetti 2017, Pedwell 2019)

References

Abers, Rebecca Neaera. 2019. "Bureaucratic activism: Pursuing environmentalism inside the Brazilian State." *Latin American Politics and Society* 61 (2):21–44.

Abers, Rebecca Neaera, and Margaret E. Keck. 2009. "Mobilizing the state: The erratic partner in Brazil's participatory water policy." *Politics and Society* 37 (2):289–314.

Abidin, Crystal, Dan Brockington, Michael K. Goodman, Mary Mostafanezhad, and Lisa Ann Richey. 2020. The tropes of celebrity environmentalism. *Annual Review of Environment and Resources* 45 (1):387–410.

Activist Insight. 2018. The activist invest annual review. www.activistinsight.com/research/TheActivistInvesting.AnnualReview.2018.pdf

Adger, W. Neil, and Andrew Jordan, eds. 2009. *Governing sustainability*. Cambridge: Cambridge University Press.

Adler, Paul S. 2015. "Community and innovation: From Tönnies to Marx." *Organization Studies* 36 (4):445–471.

Adsit-Morris, Chessa. 2017. *Restoring environmental education: Figurations, fictions, and feral subjectivities*. Cham: Palgrave Macmillan.

Agamben, Giorgio. 1993. *The coming community*. Minneapolis: University of Minnesota Press.

Ahl, Helene, Karin Berglund, Katarina Pettersson, and Malin Tillmar. 2016. "From feminism to FemInc.ism: On the uneasy relationship between feminism, entrepreneurship and the Nordic welfare state." *International Entrepreneurship and Management Journal* 12 (2):369–392.

Alinsky, Saul. 1971. *Rules for radicals: A pragmatic primer for realistic radicals*. New York: Vintage Books.

Allen, Stephen, Judi Marshall, and Mark Easterby-Smith. 2015. "Living with contradictions: The dynamics of senior managers' identity tensions in relation to sustainability." *Organization & Environment* 1–21.

Alnoor, Ebrahim, Julie Battilana, and Johanna Mair. 2014. "The governance of social enterprises: Mission drift and accountability challenges in hybrid organizations." *Research in Organizational Behavior* 34:81–100.

Alvesson, Mats, and Maxine Robertson. 2015. "Money matters: Teflonic identity manoeuvring in the investment banking sector." *Organization Studies* 1–28.

Anderson, Benedict. 2006. *Imagined communities: Reflections on the origin and spread of nationalism.* Revised ed. London and New York: Verso.

Antorini, Yun Mi, Albert M. Muñiz Jr, and Tormod Askildsen. 2012. "Collaborating with customer communities: Lessons from the LEGO Group." *MIT Sloan Management Review* 53 (3):73.

Appadurai, Arjun. 1996. *Modernity at large: Cultural dimensions of globalization.* Minneapolis and London: University of Minnesota Press.

Appadurai, Arjun. 2013. *The future as cultural fact.* London and New York: Verso.

Asplund, Jonas. 1991. *Essä om Gemeinschaft och Gesellschaft.* Gothenburg: Bokförlaget Korpen.

Aust, Ina, Michael Muller-Camen, and Erik Poutsm. 2018. "Sustainable HRM: A comparative and international perspective." In *Handbook of research on comparative human resource management,* edited by Chris Brewster, Wolfgang Mayrhofer, and Elaine Farndale, 358–372. Cheltenham: Edward Elgar Publishing.

Bäckstrand, Karin. 2003. "Civic science for sustainability: Reframing the role of experts, policy-makers and citizens in environmental governance." *Global Environmental Politics* 3 (4):24–41.

Bäckstrand, Karin, Jamil Khan, Annica Kronsell, and Eva Lövbrand. eds. 2010. *Environmental politics and deliberative democracy: Examining the promise of new modes of governance.* Cheltenham: Edward Elgar Publishing.

Bacq, Sophie, and Frank Janssen. 2011. "The multiple faces of social entrepreneurship: A review of definitional issues based on geographical and thematic criteria." *Entrepreneurship and Regional Development* 23 (5–6):373–403.

Bain, Peter, and Phil Taylor. 2000. "Entrapped by the 'electronic panopticon'? Worker resistance in the call centre." *New Technology, Work and Employment* 15 (1):2–18.

Baker, Lucy, and Jon Phillips. 2019. "Tensions in the transition: The politics of electricity distribution in South Africa." *Environment and Planning C: Politics and Space* 37 (1):177–196.

Baldwin, Rosecrans. 2018. "Patagonia vs. Donald Trump." GQ, 5 April. www.gq.com/story/patagonia-versus-donald-trump

Balibar, Étienne, Antonio Negri, Anna Curcio, and Ceren Özselcuk. 2010. "On the common, universality, and communism: A conversation between Étienne Balibar and Antonio Negri, introduction by Anna Curcio and Ceren Özselcuk." *Rethinking Marxism* 22 (3):312–328.

Banerjee, Bobby Subhabrata. 1998. "Corporate environmentalism: Perspectives from organizational learning." *Management Learning* 29 (2):147–164.

Banerjee, Bobby Subhabrata. 2002. "Corporate environmentalism: The construct and its measurement." *Journal of Business Research* 55 (3):177–191.

Bansal, Pratima, Jijun Gao, and Israr Qureshi. 2014. "The extensiveness of corporate social and environmental commitment across firms over time." *Organization Studies* 35 (7):949–966.

Barinaga, Ester. 2013. "Politicising social entrepreneurship–three social entrepreneurial rationalities toward social change." *Journal of Social Entrepreneurship* 4 (3):347–372.

Barratt, Ed. 2001. "Foucault, Foucauldianism and human resource management." *Personnel Review* 31 (2):189–204.

Bauwens, Thomas, Daan Schraven, Emily Drewing, Jörg Radtke, Lars Holstenkamp, Boris Gotchev, and Özgür Yildiz. 2022 in press. Conceptualizing community in energy systems: A systematic review of 183 definitions. Renewable & sustainable energy reviews 156:111999. doi: 10.1016/j.rser.2021.111999

Baysinger, Barry D. 1994. "Domain maintenance as an objective of business political activity: An expanded typology." *Academy of Management Review* 9 (2): 248–258.

Beder, Sharon. 2002. "bp: Beyond petroleum?" In *Battling big business: Countering greenwash, infiltration and other forms of corporate bullying*, edited by Eveline Lubbers, 26–32. Devon: Green Books.

Beder, Sharon. 2005. "Corporate propaganda and global capitalism: Selling free enterprise?" In *Global politics in the information age*, edited by J. Mark Lacy, and Peter Wilkin, 116–130. Manchester: Manchester University Press.

BEIS (The Department for Business, Energy and Industrial Strategy). 2018. "Digest of UK Energy Statistics (DUKES) 2018: Main report." Published 26 July 2018. https://assets.publishing.service.gov.uk/government/uploads/system/uploads/attachment_data/file/731235/DUKES_2018.pdf

Belfiore, Peter. 2021. Green activists win third seat on Exxon's 12-member board and will now try to force oil giant to reduce emissions and overhaul pay. *Daily Mail*, 3 June. www.dailymail.co.uk/news/article-9646515/Green-activist-investors-score-seat-Exxons-12-member-board.html

Benjamin, Walter. 1997. *Charles Baudelaire: A lyric poet in the era of high capitalism*. New York: Verso Books.

Bennett, Jane. 2010. *Vibrant matter: A political ecology of things*. Durham, NC, and London: Duke University Press.

Bennett, W. Lance, and Alexandra Segerberg. 2011. "Digital media and the personalization of collective action: Social technology and the organization of protests against the global economic crisis." *Information, Communication & Society* 14 (6):770–799.

Benton, Ted. 2017. "Part three: Beyond neoliberalism, or life after capitalism? A red-green debate. Alternatives to neoliberalism: Towards equality and democracy." In *Beyond neoliberalism, or life after capitalism? A red-green debate. Alternatives to neoliberalism: Towards equality and democracy*, edited by Bryn Jones and Mike O'Donnell, 59–78. Bristol: Policy Press.

Bershady, J. Harold. 2020. "Gemeinschaft and Gesellschaft." In *Encyclopedia of community from the village to the virtual world*, edited by Karen Christensen, and David Levinson. London: SAGE Publications.

Bertels, Stephanie, J. Andrew Hoffman, and Rich DeJordy. 2014. "The varied work of challenger movements: Identifying challenger roles in the US environmental movement." *Organization Studies* 35 (8):1171–1210.

Beverungen, Armin, Anna-Maria Murtola, and Gregory Schwartz. 2013. "The communism of capital?" *Ephemera, Theory & Politics in Organization* 13 (3):483–495.

Billig, Michael. 1995. "Rhetorical psychology, ideological thinking and imagining nationhood." In *Social movements and culture*, edited by Hank Johnston, and Bert Klandermans. Minneapolis: University of Minnesota Press.

Bobel, Chris. 2007. "'I'm not an activist, though I've done a lot of it': Doing activism, being activist and the 'Perfect Standard' in a contemporary movement." *Social Movement Studies* 6 (2):147–159.

Boggs, Carl. 1977. "Marxism, prefigurative communism, and the problem of workers' control." *Radical America* 11 (6):99–122.

Boggs, Carl. 2000. *The end of politics: Corporate power and the decline of the public sphere*. New York and London: The Guilford Press.

Böhm, Steffen. 2005. "Fetish failures: Interrupting the subject and the other." In *Organization and identity*, edited by Alison Pullen and Stephen Linstead, 127–161. London: Routledge.

Böhm, Steffen, Ana C. Dinerstein, and André Spicer. 2010. "(Im)possibilities of autonomy: Social movements in and beyond capital, the state and development." *Social Movement Studies* 9 (1):17–32.

Böhm, Steffen, Zareen Pervez Bharucha, and Jules Pretty, eds. 2015. *Ecocultures: Blueprints for sustainable communities*. New York: Routledge.

Böhm, Steffen, and Annika Skoglund. 2015. "Why some companies are becoming environmental activists." *The Conversation*, 12 October. www.theconversation.com/why-some-companies-are-becoming-environmental-activists-42510

Böhm, Steffen, Annika Skoglund, and Dan Eatherley. 2018. "What's behind the current wave of 'corporate activism'?" *The Conversation*, 13 September. https://theconversation.com/whats-behind-the-current-wave-of-corporate-activism-102695

Bonanni, Carole, François Lépineux, and Julia Roloff, eds. 2012. *Social responsibility, entrepreneurship and the common good: International and interdisciplinary perspectives*. Basingstoke and New York: Palgrave Macmillan.

Bowen, Frances. 2014. *After greenwashing: Symbolic corporate environmentalism and society*. Cambridge: Cambridge University Press.

Boyd, Emily, and Carl Folke, eds. 2012. *Adapting institutions: Governance, complexity and social-ecological resilience*. Cambridge: Cambridge University Press.

Bracken, M. Harry. 1994. *Freedom of speech: Words are not deeds*. Westport and London: Praeger.

Braidotti, Rosi. 2013. *The Posthuman*. Cambridge, MA and Malden: Polity.

Branicki, Layla, Stephen Brammer, Alison Pullen, and Carl Rhodes. 2020. "The morality of "new" CEO activism." *Journal of Business Ethics* 170 (2):269–285.

Brenton, Scott. 2013. "The political motivations of ethical consumers." *International Journal of Consumer Studies* 37:490–497.

Briscoe, Forrest, and Abhinav Gupta. 2016. "Social activism in and around organizations." *Academy of Management Annals* 10 (1):671–727.

Brown, Lucy. 2020. Record number of electricity switches in 2019. Choose, fair price comparison. www.choose.co.uk/news/2020/6-4-million-customers-switched-electric-supplier-2019/

Burke, J. Matthew, and C. Jennie Stephens. 2017. "Energy democracy: Goals and policy instruments for sociotechnical transitions." *Energy Research and Social Science* 33:35–48.

Butler, Judith. 1997. *Excitable speech – a politics of the performative*. New York and London: Routledge.

Butler, Judith. 2002. "Afterword." In *The scandal of the speaking body. Don Juan with JL Austin, or seduction in two languages*, Shoshana Felman, 113–124. Stanford: Stanford University Press.

Butler, Judith. 2015. *Notes toward a performative theory of assembly*. Cambridge, MA: Harvard University Press.

Butler, Judith. 2017. *Judith Butler: This is what resistance looks like*. YouTube. UCLA Luskin. www.youtube.com/watch?reload=9&v=zRz0YTIw62k

Byford, Iona, and Susan Wong. 2016. "Union formation and worker resistance in a multinational: A personal account of an Asian cabin crew member in UK civil aviation." *Work, Employment and Society* 30 (6):1030–1038.

Camden Council, 2019. "Citizens' Assembly on the climate crisis." https://www.camden.gov.uk/citizens-assembly-climate-crisis

Cahalane, Claudia. 2006. "I believe they are honourable and the work they do is honourable." *The Guardian.* www.theguardian.com/business/2006/nov/03/ethicalliving.environment

Calandro, Tony. 2017. "The rise of activist employees." *Huffpost.* www.huffingtonpost.com/entry/the-rise-of-activist-employees_us_591b2001e4b086d2d0d8d2d6

Calás, B. Marta, Linda Smircich, and Kristina A. Bourne. 2009. "Extending the boundaries: Reframing 'entrepreneurship as social change' through feminist perspectives." *Academy of Management Review* 34 (3):552–569.

Capstick, Stuart Bryce, and Nicholas Frank Pidgeon. 2014. "What is climate change scepticism? Examination of the concept using a mixed methods study of the UK public." *Global Environmental Change*, 24:389–401.

Caputo, D. John. 1996. "A community without truth: Derrida and the impossible community." *Research in Phenomenology* 26:25–37.

Carbon Neutral Cornwall. 2020. "Climate emergency." www.cornwall.gov.uk/environment-and-planning/climate-emergency/

Carrington, Damian. 2019. "Why the Guardian is changing the language it uses about the environment." *The Guardian*, 17May.

Castells, Manuel. 2018. *Rupture: The crisis of liberal democracy.* Trans. Rosie Marteau. Cambridge: Polity Press.

Catney, Philip, Sherilyn MacGregor, Andrew Dobson, et al. 2014. "Big society, little justice? Community renewable energy and the politics of localism." *Local Environment* 19 (7):715–730.

Cedamia. 2019. "Why declare a climate emergency?"www.cedamia.org/why-declare/

Cederström, Carl, and Michael Marinetto. 2013. "Corporate social responsibility à la the liberal communist." *Organization* 20 (3):416–432.

Certified B Corporations. 2020. "About B Corps." https://bcorporation.net/about-b-corps

CGTN America (China Global Television Network). 2015. "In the middle of the Amazon, the haunted remains of Fordlandia." YouTube. https://www.youtube.com/watch?v=EbFY94d51Tw

Chamorel, P. 2019. "Macron versus the yellow vests." *Journal of Democracy* 30 (4):48–62.

Chandler, David, and Julian Reid. 2016. *The neoliberal subject: Resilience, adaptation and vulnerability.* London and New York: Rowman & Littlefield.

Chandler, David, and Julian Reid. 2019. *Becoming indigenous – governing imaginaries in the Anthropocene.* London and New York: Rowman & Littlefield.

Chatterji, K. Aaron, and W. Michael Toffel. 2015. "Starbucks' 'race together' campaign and the upside of CEO activism." Harvard Business Review. https://hbr.org/2015/03/starbucks-race-together-campaign-and-the-upside-of-ceo-activism

Chatterji, K. Aaron, and W. Michael Toffel. 2016. "Do CEO activists make a difference? Evidence from a field experiment." Harvard Business School Working Paper (16–100, March).

Chatterji, K. Aaron, and W. Michael Toffel. 2018. "The new CEO activists." *Harvard Business Review* (January–February):47–65.

Chatterji, K. Aaron, and W. Michael Toffel. 2019. Assessing the impact of CEO activism. *Organization & Environment* 32 (2):159–185.

Chia, C. H. Robert, and Robin Holt. 2009. *Strategy without design: The silent efficacy of indirect action.* New York: Cambridge University Press.

Chin, Mun Kyun, Donald C. Hambrick, and Linda K. Treviño. 2013. "Political ideologies of CEOs: The influence of executives' values on corporate social responsibility." *Administrative Science Quarterly* 58 (2):197–232.

Chouinard, Yvon 2016. "Introduction." In *Patagonia tools for grassroots activists: Best practices for success in the environmental movement*, edited by Nora Gallagher and Lisa Myers, n.p. New York: Patagonia.

Christensen, Karen, and David Levinson. 2020. *Encyclopedia of community from the village to the virtual world.* London: Sage Publications.

Christiansen, Atle Christer. 2002. "Beyond petroleum: Can BP deliver?" In *Fridtjof nansens institutt.* Lysaker. https://citeseerx.ist.psu.edu/viewdoc/download?doi=10.1.1.585.4865&rep=rep1&type=pdf

Citizenergy. 2018. "Your power." https://citizenergy.eu

Clean Government. 2018. "Smart living." Welsh Government. https://gov.wales/topics/businessandeconomy/creating-a-sustainable-economy/smart-living/?lang=en

ClientEarth. 2020. "Responding to investor pressure, Barclays presents new, beefed up climate policy." www.clientearth.org/responding-to-investor-pressure-barclays-presents-new-climate-policy/

Declare a climate emergency. 2020. "List of councils who have declared a climate emergency." www.climateemergency.uk/blog/list-of-councils/

Climate Change Act. 2008. www.legislation.gov.uk/ukpga/2008/27/contents

Climate Emergency UK. 2019. "Climate Emergency Declarations with a target date by 2030." https://climateemergency.uk

Climate Greenwash Award. 2009. www.climate greenwash.org/climate-greenwash-winner-revealed

Cole, Alistair. 2019. *Emmanuel Macron and the two years that changed France.* Manchester: Manchester University Press.

Comor, Edward. 2011. "Contextualizing and critiquing the fantastic prosumer: Power, alienation and hegemony." *Critical Sociology* 37 (3):309–327.

Conklin Frederking, Lauretta. 2010. "Government entrepreneurship and the arts: The politics of the National Endowment for the arts." In *The politics and aesthetics of entrepreneurship: A fourth movements in entrepreneurship book*, edited by Daniel Hjorth, and Chris Steyaert, 55–74. Cheltenham: Edward Elgar Publishing.

Cooke, Bill, and Uma Kothari, eds. 2001. *Participation: The new tyranny?* London and New York: Zed books.

Cornish, Flora, Jan Haaken, Liora Moskovitz, and Sharon Jackson. 2016. "Rethinking prefigurative politics: Introduction to the special thematic section." *Social and Political Psychology* 4 (1):114–127.

Country Guardian. 2018. "Country Guardian's website." www.countryguardian.net

Courpasson, David, Françoise Dany, and Stewart Clegg. 2012. "Resisters at work: Generating productive resistance in the workplace." *Organization Science* 23 (3):801–819.

Coyne, Brendan. 2018. "Ecotricity touts 'vegan' electricity, plans vegan green gas." https://theenergyst.com/ecotricity-launches-vegan-electricity/

Crane, Andrew, Dirk Matten, and Jeremy Moon. 2008a. *Corporations and citizenship*. New York: Cambridge University Press.

Crane, Andrew, Dirk Matten, and Jeremy Moon. 2008b. "Ecological citizenship and the corporation. Politicizing the new corporate environmentalism." *Organization & Environment* 21 (4):371–389.

Crane, Andrew, Guido Palazzo, Laura J. Spence, and Dirk Matten. 2014. "Contesting the value of 'Creating Shared Value'." *California Management Review* 56 (2):130–153.

Creed, W. E. Douglas, and A. Maureen Scully. 2000. "Songs of ourselves: Employees' deployment of social identity in workplace encounters." *Journal of Management Inquiry* 9 (4):391–412.

Creed, W. E. Douglas, A. Maureen Scully, and R. John Austin. 2002. "Clothes make the person? The tailoring of legitimating accounts and the social construction of identity." *Organization Science* 13 (5):475–496.

Crisafulli, Patricia. 2018. "When having activist employees is good." *On the horizon.* https://www.kornferry.com/insights/briefings-magazine/issue-28/on-the-horizon-survey-says

Cronin, J. Joseph, S. Jeffery Smith, R.- Mark Gleim, Edward Ramirez, and Dawn Jennifer Martinez. 2011. "Green marketing strategies: An examination of stakeholders and the opportunities they present." *Journal of the Academy of Marketing Science* 39 (1):158–174.

Crow, Graham, and Graham Allan. 2014. *Community life*. London: Routledge.

CSE. 2010. "Green communities." www.cse.org.uk/projects/view/13

Cundill, Gary J., Palie Smart, and Hugh N. Wilson. 2018. "Non-financial shareholder activism: A process model for influencing corporate environmental and social performance." *International Journal of Management Reviews* 20 (2):606–626.

Curran, Giorel. 2015. *Sustainability and energy politics: Ecological modernisation and corporate social responsibility*. Basingstoke and New York: Palgrave Macmillan.

Curtin, Deane. 1999. *Chinnagounder's challenge: The question of ecological citizenship*. Bloomington: Indiana University Press.

Curtin, Nicola, and Craig McGarty. 2016. "Expanding on psychological theories of engagement to understand activism in context (s)." *Journal of Social Issues* 72 (2): 227–241.

Daniel, Klooster J. 2006. "Forest struggles and forest policy: Villagers' environmental activism in Mexico." In *Shades of green: Environmental activism around the globe*, edited by Christ of Mauch, Nathan Stoltzfus, and R. Douglas Weiner, 183. Lanham: Rowman & Littlefield.

Darier, Éric, ed. 1999. *Discourses of the environment*. Malden: Blackwell Publishers.

Daskalaki, Maria, Daniel Hjorth, and Johanna Mair. 2015. "Are entrepreneurship, communities, and social transformation related?" *Journal of Management Inquiry* 24 (4):419–423.

Dauvergne, Peter, and Jane Lister. 2013. *Eco-business: A big-brand takeover of sustainability*. Cambridge, MA: MIT Press.

Dauvergne, Peter. 2016. *Environmentalism of the rich*. Cambridge, MA: MIT Press.

Davis Cross, K. Mai'a. 2013. "Rethinking epistemic communities twenty years later." *Review of International Studies* 39 (1):137–160.

Davis, F. Gerald, and Doug McAdam. 2000. "Corporations, classes, and social movements after managerialism." *Research in Organizational Behaviour* 22:195–238.

Davis, F. Gerald, and Christopher J. White. 2015. "The new face of corporate activism." *Stanford Social Innovation Review* 13 (4): 40–45.

Davis, Jerry. 2016. "What's driving corporate activism?" *The New Republic*, 7 September. https://newrepublic.com/article/137252/whats-driving-corporate-activism

de Bakker, G. A. Frank, Frank den Hond, Brayden King, and Klaus Weber. 2013. "Social movements, civil society and corporations: Taking stock and looking ahead." *Organization Studies* 34 (5–6):573–593.

Dean, Jodi. 2019. "Critique or collectivity? Capitalism and the subject of politics." In *Digital objects digital subjects: Interdisciplinary perspectives on capitalism, labour and politics in the age of big data*, edited by David Chandler, and Christian Fuchs, 171–182. London: University of Westminster Press.

DECC (Department for Energy and Climate Change). 2009. *The UK low carbon transition plan: National strategy for climate and energy.* Department of Energy & Climate Change. https://assets.publishing.service.gov .uk/government/uploads/system/uploads/attachment_data/file/486084/ IA_-_FITs_consultation_response_with_Annexes_-_FINAL_SIGNED .pdf

Decreus, Thomas, Matthias Lievens, and Antoon Braeckman. 2014. "Building collective identities: How new social movements try to overcome post-politics." *Parallax: Chantal Mouffe: Agonism and the Politics of Passion* 20 (2):136–148.

Deichmann, Uwe, and Fan Zhang. 2013. *Growing green, the economic benefits of climate action.* Washington, DC: The World Bank.

Deleuze, Gilles, and Felix Guattari. 1988. *A thousand plateaus: Capitalism and schizophrenia.* London: Bloomsbury Publishing.

Delmas, A. Magali, and W. Michael Toffel. 2011. "Institutional pressures and organizational characteristics: Implications for environmental strategy." In *The Oxford handbook of business and the natural environment,* edited by Pratima Bansal, and J. Andrew Hoffman, 229–247. Oxford: Oxford University Press.

den Hond, Frank, and Frank G. A. de Bakker. 2007. "Ideologically motivated activism: How activist groups influence corporate social change activities." *Academy of Management Review* 32 (3):901–924.

den Hond, Frank, Frank G. A. de Bakker, and Nikolai Smith. 2015. "Social movements and organizational analysis." In *The Oxford handbook of social movements,* edited by Donatella Della Porta, and Mario Diani, 291–305. New York: Oxford University Press.

Department for Business, Energy & Industrial Strategy. 2018. "Clean growth – transforming heating." https://assets.publishing.service.gov .uk/government/uploads/system/uploads/attachment_data/file/766109/ decarbonising-heating.pdf

Department of Energy. 1988. *Renewable energy in the UK: The way forward, energy paper 55.* London: HMSO.

Department of the Environment. 1990. *This common inheritance: Britain's environmental strategy.* London: HMSO Publications.

Deutsche Welle, made for minds. 2015. "Greenpeace plans bid for Vattenfall's German coal business." www.dw.com/en/greenpeace-plans-bid-for-vattenfalls-german-coal-business/a-18763586

Devine-Wright, Patrick, ed. 2014. *Renewable energy and the public: From NIMBY to participation.* London: Routledge.

Dewey, Scott. 1998. "Working for the environment: Organized labor and the origins of environmentalism in the United States, 1948–1970." *Environmental History* 3 (1):45–63.

Dey, Pascal, and Chris Mason. 2018. "Overcoming constraints of collective imagination: An inquiry into activist entrepreneuring, disruptive truth-telling and the creation of 'possible worlds." *Journal of Business Venturing* 33 (1):84–99.

Dixon, Christopher Andrew. 2014. *Another politics – talking across today's transformative movements*. Oakland: University of California Press.

Dixon, Sarah, and Anne Clifford. 2007. "Ecopreneurship – a new approach to managing the triple bottom line." *Journal of Organizational Change Management* 20 (3):326–345.

Dobek, Mariusz Mark. 1993. "Privatization as a political priority: The British experience." *Political Studies* 41 (1):24–40.

Doh, P. Jonathan, and R. Terrence Guay. 2006. "Corporate social responsibility, public policy, and NGO activism in Europe and the United States: An institutional-stakeholder perspective." *Journal of Management Studies* 43 (1):47–73.

Doherty, Brian, and Timothy Doyle. 2013. *Environmentalism, resistance and solidarity: the politics of friends of the earth international*. New York: Palgrave Macmillan.

Dolezal, Martin. 2010. "Exploring the stabilization of a political force: The social and attitudinal basis of green parties in the age of globalization." *West European Politics* 33 (3):534–552.

Dowling, Robyn. 2010. "Geographies of Identity: Climate change, governmentality and activism." *Progress in Human Geography* 34 (4): 488–495.

Dryzek, S. John. 2013. *The politics of the Earth: Environmental discourses*: Oxford: Oxford University Press.

DuBois, L. Z. Cathy, and A. David Dubois. 2012. "Strategic HRM as social design for environmental sustainability in organization." *Human Resource Management* 51 (6):799–826.

Dubuisson-Quellier, Sophie. 2013. "A market mediation strategy: How social movements seek to change firms' practices by promoting new principles of product valuation." *Organization Studies* 34 (5–6):683–703.

Duffield, Mark. 2010. "The liberal way of development and the development-security impasse: Exploring the global life-chance divide." *Security Dialogue* 41 (1):53–76.

Eckersley, Robyn. 1992. *Environmentalism and political theory: Toward an ecocentric approach*. Albany: State University of New York Press.

Ecotalk. 2018. "We're moving to a new network." www.ecotalk.co.uk

Ecotricity. 2022. "Britain's greenest energy company." www.ecotricity.co.uk

Edward, Peter, and Hugh Willmott. 2013. "Discourse and normative business ethics. In *Handbook of the philosophical foundations of business ethics*, edited by Christoph Lütge, 549–580. Dordrecht: Springer.

Ehnert, Ina, Harry Wes, and J. Klaus Zink, eds. 2013. *Sustainability and human resource management: Developing sustainable business organizations.* Berlin: Springer Science & Business Media.

Ekman, Susanne. 2014. "Is the high-involvement worker precarious or opportunistic? Hierarchical ambiguities in late capitalism." *Organization* 21:141–158.

Eleftheriadis, Konstantinos. 2015. "Organizational practices and prefigurative spaces in European queer festivals." *Social Movement Studies* 14 (6):651–667.

Elias, Norbert. 1987/2001. *The society of individuals.* Translated by Edmund Jephcott. New York and London: Continuum.

Elliott, David. 2016. "The alternative technology movement: An early green radical challenge." *Science as Culture* 25(3):386–399.

Endrissat, Nada, Dan Kärreman, and Claus Noppeney. 2017. "Incorporating the creative subject: Branding outside–in through identity incentives." *Human Relations* 70 (4):488–515.

Énergies, Planète. 2015. "The history of energy in the United Kingdom." www.planete-energies.com/en/medias/saga-energies/history-energy-united-kingdom

Epstein, Barbara. 1991. *Political protest and cultural revolution: Nonviolent direct action in the 1970s and 1980s.* Berkeley: University of California Press.

Epstein, J. Mark. 2008. *Making sustainability work, best practices in managing and measuring corporate social, environmental and economic impacts.* Sheffield: Greenleaf Publishing Limited.

Esposito, Roberto. 2010. *Community, the origin and destiny of community.* Translated by Timothy Campbell. Stanford: Stanford University Press.

Etzioni, Amitai. 2004. *From empire to community, a new approach to international relations.* New York: Palgrave Macmillan.

European Commission. 2018a. "EU Clean energy package: More chance for 'energy citizens'?". CORDIS. https://cordis.europa.eu/news/rcn/141934_en.html

European Commission. 2018b. "The European platform for citizen investment in renewable energy (CITIZENERGY)." Citizenergy Project. https://ec.europa.eu/energy/intelligent/projects/en/projects/citizenergy

European Commission. 2019. "Citizen support for climate action." https://ec.europa.eu/clima/citizens/support_en

European Greens. 2009. "Vattenfall wins greenwashing award." https://europeangreens.eu/news/swedish-energy-giant-vattenfall-wins-climate-greenwash-award

Evans, Brad, and Julian Reid. 2014. *Resilient life, the art of living dangerously.* Cambridge: Polity Press.

Eyerman, Ron, and Andrew Jamison. 1991. *Social movements, a cognitive approach* Cambridge: Polity Press.

Farias, Carine. 2017. "That's what friends are for: Hospitality and affective bonds fostering collective empowerment in an intentional community." *Organization Studies* 38 (5):577–595.

Fast, Stewart. 2013. "A Habermasian analysis of local renewable energy deliberations." *Journal of Rural Studies* 30:86–98.

Fawcett, Leesa. 2009. "Feral sociality and (Un)natural histories: On nomadic ethics and embodied learning." In *Fields of green: Restorying culture, environment, and education*, edited by Marcia McKenzie, Paul Hart, Heesoon Bai, and Bob Jickling, 227–237. Cresskill: Hampton Press.

Felicetti, Andrea. 2017. *Deliberative democracy and social movements: Transition initiatives in the public sphere*. New York and London: Rowman & Littlefield.

Felman, Shoshana. 2002. *The scandal of the speaking body. Don Juan with JL Austin, or seduction in two languages*. Stanford: Stanford University press.

Fileborn, Bianca, and Rachel Loney-Howes, eds. 2019. *#MeToo and the politics of social change*. Cham: Palgrave Macmillan.

Fineman, Stephen. 1998. "Street-level bureaucrats and the social construction of environmental control." *Organization Studies* 19 (6):953–974.

Fisher, Dana R., and Sohana Nasrin. 2021. "Climate activism and its effects. Wiley interdisciplinary reviews." *Climate change* 12 (1): 1–11.

Fitzgerald, Joan. 2020. *Greenovation: Urban leadership on climate change*. New York: Oxford University Press.

Fleming, Peter. 2009. *Authenticity and the cultural politics of work: New forms of informal control*. Oxford: Oxford Scholarship Online.

Fleming, Peter. 2014. *Resisting work – the corporatization of life and its discontents*. Philadelphia: Temple University Press.

Fleming, Peter, and Andrew Sturdy. 2009. "'Just be yourself!': Towards neo-normative control in organisations?" *Employee Relations* 31:569–583.

Fleming, Peter, and André Spicer. 2004. "You can checkout anytime, but you can never leave': Spatial boundaries in a high commitment organization." *Human Relations* 57 (1):75–94.

Fleming, Peter, and André Spicer. 2007. *Contesting the corporation, struggle, power, and resistance in organizations*. New York: Cambridge University Press.

Fogarty, Molly, and Dely Lazarte Elliot. 2020. "The role of humour in the social care professions: An exploratory study." The British Journal of Social Work 50 (3):778–796.

Folke, Carl, Stephen R. Carpenter, Brian Walker, Marten Scheffer, Terry Chapin, and Johan Rockström. 2010. "Resilience thinking: Integrating resilience, adaptability and transformability." *Ecology and Society* 15 (4):20.

Fondas, Nanette. 2000. "Women on boards of directors: Gender bias or power threat?" In *Women on corporate boards of directors. Issues in business ethics*, edited by J. Ronald Burke, and Mary C. Mattis, 171–177. Dordrecht: Springer.

Forester, John. 1999. *The deliberative practitioner: Encouraging participatory planning processes*. Cambridge, MA: MIT Press.

Foucault, Michel. 1966/2002. *The order of things*. New York: Routledge.

Foucault, Michel. 1980. *Power/knowledge: Selected interviews and other writings 1972–1977*, edited by Colin Gordon. New York: Pantheon Books.

Foucault, Michel. 1984/2011. *The courage of truth*. Translated by Gramham Burchell, edited by Francois Ewald, Allessandro Fontana, Frédéric Gros, and Arnold I. Davidson. New York: Palgrave Macmillan.

Foxon, J. Timothy, Robert Gross, Adam Chase, Jo Howes, Alex Arnall, and Dennis Anderson. 2005. "UK innovation systems for new and renewable energy technologies: Drivers, barriers and systems failures." *Energy Policy* 33 (16):2123–2137.

Frederick, C. William. 2008. "Corporate social responsibility, deep roots, flourishing growth, promising future." In *The Oxford handbook of corporate social responsibility*, edited by Andrew Crane, Abagail McWilliams, Dirk Matten, Jeremy Moon, and S. Donald Siegel, 522–531. New York: Oxford University Press.

Friends of the Earth. 2018. "Switch to green energy now." https://friendsoftheearth.uk/business-partnerships/take-part-switch-renewable-energy

FSL, Föreningen för svensk landskapsskydd. 2018. "Välkommen till Föreningen Svenskt Landskapsskydd." http://landskapsskydd.se

Garside, Nick. 2013. *Democratic ideals and the politicization of nature: The roving life of a feral citizen*. New York: Palgrave Macmillan.

George, Gerard, Jennifer Howard-Grenville, Aparna Joshi, and Laszlo Tihanyi. 2016. "Understanding and tackling societal grand challenges through management research." *Academy of Management Journal* 59 (6):1880–1895.

Gillan, L. Stuart, and T. Laura Starks. 2000. "Corporate governance proposals and shareholder activism: The role of institutional investors." *Journal of Financial Economics* 57:275–305.

Giroux, A. Henry. 1994. "Consuming social change: The 'united colors of Benetton'." *Cultural Critique* 26:5–32.

Girschik, Verena. 2020. "Shared responsibility for societal problems: The role of internal activists in reframing corporate responsibility." *Business & Society* 59 (1):34–66.

Glezos, Simon. 2012. *The politics of speed. Capitalism, the state and war in an accelerating world.* London and New York: Routledge.

Glickman, B. Lawrence 2009. *Buying power: A history of consumer activism in America.* Chicago: University of Chicago Press.

Goh, Irving. 2006. "The question of community in Deleuze and Guattari (I): Anti-community." *Symplokē* 14 (1/2):216–231.

Goldman, Robert, and Stephen Papson. 2006. "Capital's brandscapes." *Journal of Consumer Culture* 6 (3):327–353.

Good Energy. 2018. "Our blog." www.goodenergy.co.uk/blog/

Good Energy. 2022. "Climate action is non-negotiable." www.goodenergy.co.uk/

Good Energy. 2019. "Corporations must pursue purpose and not just profit, for people and planet." www.goodenergy.co.uk/blog/2019/12/20/corporations-must-pursue-purpose-and-not-just-profit-for-people-and-planet/

Goranova, Maria, and Lori Verstegen Ryan. 2014. "Shareholder activism: A multidisciplinary review." *Journal of Management* 40 (5):1230–1268.

Gough, Clair, and Simon Shackley. 2001. "The respectable politics of climate change: The epistemic communities and NGOs." *International Affairs*, 77(2): 329–346.

Gould, B. Deborah. 2009. *Moving politics: Emotion and ACT UP's fight against AIDS.* Chicago: University of Chicago Press.

Gould, Deborah. 2010. "On affect and protest." In *Political emotions – new agendas in communication*, edited by Janet Staiger, Ann Cvetkovich, and Ann Reynolds, 18–44. New York and London: Routledge.

Graham, Helen. 2012. "Scaling governmentality: Museums, co-production and re-calibrations of the 'logic of culture'." *Cultural Studies* 26 (4):565–592.

Graz, Jean-Christophe, and Andreas Nölke, eds. 2008. *Transnational private governance and its limits.* New York: Routledge.

Greenpeace. 2018a. "Five reasons we're making a fuss about finance." https://medium.com/greenpeace/five-reasons-were-making-a-fuss-about-finance-ada9b56e33ec

Greenpeace. 2018b. "How Greenpeace changed an industry: 25 years of GreenFreeze to cool the planet." https://www.greenpeace.org/international/story/15323/how-greenpeace-changed-an-industry-25-years-of-greenfreeze-to-cool-the-planet/.

Greenpeace Energy. 2020. "Entschlossen. Energisch. Echt." www.greenpeace-energy.de/privatkunden.html

Grefe, A. Edward, and Martin Linsky. 1995. *The new corporate activism: Harnessing the power of grassroots tactics for your organization.* New York: McGraw-Hill Companies.

Grewal, Jody, George Serafeim, and Aaron Yoon. 2016. Shareholder Activism on Sustainability Issues. In Working Paper no. 17–003, edited by Harvard Business School. https://dash.harvard.edu/bitstream/handle/1/27864360/17-003.pdf?sequence=1

Grim, John, and Evelyn Tucker. 2014. *Ecology and religion.* Washington, DC: Island Press.

Grover, David. 2013. The British Feed-in Tariff for small renewable energy systems: Can it be made fairer? Centre for Climate Change Economics and Policy, Grantham Research Institute on Climate Change and the Environment. http://www.lse.ac.uk/GranthamInstitute/wp-content/uploads/2014/02/british-feed-in-tariff-renewable-energy.pdfhttp://www.lse.ac.uk/GranthamInstitute/wp-content/uploads/2014/02/british-feed-in-tariff-renewable-energy.pdf

Grubor, Aleksandar, and Olja Milovanov. 2017. "Brand strategies in the era of sustainability". *Interdisciplinary Description of Complex Systems, INDECS,* 15(1): 78–88.

Guattari, Félix, and Antonio Negri. 1985/2010. *New lines of alliance, new spaces of liberty.* Translated by Michael Ryan, Jared Becker, Arianna Bove and Noe Le Blanc. London and New York: Minor compositions, MayFlyBooks.

Guay, Terrence, Jonathan P. Doh, and Graham Sinclair. 2004. "Non-governmental organizations, shareholder activism, and socially responsible investments: Ethical, strategic, and governance implications." *Journal of Business Ethics* 52 (1):125–139.

Gumbel, Peter. 2005. "Industrious Activist." *Time,* 2 October. http://content.time.com/time/magazine/article/0,9171,1112767,00.html

Guy, Simon, and Elizabeth Shove. 2000. *The sociology of energy, buildings and the environment: Constructing knowledge, designing practice.* London: Routledge.

Haas, M. Peter. 1992. "Introduction: Epistemic communities and international policy coordination." *International Organization* 46 (1):1–35.

Haas, M. Peter. 2004. "When does power listen to truth? A constructivist approach to the policy process." *Journal of European Public Policy* 11 (4):569–592.

Haas, M. Peter. 2015. *Epistemic communities, constructivism, and international environmental politics.* London: Routledge.

Hambrick, C. Donald, and Adam Wowak. 2021. CEO sociopolitical activism: A stakeholder alignment model. *Academy of Management Review* 46 (1):33–59.

Harper, Peter, and Björn Eriksson. 1972. "Alternative Technology: A Guide to Sources and Contacts." *Undercurrents* (3)

Hajer, Maarten, and Wytske Versteeg. 2005. "A decade of discourse analysis of environmental politics: Achievements, challenges, perspectives." *Journal of Environmental Policy & Planning* 7 (3):175–184.

Hajer, Marten. 1995. *The politics of environmental discourse, ecological modernization and the policy process.* Oxford: Clarendon Press.

Hampton, Paul. 2015. *Workers and trade unions for climate solidarity: Tackling climate change in a neoliberal world.* New York: Routledge.

Hansson, Stina, Sofie Hellberg, and Maria Stern, eds. 2015. *Studying the agency of being governed.* New York: Routledge.

Haraway, Donna. 2015. "Anthropocene, capitalocene, plantationocene, chthulucene: Making kin." *Environmental Humanities* 6 (1):159–165.

Hardt, Michael, and Antonio Negri. 2000. *Empire.* Cambridge, MA and London: Harvard University Press.

Hardt, Michael, and Antonio Negri. 2005. *Multitude: War and democracy in the age of empire*: London: Penguin.

Hardt, Michael, and Antonio Negri. 2009. *Commonwealth.* Cambridge, MA: Harvard University Press.

Hargreaves, Tom. 2016. "Interacting for the environment: Engaging Goffman in pro-environmental action." *Society & Natural Resources: An International Journal* 29 (1):53–67.

Harrigan, Nicholas, Palakorn Achananuparp, and Ee-Peng Lim. 2012. "Influentials, novelty, and social contagion: The viral power of average friends, close communities, and old news." *Social Networks* 34 (4):470–480.

Hartman, L. Cathy, and L. Caryn Beck-Dudley. 1999. "Marketing strategies and the search for virtue: A case analysis of the body shop, international." *Source: Journal of Business Ethics* 20 (3):249–263.

Hartmann, Patrick, Vanessa Apoalaza Ibanez, and F. J. Forcada Sainz. 2005. Green branding effects on attitude: Functional versus emotional positioning strategies. *Market Intelligence and Planning* 1 (23):9–29.

Harvey, David. 2007. *A brief history of neoliberalism.* Oxford and New York: Oxford University Press.

Hatch, Jo. Mary, and Majken Schultz. 2008. *Taking brand initiative: How companies can align strategy, culture, and identity.* San Fransisco: Jossey-Bass.

Haug, Christoph. 2013. "Organizing spaces: Meeting arenas as a social movement infrastructure between organization, network, and institution." *Organization Studies* 34 (5–6):705–732.

Healy, Jonathan D. 2017. *Housing, fuel poverty and health: A pan-European analysis.* London: Routledge.

Heazle, Michael. 2010. *Uncertainty in policy making: Values and evidence in complex decisions.* London: Routledge.

Hejjas, Kelsy, Graham Miller, and Caroline Scarles. 2018. "'It's like hating puppies!' Employee disengagement and corporate social responsibility." *Journal of Business Ethics* 157 (2):1–19.

Hemingway, A. Christine. 2005. "Personal values as a catalyst for corporate social entrepreneurship." *Journal of Business Ethics* 60 (3):233–249.

Hemingway, A. Christine. 2013. *Corporate social entrepreneurship: Integrity within the socially responsible organisation*. New York: Cambridge University Press.

Hemingway, A. Christine, and W. Patrick Maclagan. 2004. "Managers' personal values as drivers of corporate social responsibility." *Journal of Business Ethics* 50 (1):33–44.

Hemmati, Minu. 2002. *Multi-stakeholder processes for governance and sustainability: Beyond deadlock and conflict*. London: Routledge.

Hensby, Alexander, Johanne Sibthorpe, and Stephen Drvier. 2011. "Resisting the 'protest business': Bureaucracy, postbureaucracy and active membership in social movement organizations." *Organization* 19 (6):809–823.

Heyley, Stevenson. 2014. "Representing green radicalism: The limits of state-based representation in global climate governance." *Review of International Studies* 40 (1):177–201.

Hiatt, R. Shon, D. Wesley Sine, and S. Pamela Tolbert. 2009. "From Pabst to Pepsi: The deinstitutionalization of social practices and the creation of entrepreneurial opportunities." *Administrative Science Quarterly* 54:635–667.

Higginbottom, Karen. 2014. "Social media ignites employee activism." *Forbes*, 14 April. www.forbes.com/sites/karenhigginbottom/2014/04/14/social-media-ignites-employee-activism/#2d2fbc076de4

Hill, A. Kevin, and E. John Hughes. 1998. *Cyberpolitics: Citizen activism in the age of the Internet*. Oxford: Rowman & Littlefield.

Hillman, Amy J., Gerald D. Keim, and Douglas Schuler. 2004. "Corporate political activity: A review and research agenda." *Journal of Management* 30 (6):837–857.

Hilton, M. 2009. *Prosperity for all: Consumer activism in an era of globalization*. Ithaca: Cornell University Press.

Hinterecker, Harald, Michael Kopel, and Anna Ressi. 2018. "CEO activism and supply chain interactions." *Annals of Public and Cooperative Economics* 89 (1):235–249.

Hjorth, Daniel, and Robin Holt. 2016. "It's entrepreneurship, not enterprise: Ai Weiwei as entrepreneur." *Journal of Business Venturing Insights* 5:50–54.

Hobson, Kersty. 2009. "On a governmentality analytics of the 'deliberative turn': Material conditions, rationalities and the deliberating subject." *Space and Polity* 13 (3):175–191.

Hochstetler, Kathryn, and E. Margaret Keck. 2007. *Greening Brazil: Environmental activism in state and society*. Durham, NC: Duke University Press.

Hockerts, Kai. 2006. "Entrepreneurial opportunity in social purpose business ventures." In *Social entrepreneurship*, edited by Johanna Mair, Jeffrey A. Robinson, and Kai Hockerts, 142–154. Basingstoke and New York: Palgrave Macmillan.

Hoffman, J. Andrew. 1996. "A strategic response to investor activism." *Sloan Management Review* 37 (2):51–64.

Hoffman, J. Andrew. 2001. *From heresy to dogma: An institutional history of corporate environmentalism*. Standford: Stanford University Press.

Hoggett, Paul. 2011. "Climate change and the apocalyptic imagination." *Psychoanalysis, Culture & Society* 16 (3):261–275.

Hoggett, Richard. 2010. Community-owned renewable energy projects. Evidence for their development, funding and sustainability. In *Report produced on behalf of Community Energy Plus*. http://www.communitypowercornwall.coop/downloads/community_renewables_--_richard_hoggett.pdf

Höijer, Birgitta. 2010. "Emotional anchoring and objectification in the media reporting on climate change." *Public Understanding of Science* 19 (6):717–731.

Holston, James. 2014. "'Come to the street!': Urban protest, Brazil 2013." *Anthropological Quarterly* 87 (3):887–900.

Holt, B. Douglas. 2002. "Why do brands cause trouble? A dialectical theory of consumer culture and branding." *Journal of Consumer Culture* 29 (1):70–90.

Holt, Diane. 2011. "Where are they now? Tracking the longitudinal evolution of environmental businesses from the 1990s." *Business Strategy and the Environment* 20 (4):238–250.

Horrigan, Bryan. 2010. *Corporate social responsibility in the 21st century: Debates, models and practices across government, law and business*. Cheltenham: Edward Elgar Publishing.

Horton, Dave. 2006. "Environmentalism and the bicycle." *Environmental Politics* 15 (1):41–58.

Hosie, Rachel. 2017. "Why I turned my football club vegan." Independent. www.independent.co.uk/life-style/health-and-families/forest-green-rovers-why-i-turned-my-football-club-vegan-dale-vince-a7537286.html

Howard-Grenville, A. Jennifer. 2006. "Inside the 'Black Box' how organizational culture and subcultures inform interpretations and actions on environmental issues." *Organization & Environment* 19 (1):46–73.

Howarth, Candice, and James Painter. 2016. "Exploring the science–policy interface on climate change: The role of the IPCC in informing local decision-making in the UK." *Palgrave Communications* 2 (1):1–12.

Huault, Isabelle, Véronique Perret, and André Spicer. 2014. "Beyond macro- and micro-emancipation: Rethinking emancipation in organization studies." *Organization* 21 (1):22–49.

Hughes, L. Cheryl. 1998. "The primacy of ethics: Hobbes and Levinas." *Continental Philosophy Review* 31 (1):79–94.

Hulme, Mike. 2008. "The conquering of climate: Discourses of fear and their dissolution." *The Geographical Journal* 174 (1):5–16.

Humphreys, Michael, and Andrew D. Brown. 2002. "Narratives of organizational identity and identification: A case study of hegemony and resistance." *Organization Studies* 23 (3):421–448.

Hysing, Erik, and Jan Olsson. 2018. *Green inside activism for sustainable development: Political agency and institutional change.* Cham: Springer.

Icaza, Rosalba, and Rolando Vázquez. 2013. "Social struggles as epistemic struggles." *Development and Change* 44 (3):683–704.

Inagami, Takeshi, and D. Hugh Whittaker. 2005. *The new community firm: Employment, governance and management reform in Japan.* London: Cambridge University Press.

Incropera, P. Frank. 2016. *Climate change: A wicked problem: Complexity and uncertainty at the intersection of science, economics, politics, and human behavior.* New York: Cambridge University Press.

Inglis, David. 2009. "Cosmopolitan sociology and the classical canon: Ferdinand Tönnies and the emergence of global Gesellschaft." *The British Journal of Sociology* 60 (4):813–832.

IPCC (Intergovernmental Panel on Climate Change). 2011a. Mitigation, climate change. IPCC special report on renewable energy sources and climate change mitigation. Abu Dhabi, United Arab Emirates, 5–8 May. https://www.uncclearn.org/sites/default/files/inventory/ipcc15.pdf

IPCC (Intergovernmental Panel on Climate Change). 2011b. Special report on renewable energy sources and climate change mitigation and a technical summary, a report accepted by Working Group III of the IPCC but not approved in detail, edited by O. Edenhofer, R. Pichs-Madruga, Y. Sokona, K. Seyboth, P. Matschoss, S. Kadner, T. Zwickel, P. Eickemeier, G. Hansen, S. Schlömer and C.von Stechow. Cambridge University Press, Cambridge, United Kingdom and New York, NY, USA. https://www.ipcc.ch/site/assets/uploads/2018/03/SRREN_FD_SPM_final-1.pdf

IPCC (Intergovernmental Panel on Climate Change). 2014. AR5 climate change 2014: Mitigation of climate change. https://www.ipcc.ch/report/ar5/wg3/

Jacobsson, Kerstin, and Adrienne Sörbom. 2015. "After a cycle of contention: Post-Gothenburg strategies of left-libertarian activists in Sweden." *Social Movement Studies* 14 (6):713–732.

Jacques, Peter. 2006. "The rearguard of modernity: Environmental skepticism as a struggle of citizenship." *Global Environmental Politics* 6 (1):76–101.

Jaffe, Sarah. 2016. *Necessary trouble: Americans in revolt*. New York: Nation Books.

Jamison, Andrew. 2001. *The making of green knowledge – environmental politics and cultural transformation*. Cambridge: Cambridge University Press.

Jan, Inayatullah, Shazia Farhat Durrani, and Khan Himayatullah. 2021. "Does renewable energy efficiently spur economic growth? Evidence from Pakistan." *Environment, Development and Sustainability* 23 (1):373–387.

Jasper, M. James. 2011. "Emotions and social movements: Twenty years of theory and research." *Annual Review of Sociology* 37:285–303.

Jasper, M. James, and D. Jane Poulsen. 1995. "Recruiting strangers and friends: Moral shocks and social networks in animal rights and anti-nuclear protests." *Social problems* 42 (4):493–512.

Jeanes, L. Emma. 2013. The construction and controlling effect of a moral brand. *Scandinavian Journal of Management* 29 (2):163–172.

Kandpal, C. Tara, and Lars Broman. 2014. "Renewable energy education: A global status review." *Renewable and Sustainable Energy Reviews* 34:300–324.

Kant, Immanuel. 1899/2003. *On education*. Minneola: Dover Publications.

Kant, Immanuel. 2013. *An answer to the question: 'What is enlightenment?*. Translated by Hugh B. Nisbet. London: Penguin.

Kanter, Moss Rosabeth. 1972. *Commitment and community: Communes and utopias in sociological perspective*. Cambridge and London: Harvard University Press.

Kanter, Moss Rosabeth. 1977. *Men and women of the corporation*. 2nd ed. New York: Basic Books.

Kao, W. Y. Raymond, ed. 2010. *Sustainable economy: Corporate, social and environmental responsibility*. Singapore: World Scientific Publishing Co. Pte. Ltd.

Katzenstein Fainsod, Mary. 1998. "Stepsisters: Feminist movement activism in different institutional spaces." In *The social movement society: Contentious politics for a new century*, edited by S. David Meyer, and G. Sidney Tarrow, 195–216. Oxford: Rowman & Littlefield.

Kaufman, Cynthia. 2016. *Ideas for action: Relevant theory for radical change*. 2nd ed. Oakland: PM Press.

Keck, E. Margaret, and Kathryn Sikkink. 2014. *Activists beyond borders: Advocacy networks in international politics*. Ithaca: Cornell University Press.

Kern, Kristine, and Harriet Bulkeley. 2009. "Cities, Europeanization and multi-level governance: Governing climate change through transnational municipal network." *Journal of Common Market Studies* 47 (2):309–332.

Knorr Cetina, Karin. 1999. *Epistemic cultures: How the sciences make knowledge.* Cambridge, MA and London: Harvard University Press.

Kohn, Margaret. 2000. "Language, power, and persuasion: Toward a critique of deliberative democracy Kohn, Margaret." *Constellations* 7 (3):408–429.

Kokkinidis, George. 2015. "Spaces of possibilities: Workers' self-management in Greece." *Organization* 22 (6):847–871.

Kornberger, Martin. 2010. *Brand society: How brands transform management and lifestyle.* Cambridge: Cambridge University Press.

Kornwachs, Klaus. 2000. "Data—information—knowledge. A trial of a technological enlightenment." In *Towards the information society. The case of Central and Eastern European Countries*, edited by Gerhard Banse, J.Christian Langenbach, Petr Machleidt, and Dagmar Uhl, 109–124. Berlin, Heidelberg: Springer.

Kotilainen, Kirsi. 2020. "Energy prosumers' role in the sustainable energy system." In *Encyclopeadia of the UN sustainable development goals: Affordable and clean energy*, edited by Walter Leal Filho, 1–14. Cham: Springer.

Kourula, Arno, and Minna Halme. 2008. "Types of corporate responsibility and engagement with NGOs: An exploration of business and societal outcomes". *Corporate Governance: The International Journal of Business in Society* 8 (4):557–570.

Kraemer, Romy, Gail Whiteman, and Bobby Banerjee. 2013. "Conflict and astroturfing in Niyamgiri: The importance of national advocacy networks in anti-corporate social movements." *Organization Studies* 34 (5–6):823–852.

Kryger Aggerholm, Helle, Sophie Esmann Andersen, and Christa Thomsen. 2010. "Conceptualising employer branding in sustainable organisations." *Corporate Communications: An International Journal* 16 (2):105–123.

Kuhn, Timothy, and Stanley Deetz. 2008. "Critical theory and corporate social responsibility, can/should we get beyond cynical reasoning?" In *The Oxford handbook of corporate social responsibility*, edited by Andrew Crane, Abgail McWilliams, Dirk Matten, Jeremy Moon, and S. Donald Siegel, 173–196. New York: Oxford University Press.

Kurtz, Lloyd. 2008. "Socially responsible investment and shareholder activism." In *The Oxford handbook of corporate social responsibility*, edited by Andrew Crane, Abgail McWilliams, Dirk Matten, Jeremy Moon, and S. Donald Siegel, 249–280. New York: Oxford University Press.

Land, Christopher, and Daniel Robert King. 2014. "Organizing otherwise: Translating anarchism in a voluntary sector organization." *Ephemera, Theory & Politics in Organization* 14: 923–950.

Langley, Ann, Kajsa Lindberg, Bjørn Erik Mørk, Davide Nicolini, Elena Raviola, and Lars Walter. 2019. "Boundary work among groups, occupations, and organizations: From cartography to process." *Academy of Management Annals* 13 (2):704–736.

Larcker, F. David, Stephen Miles, Brian Tayan, and Kim Wright-Violich. 2018. The double-edged sword of CEO activism. In *Stanford University Graduate School of Business Research Paper No. 19-5*: Rock Center for Corporate Governance at Stanford University Closer Look Series: Topics, Issues and Controversies in Corporate Governance No. CGRP-74.

Latour, Bruno. 2018. *Down to earth: Politics in the new climatic regime.* Cambridge UK and Medford US: Polity Press.

Latour, Bruno, Denise Milstein, Isaac Marrero-Guillamón, and Israel Rodríguez-Giralt. 2018. "Down to earth social movements: An interview with Bruno Latour." *Social Movement Studies* 17 (3):353–361.

Lawton, Thomas, Steven McGuire, and Tazeeb Rajwani. 2013. "Corporate political activity: A literature review and research agenda." *International Journal of Management Reviews* 15 (1):86–105.

Leach, Melissa. 2015. "What is green? Transformative imperatives and knowledge politics." In *The politics of green transformations*, edited by Ian Scoones, Melissa Leach, and Peter Newell, 43–56. New York: Routledge, Earthscan.

Leach, Melissa, and Ian Scoones. 2015. "Mobilizing for green transformations." In *The politics of green transformations*, edited by Ian Scoones, Melissa Leach, and Peter Newell, 119–133. New York: Routledge, Earthscan.

LEG, (pseudonym). 2018. "About local energy group." www.plymouthenergycommunity.com/about/story

Leggett, Will. 2014. "The politics of behaviour change: Nudge, neoliberalism and the state." *Policy and Politics* 42 (1):3–19.

Levitt, Tom. 2016. "How badger bombs and politics brought Lush sales of £500m." *The Guardian*, 10 May. www.theguardian.com/sustainable-business/2016/may/10/badger-bombs-politics-lush-sales-500m

Levy, L. David, and Rami Kaplan. 2008. "Corporate social responsibility and theories of global governance, strategic contestation in global issue arenas." In *The Oxford handbook of corporate social responsibility*, edited by Andrew Crane, Abagail McWilliams, Dirk Matten, Jeremy Moon, and S. Donald Siegel, 432–451. New York: Oxford University Press.

Lewis, Camilla. 2016. "'Regenerating community'? Urban change and narratives of the past." *The Sociological Review* 64:912–928.

Lichterman, Paul, and Nina Eliasoph. 2014. "Civic action." *The American Journal of Sociology* 120 (3):798–863.

Lockwood, Matthew. 2013. "The political sustainability of climate policy: The case of the UK Climate Change Act." *Global Environmental Change* 23 (5):1339–1348.

Lövbrand, Eva, and Johannes Stripple. 2013. "Part I: Governmentality, critical theory and climate change, bringing governmentality to the study of global climate governance." In *Governing the climate, new approaches to rationality, power and politics*, edited by Johannes Stripple, and Harriet Bulkeley, 27–41. New York: Cambridge University Press.

Lush. 2018. "Lavender hill mob, Gorilla perfume incense." https://mena.lush.com/products/lavender-hill-mob

Lux, Sean, T. Russell Crook, and David J. Woehr. 2011. "Mixing business with politics: A meta-analysis of the antecedents and outcomes of corporate political activity." *Journal of Management* 37 (1):223–247.

MacArthur, L. Julie. 2016. "Challenging public engagement: participation, deliberation and power in renewable energy policy." *Journal of Environmental Studies and Sciences* 6 (3):631–640.

MacGregor, Sherilyn. 2019. "Finding transformative potential in the cracks? The ambiguities of urban environmental activism in a neoliberal city." *Social Movement Studies* 20 (3):1–17.

MacKay, Brad, and Iain Munro. 2012. "Information warfare and new organizational landscapes: An in quity into the ExxonMobil – Greenpeace dispute over climate change." *Organization Studies* 33 (11):1507–1536.

Maeckelbergh, Marianne. 2011. "Doing is believing: Prefiguration as strategic practice in the alter globalization movement." *Social Movement Studies* 10 (1):1–20.

Maeckelbergh, Marianne. 2016. "The prefigurative turn: The time and place of social movement practice." In *Social sciences for an other politics. Women theorizing without parachute*, edited by Anna Cecilia Dinerstein, 121–134. Basingstoke: Palgrave Macmillan.

Maize, Kennedy. 2017. "The seep dispute over 'Deep Decarbonization'." Power. www.powermag.com/the-deep-dispute-over-deep-decarbonization/

Măntescu, Liviu. 2016. "Ecoporn, irrationalities and radical environmentalism." *THESys Discussion Paper No. 2016-3 for Integrative Research Institute on Transformations of Human-Environment Systems, Humboldt-Universität zu Berlin*.

Marens, Richard. 2013. "What comes around: The early 20th century American roots of legitimating corporate social responsibility." *Organization* 20 (3):454–476.

Marres, Noortje. 2012. *Material participation, technology, the environment and everyday publics*. London: Palgrave Macmillan.

Mason, Paul. 2013. *Why it's still kicking off everywhere: The new global revolutions*. London: Verso.

Matten, Dirk, Andrew Crane, and Wendy Chapple. 2003. "Behind the mask: Revealing the true face of corporate citizenship." *Journal of Business Ethics* 45 (1–2):109–120.

Maxey, Ian. 1999. "Beyond boundaries? Activism, academia, reflexivity and research." *Area* 31 (3):199–208.

Mayer, D. 2017. The law and ethics of CEO social activism. *Journal of Law, Business & Ethics* 23:21–44.

Mazzucato, Mariana. 2015a. *The entrepreneurial state – Debunking public vs. private sector myths*. London: Anthem Press.

Mazzucato, Mariana. 2015b. "The green entrepreneurial state." In *The politics of green transformations*, edited by Ian Scoones, Melissa Leach, and Peter Newell, 134–152. New York: Routledge, Earthscan.

McCormick. 2006. "The Brazilian anti-dam movement: Knowledge contestation as communicative action." *Organization & Environment* 19 (3):321–346.

McEachern, Morven G. 2015. "Corporate citizenship and its impact upon consumer moralisation, decision-making and choice." *Journal of Marketing Management* 31 (3–4):430–452.

McKee, Ian. 2018. "Do your eco actions speak louder than words?" Good Energy. www.goodenergy.co.uk/do-your-eco-actions-speak-louder-than-words/

Medium. 2017. "The rise of brand activism in business." https://medium.com/@TheBodyShop/the-rise-of-brand-activism-in-business-66436d000b3e

Mena, Sébastien, and Daniel Waeger. 2014. "Activism for corporate responsibility: Conceptualizing private regulation opportunity structures." *Journal of Management Studies* 51 (7):1091–1117.

Menon, Ajay, and Anil Menon. 1997. "Enviropreneurial marketing strategy: The emergence of corporate environmentalism as market strategy." *The Journal of Marketing* 61 (1):51–67.

Mercea, Dan. 2016. *Civic participation in contentious politics – the digital foreshadowing of protest*. London: Palgrave Macmillan.

Mey, Franziska, and Mark Diesendorf. 2018. "Who owns an energy transition? Strategic action fields and community wind energy in Denmark." *Energy Research & Social Science* 35:108–117.

Meyer, S. David, and G. Sidney Tarrow, eds. 1998. *The social movement society: Contentious politics for a new century*. Oxford: Rowman & Littlefield.

Meyerson, E. Debra, and A. Maureen Scully. 1995. "Tempered radicalism and the politics of ambivalence and change." *Organization Science* 6 (5):585–600.

Mieder, Wolfgang. 2009. 'Yes we can': Barack Obama's proverbial rhetoric. New York: Peter Lang.

Mirvis, H. Philip. 1994. "Environmentalism in progressive businesses." Journal of Organizational Change Management 7 (4):82–100.

Mitchell, Catherine, and Peter Connor. 2004. "Renewable energy policy in the UK 1990–2003." Energy Policy 32 (17):1935–1947.

Mitchell, Catherine, Jim Watson, Jessica Whiting, and Jessica Britton. 2013. New challenges in energy security: The UK in a multipolar world. London: Palgrave Macmillan.

Mitchell, Catherine. 2008. The political economy of sustainable energy. Basingstoke: Palgrave Macmillan.

Mitlin, Diana. 2008. "With and beyond the state—co-production as a route to political influence, power and transformation for grassroots organizations." Environment and Urbanization 20 (2):339–360.

Montgomery, Nina, ed. 2019. Perspectives on purpose: Leading voices on building brands and businesses for the twenty-first century. London: Routledge.

Moog, Sandra, André Spicer, and Steffen Böhm. 2015. "The politics of multi-stakeholder initiatives: The crisis of the Forest Stewardship Council." Journal of Business Ethics 128 (3):469–493.

Moon, Jeremy, Andrew Crane, and Dirk Matten. 2005. "Can corporations be citizens? Corporate citizenship as a metaphor for business participation in society." Business Ethics Quarterly 15:427–451.

Moon, Jeremy, and David Vogel. 2008. "Corporate social responsibility, government, and civil society." In The Oxford handbook of corporate social responsibility, edited by Andrew Crane, Abagail McWilliams, Dirk Matten, Jeremy Moon, and S. Donald Siegel, 303–326. New York: Oxford University Press.

Moravec, Lukáš. 2017. The role of the epistemic community in socio-economic development. Zeszyty Naukowe politechniki Slaskiej 110:151–157.

Morgan, David H. 2005. "Revisiting 'communities in Britain." The Sociological Review 53 (4):641–657.

Morsing, Mette. 2006. Corporate moral branding. Corporate Communication: An International Journal 11 (2):97–108.

Morton, Timothy. 2018. Being ecological. London: Penguin Books.

Moselle, Boaz, Jorge Padilla, and Richard Schmalensee. 2010. Harnessing renewable energy in electric power systems: Theory, practice, policy. London: Routledge.

Mouffe, Chantal. 1999. "Deliberative democracy or agonistic pluralism?" Social Research 66 (3):745–758.

Muhr, Sara Louise, and Alf Rehn. 2014. "Branding atrocity: Narrating dark sides and managing organizational image." Organization Studies 35 (2):209–231.

Muinzer, L. Thomas. 2018. *Climate and energy governance for the UK low carbon transition: The Climate Change Act 2008*. Cham: Springer.

Mukherjee, Roopali, and Sarah Banet-Weiser, eds. 2012. *Commodity activism: Cultural resistance in neoliberal times*. New York: New York University Press.

Muralidharan, Sidharth. 2011. "The Gulf Coast oil spill: Extending the theory of image restoration discourse to the realm of social media and beyond petroleum." *Public Relations Review* 37 (3):226–232.

Musacchio, Aldo Farias, and Sergio G. Lazzarini. 2014. "Investor activism." In *Reinventing state capitalism, 53*. Cambridge, MA and London: Harvard University Press.

Myers, C. Daniel, Tara Ritter, and Andrew Rockway. 2017. "Community deliberation to build local capacity for climate change adaptation: The rural climate dialogues program." In *Climate change adaptation in North America*, edited by Walter Leal Filho, and M. Jesse Keenan, 9–26. Cham: Springer.

Nancy, Jean-Luc. 1991. *The inoperative community*. Minneapolis: University of Minnesota Press.

National Opposition to Windfarms. 2018. "Our Aim." www.nowind.org.uk

New Scientist. 2019a. "The musicians helping make climate change a cultural movement." www.newscientist.com/article/2206461-the-musicians-helping-make-climate-change-a-cultural-movement/

New Scientist. 2019b. "David Attenborough on climate change: 'We cannot be radical enough'." https://www.newscientist.com/article/2209126-david-attenborough-on-climate-change-we-cannot-be-radical-enough/#ixzz6Gy0u6Oan

Newell, Peter. 2020. "The business of rapid transition." *Wiley Interdisciplinary Reviews: Climate Change, e670*.

Nolden, Colin. 2015. "Performance and impact of the feed-in tariff scheme: Review of evidence." Department of Energy and Climate Change. https://assets.publishing.service.gov.uk/government/uploads/system/uploads/attachment_data/file/456181/FIT_Evidence_Review.pdfhttps://assets.publishing.service.gov.uk/government/uploads/system/uploads/attachment_data/file/456181/FIT_Evidence_Review.pdf

Norgaard, Kari Marie. 2011. *Living in denial: Climate change, emotions, and everyday life*. Cambridge, MA and London: MIT Press.

Norgaard, Kari Marie. 2006. "'People want to protect themselves a little bit': Emotions, denial, and social movement nonparticipation." *Sociological Inquiry* 76 (3):372–396.

Norström, V. Albert, Christopher Cvitanovic, and Marie F. Löf, et al. 2020. "Principles for knowledge co-production in sustainability research." *Nature Sustainability* 3 (3):1–9.

Nyberg, Daniel, André Spicer, and Christopher Wright. 2013. "Incorporating citizens: Corporate political engagement with climate change in Australia." *Organization* 20 (3):433–453.

O'Brien, Martin, and Sue Penna. 1998. *Theorising welfare: Enlightenment and modern society.* London: Sage Publications.

O'Neill, Maggie. 2012. "Ethno-mimesis and participatory arts." In *Advances in visual methodology,* edited by Sarah Pink, 153–172. London: Sage Publications.

Ockwell, David, Whitmarsh Lorraine, and Saffron O'Neill. 2009. "Reorienting climate change communication for effective mitigation." *Science Communication* 30 (3):305–327.

Ofgem. 2020. "Electricity supply market shares by company: Domestic (GB)". www.ofgem.gov.uk/data-portal/electricity-supply-market-shares-company-domestic-gb

Oldfield, Sophie, and Kristian Stokke. 2007. "Political polemics and local practices of community organizing and neoliberal politics in South Africa." In *Contesting neoliberalism,* edited by Helga Leitner, Jamie Peck, and S. Eric Sheppard, 139–156. New York and London: The Guilford Press.

Olofsson, Gunnar. 1999. "Embeddedness and integration." In *Capitalism and social cohesion: Essays on exclusion and integrationGough,* edited by Ian Gough and Gunnar Olofsson, 38–59. London: Palgrave MacMillan.

Olsen, P. Johan. 2017. *Democratic accountability, political order, and change: Exploring accountability processes in an Era of European transformation.* Oxford: Oxford University Press.

Olsson, Jan, and Erik Hysing. 2012. "Theorizing inside activism: Understanding policymaking and policy change from below." *Planning Theory and Practice* 13 (2):257–273.

Omnom. 2018. "Ecotricity founder Dale Vince on building a bright, green future." www.readomnom.com/ideas/ecotricity-dale-vince

Orihuela, Rodrigo, and Landberg Reed. 2018. "Renewable energy giant shifts toward grids to shore up returns." *Bloomberg News,* 26 July. www.bloomberg.com/news/articles/2018-07-26/renewable-energy-giant-shifts-toward-grids-to-shore-up-returns

Össbo, Åsa. 2018. "Recurring colonial ignorance: A genealogy of the Swedish energy system." *Journal of Northern Studies* 12 (2):63–80.

OTL. 2011. One Tonne Life, Vattenfall. Test family will live climate-smart without affecting standard of living. www.onetonnelife.com/newsroom/test-family-will-live-climate-smart-without-affecting-standard-of-living/

Ottman, A. Jacquelyn. 2011. *The new rules of green marketing: Strategies, tools and inspiration for sustainable branding.* San Fransisco: Berett-Koehler.

Ottum, Lisa, and Seth Reno. 2016. *Wordsworth and the green romantics. Affect and ecology in the nineteenth century*. Durham: University of New Hampshire Press.

Pacheco, Desirée F., Jeffrey G. York, and Timothy J. Hargrave. 2014. "The coevolution of industries, social movements, and institutions: Wind power in the United States." *Organization Science* 25 (6):1609–1632.

Painter, James. 2013. *Climate change in the media: Reporting risk and uncertainty*. London: Bloomsbury.

Parker, Simon, and Martin Parker. 2017. "Antagonism, accommodation and agonism in critical management studies: Alternative organizations as allies." *Human Relations* 70 (11):1366–1387.

Parliament UK. 2019. "Parliament sends 30,000 invitations for citizens' assembly on climate change." www.parliament.uk/business/committees/committees-a-z/commons-select/business-energy-industrial-strategy/news-parliament-2017/citizens-assembly-climate-change-19-20/

Pastakia, Astad. 1998. "Grassroots ecopreneurs: Change agents for a sustainable society." *Journal of Organizational Change Management* 11 (2):157.

Patagonia. 2018. "Employee Activism." www.patagonia.com/employee-activism.html

Patagonia. 2020. "We are in business to save our home planet." www.patagonia.com/activism/

Paterson, Matthew, and Johannes Stripple. 2010. "My Space: Governing individuals' carbon emissions." *Environment and Planning D: Society and Space* 28 (2):341–362.

Pattberg, Philipp, and Johannes Stripple. 2008. "Beyond the public and private divide: Remapping transnational climate governance in the 21st century." *International Environmental Agreements* 8:367–388.

Paulas, Rick. 2017. "The limits of corporate activism." Pacific Standard, 17 December. https://psmag.com/economics/the-limits-of-corporate-activism

Pearce, Fred. 2009. "Greenwash: Why 'clean coal' is the ultimate climate change oxymoron." The Guardian. www.theguardian.com/environment/2009/feb/26/greenwash-clean-coal

Peck, Jamie, Neil Brenner, and Nik Theodore. 2018. "Actually existing neoliberalism." In *The Sage handbook of neoliberalism*, edited by Damien Cahill, Melinda Cooper, Martijn Konings, and David Primrose, 3–15. London: SAGE Publications.

Peck, Jamie, and Nik Theodore. 2012. "Reanimating neoliberalism: Process geographies of neoliberalisation." *Social Anthropology* 20 (2):177–185.

Pedwell, Carolyn. 2019. "Digital tendencies: Intuition, algorithmic thought and new social movements." *Culture, Theory and Critique* 60 (2):123–138.

Peredo, Ana Maria, and James J. Chrisman. 2006. "Toward a theory of community-based enterprise." *Academy of Management Review* 31 (2):309–328.

Perrault, Elise, and Cynthia Clark. 2016. "Environmental shareholder activism: Considering status and reputation in firm responsiveness." *Organization & Environment* 29 (2):194–211.

Petschow, Ulrich, James Rosenau, and Ernst Ulrich von Weizsäcker. 2005. *Governance and sustainability: New challenges for states, companies and civil society.* Sheffield: Greenleaf Publishing Limited.

Phillips, Mary. 2013. "On being green and being enterprising: Narrative and the ecopreneurial self." *Organization* 20 (6):794–817.

Pink, Sarah. 2008. "Re-thinking contemporary activism: From community to emplaced sociality." *Ethnos – Journal of Anthropology* 73 (2):163–188.

Pohjanpalo, Kati. 2021. "Engine No. 1 Exxon Pick is a different kind of climate activist." *Bloomberg Green.* https://www.bloomberg.com/news/articles/2021-06-05/exxon-activist-director-says-she-s-no-climate-radical

Polanyi, Karl. 1944/2001. *The great transformation: The political and economic origins of our time.* Boston: Beacon Press.

Polletta, Francesca, and Katt Hoban. 2016. "Why consensus? Prefiguration in three activist eras." *Journal of Social and Political Psychology* 4 (1):286–301.

Poortinga, Wouter, Alexa Spence, Lorraine Whitmarsh, Stuart Capstick, and F. Nick Pidgeon. 2011. "Uncertain climate: An investigation into public scepticism about anthropogenic climate change." *Global Environmental Change* 21 (3):1015–1024.

Porter, E. Michael, and R. Mark Kramer. 2011. "The big idea: Creating shared value." *Harvard Business Review* 89 (1/2):62–77.

Postill, John. 2018. *The rise of nerd politics: Digital activism and political change.* London: Pluto Press.

Powell, W. Walter, and Kaisa Snellman. 2004. "The knowledge economy." *Annual Review of Sociology* 30:199–220.

Proffitt, W. Trexler, and Andrew Spicer. 2006. "Shaping the shareholder activism agenda: Institutional investors and global social issues." *Strategic organization* 4 (2):165–190.

Purewal, Vicki. 2013. "Big Green Challenge finalists booklet." Published 11 November 2013. Nesta www.nesta.org.uk/report/big-green-challenge-finalists-booklet/

Purkayastha, Debapratim, and Rajiv Fernando. 2007. "The body shop: Social responsibility or sustained greenwashing." In *Case studies in sustainability management and strategy,* edited by Jost Hamschmidt. 226–251. London: Routledge.

Raeburn, Nicole Christine. 2004. *Changing corporate America from inside out: Lesbian and gay workplace rights.* Vol. 20. Minneapolis: University of Minnesota Press.

Rancière, Jacques. 1992/2007. *On the shores of politics.* Translated by Liz Heron. London and New York: Verso.

Rancière, Jacques. 2005/2014. *Hatred of democracy.* London and New York: Verso.

Rancière, Jacques. 2016. *The method of equality.* Cambridge: Polity Press.

Rasche, Andreas. 2015. "The corporation as a political actor – European and North American perspectives." *European Management Journal* 33 (1):4–8.

Rauwald, Christoph. 2020. "VW will hire 'aggressive' climate activist to scrutinize policies." Automotive News. www.autonews.com/automakers-suppliers/vw-will-hire-aggressive-climate-activist-scrutinize-policies

Ravazzi, Stefania. 2016. "When a government attempts to institutionalize and regulate deliberative democracy: The how and why from a process-tracing perspective." *Critical Policy Studies* 11 (1):1–22.

Reedy, Patrick, Daniel King, and Christine Coupland. 2016. "Organizing for individuation: Alternative organizing, politics and new identities." *Organization Studies* 37 (11):1553–1573.

Rehbein, Kathleen, Sandra Waddock, and Samuel Graves. 2004a. "Understanding shareholder activism: Which corporations are targeted?" *Business & Society* 43 (3):239–267.

Rehbein, Kathleen, Sandra Waddock, and B. Samuel Graves. 2004b. "Understanding shareholder activism: Which corporations are targeted?" *Business & Society* 43 (3):239–267.

Reichenbach, Roland. 2002. "On irritation and transformation: A-teleological bildung and its significance for the democratic form of living." *Journal of Philosophy of Education* 36 (3):409–419.

Reilly, Kaitlin. 2019. "Celebrity activists fighting the climate change crisis." Refinery29. www.refinery29.com/en-us/2019/09/8467975/celebrities-climate-change-activist

Reinecke, Juliane. 2018. "Social movements and prefigurative organizing: Confronting entrenched inequalities in occupy London." *Organization Studies* 39 (9):1299–1321.

Reitan, Ruth. 2010. "Coordinated power in contemporary leftist activism." In *Power and global activism*, edited by Thomas Olesen, 51–71. London: Routledge.

Reitan, Ruth, and Shannon Gibson. 2012. "Climate change or social change? Environmental and leftist praxis and participatory action research." *Globalizations* 9 (3):395–410.

Renwick, W. S. Douglas, ed. 2018. *Contemporary developments in green human resource management research: Towards sustainability in action?* London: Routledge.

Renwick, W. S. Douglas, Tom Redman, and Stuart Maguire. 2013. "Green human resource management: A review and research agenda." *International Journal of Management Reviews* 15 (1):1–14.

Rhodes, Carl. 2022. Woke capitalism: How corporate morality is sabotaging democracy. Bristol: Bristol University Press.

Rice, Andrew. 2014. "The gavel drops at Sotheby's." *New York Magazine*, 11 March. http://nymag.com/news/features/sothebys-daniel-loeb-2014-3/

Ritzer, George. 2015. "Prosumer capitalism." *The Sociological Quarterly* 56 (3):413–445.

Roberts, Josh. 2016. Prosumer Rights: Options for an EU legal framework post-2020. ClientEarth.

RobinHoodEnergy. 2018. "Tackling fuel poverty." https://robinhoodenergy.co.uk/about/tackling-energy-poverty/

Rockström, Johan, Will Steffen, and Kevin Noone, et al. 2009. "Planetary boundaries: Exploring the safe operating space for humanity." *Ecology and society* 14 (2):32.

Ronit, Karsten, and Volker Schneider, eds. 2013. *Private organisations in global politics*. New York: Routledge.

Rose, Nikolas. 1996. "The death of the social? Re-figuring the territory of government." *Economy and Society* 25 (3):327–356.

Rose, Nikolas. 1999. *Governing the soul: The shaping of the private self.* 2nd ed. London: Free Association Books.

Roth, Wolff-Michael. 2010. "Local matters, ecojustice and community." In *Cultural studies and environmentalism: The confluence of EcoJustice, place-based (science) education and indigenous knowledge systems*, edited by Deborah J. Tippins, P. Michael Mueller, Michiel van Eijck, and D. Jennifer Adams, 51–82. London and New York: Springer.

Roy, Ananya. 2009. "Civic governmentality: The politics of inclusion in Beirut and Mumbai." *Antipode* 41 (2):159–179.

Ruddick, Susan. 2010. "The politics of affect: Spinoza in the work of Negri and Deleuze." *Theory, Culture & Society* 27 (4):21–45.

Rumstadt, Franz, and Dominik K. Kanbach. 2022. CEO activism. What do we know? What don't we know? A systematic literature review. Society and business review 17 (2):307–330.

Räthzel, Nora, and David Uzzell. 2011. "Trade unions and climate change: The jobs versus environment dilemma." *Global Environmental Change* 21 (4):1215–1223.

Rönnerman, Karin, and Petri Salo. 2017. "Action research within the tradition of Nordic countries." In *The Palgrave international handbook of action research*, edited by L. Lonnie Rowell, D. Catherine Bruce, M. Joseph Shosh, and M. Margaret Riel, 455–470. New York: Palgrave Macmillan.

Sabatier, A. Paul. 1988. "An advocacy coalition framework of policy change and the role of policy-oriented learning therein." *Policy Sciences* 21 (2–3):129–168.

Sakip, Siti Rasidah Md, Noraini Johari, and Mohd Najib Mohd Salleh. 2012. "Sense of community in gated and non-gated residential neighborhoods." *Procedia-Social and Behavioral Sciences* 50:818–826.

Sanford, Carol. 2011. *The responsible business: Reimagining sustainability and success*. San Francisco: John Wiley & Sons.

Scerri, Andy. 2019. *Postpolitics and the limits of nature: Critical theory, moral authority, and radicalism in the anthropocene*. SUNY Press, 2018. New York: SUNY Press.

Scherer, Georg Andreas, and Guido Palazzo. 2007. "Toward a political conception of corporate responsibility: Business and society seen from a Habermasian perspective." *The Academy of Management Review* 32 (4):1096–1120.

Scherer, Georg Andreas, and Guido Palazzo. 2011. "The new political role of business in a globalized world: A review of a new perspective on CSR and its implications for the firm, governance and democracy." *Journal of Management Studies* 48 (4):899–931.

Schneiberg, Marc. 2013. "Movements and the spread of cooperative forms in American capitalism." *Organization Studies* 34 (5–6):653–682.

Schneider, Stephen H., and Kristin Kuntz-Duriseti. 2002. "Uncertainty and climate change policy." In *Climate Change Policy: A Survey, edited by Stephen H. Schneider, Armin Rosencranz, and John O. Niles,* 53–87. Washington, Covelo, London: Island Press.

Scoones, Ian, Melissa Leach, and Peter Newell, eds. 2015. *The politics of green transformations*. New York: Routledge, Earthscan.

Scott, C. James. 1990. *Domination and the arts of resistance: Hidden transcripts*. New Haven: Yale University Press.

Scott, C. James. 2005. "The infrapolitics of subordinate groups." In *The global resistance reader*, edited by Louise Amoore, 65–73. Oxford: Routledge.

Scott-Cato, Molly, and Jean Hillier. 2010. "How could we study climate-related social innovation? Applying Deleuzean philosophy to transition towns." *Environmental Politics* 19 (6):869–887.

Scully, Maureen, and Amy Segal. 2002. "Passion with an Umbrella: Grassroots activism in the workplace." *Social Structure and Organizations Revisited* 19:125–168.

Semuels, Alana. 2019. "'Rampant Consumerism Is Not Attractive.' Patagonia Is Climbing to the Top — and Reimagining Capitalism Along the Way." Time. 20200413. https://time.com/5684011/patagonia/

Sennero, Johan, and Jan Lopatka. 2016. "Vattenfall sells German lignite assets to Czech EPH." Reuters, 18 April. www.reuters.com/article/us-vattenfall-germany-lignite-idUSKCN0XF1DV

Sethi, S. Prakash. 1982. Corporate political activism. *California Management Review* 24 (3):32–42.

Seyfang, Gill, and Alex Haxeltine. 2012. Growing grassroots innovations: Exploring the role of community-based initiatives in governing sustainable energy transitions. *Environment and Planning C Government and Policy* 30 (3):381–400.

Seymour, Nicole. 2018. *Bad environmentalism: Irony and irreverence in the ecological age.* Minneapolis: University of Minnesota Press.

Sharon, Ori. 2019. "Fields of dreams: An economic democracy framework for addressing NIMBYism." *Environmental Law Reporter. News & Analysis* 3 (49):10264–10285.

Shaw, Eleanor, and Anne de Bruin. 2013. "Reconsidering capitalism: The promise of social innovation and social entrepreneurship?" *International Small Business Journal* 31 (7):737–746.

Sheldrick, Aaron. 2020. "Investors line up against Mizuho support for coal." 6 April. www.reuters.com/article/us-coal-japan-mizuho-climatechange/investors-line-up-against-mizuho-support-for-coal-idUSKBN21O12C

Shepherd, A. Dean, and Holger Patzelt. 2010. "The New Field of Sustainable Entrepreneurship: Studying Entrepreneurial Action Linking 'What Is to Be Sustained' With 'What Is to Be Developed'." *Entrepreneurship, Theory and Practice.*

Short, C. Jeremy, W. Todd Moss, and G. T. Lumpkin. 2009. "Research in social entrepreneurship: Past contributions and future opportunities." *Strategic Entrepreneurship Journal* 3 (2):161–194.

Shrestha, Priyanka. 2020. "SSE completes sale of retail unit to OVO Energy for £500m." Energy Live News. www.energylivenews.com/2020/01/15/sse-completes-sale-of-retail-unit-to-ovo-energy-for-500m/

Siegel, Donald. 2001. "Corporate Social Responsibility: A theory of the firm perspective." *Academy of Management Review* 26 (1):117–127.

Silver-Greenberg, Jessica. 2018. "Activist Investor Daniel Loeb Intensifies Pressure on Nestlé to Reorganize." *The New York Times*, 1st of July. *www.nytimes.com/2018/07/01/business/dealbook/nestle-daniel-loeb.html*

Silverman, Victor. 2006. "'Green unions in a grey world': Labor environmentalism and international institutions." *Organization & Environment* 19 (2):191–213.

Simon, Frédéric. 2018. "Norway's latest CCS revival attempt meets lukewarm EU response." Euractive. www.euractiv.com/section/energy/news/norways-latest-ccs-revival-attempt-meets-lukewarm-eu-response/

Simon, Karl-Heinz, and Horace Herring. 2020. "Intentional communities and sustainability." In *Encyclopedia of community from the village to the virtual world*, edited by Karen Christensen and David Levinson, 690–693. London: Sage Publications.

Simons, Arno, and Jan-Peter Voß. 2018. "The concept of instrument constituencies: Accounting for dynamics and practices of knowing governance." *Policy and Society* 37 (1):14–35.

Skagen. 2017. "Activism comes of age." www.skagenfonder.se/en/news-and-perspectives/perspectives/2017/november/activism-comes-of-age/

Skoglund, Annika. 2011. Homo Clima, Styrning genom klimatförändring som bioestetisk inramning. (PhD/Tech Dr.). Royal Institute of Technology, Stockholm.

Skoglund, Annika. 2014. "Homo Clima: The overdeveloped resilience facilitator." *Resilience: International Policies, Practices and Discourses* 2 (3):151–167.

Skoglund, Annika, and Steffen Böhm. 2016. Wind power activism: Epistemic struggles in the formation of eco-ethical selves at Vattenfall. In *Towards a cultural politics of climate change: Devices, desires and dissent*, edited by Harriet Bulkeley, Matthew Paterson and Johannes Stripple, 173. New York: Cambridge University Press.

Skoglund, Annika, and Steffen Böhm. 2020. "Prefigurative partaking: Employees' environmental activism in an energy utility." *Organization Studies* 41 (9):1257–1283.

Skoglund, Annika, and Mats Börjesson. 2020. "Juvenocracy." In *The SAGE encyclopedia of children and childhood studies*, edited by Daniel Thomas Cook, 1028–1031. London: Sage Publications.

Skoglund, Annika, and Mats Börjesson. 2014. "Mobilizing 'juvenocratic spaces' by the biopoliticization of children through sustainability." *Children's Geographies*, 12 (4): 429–446.

Slessarev-Jamir, Helene. 2011. *Prophetic activism: Progressive religious justice movements in contemporary America*. New York and London: Routledge.

Sloterdijk, Peter. 2014. "Peter Sloterdijk on the Acceleration of the Pace of Social Change." P2P Foundation. https://blog.p2pfoundation.net/peter-sloterdijk-on-the-acceleration-of-the-pace-of-social-change/2014/01/01

Smith, A. 2005. The alternative technology movement: An analysis of its framing and negotiation of technology development. *Research in Human Ecology* 12 (2):106–119.

Smith, Adrian, and Adrian Ely. 2015. "Green transformations from below? The politics of grassroots innovation." In *The politics of green transformations*, edited by Ian Scoones, Melissa Leach, and Peter Newell, 102–118. New York: Routledge, Earthscan.

Smith, Christian, ed. 1996. *Disruptive religion: The force of faith in social movement activism*. London and New York: Routledge.

Smith, Graham. 2003. *Deliberative democracy and the environment*. London and New York: Routledge.

Smith, Graham. 2009. *Democratic innovations, designing institutions for citizen participation*: Cambridge: Cambridge University Press.

Smith, Jackie, Michael Goodhart, Patrick Manning, and John Markoff, eds. 2017. *Social movements and world-system transformation*. London and New York: Routledge.

Solomon, C. Robert. 1993. *Ethics and excellence: Cooperation and integrity in business*. New York: Oxford University Press.

Sonenshein, Scott. 2016. "How corporations overcome issue illegitimacy and issue equivocality to address social welfare: The role of the social change agent." *Academy of Management Review* 41 (2):349–366.

Soule, Sarah A. 2012. "Social movements and markets, industries, and firms." *Organization Studies* 33 (12):1715–1733.

Spanning Films. 2009. Age of Stupid. https://www.youtube.com/watch?reload=9&v=vkDc7o1no2I

Spicer, André, Mats Alvesson, and Dan Kärreman. 2009. "Critical performativity: The unfinished business of critical management studies." *Human Relations* 62:537–560.

Stephens, Jennie C. 2014. "Time to stop investing in carbon capture and storage and reduce government subsidies of fossil-fuels." *Wiley Interdisciplinary Reviews: Climate Change* 5 (2):169–173.

Stern, Nicholas. 2006. Stern Review: The Economics of Climate Change.

Stevenson, T. Kathryn, M. Nils Peterson, Howard D. Bondell, Susan E. Moore, and Sarah J. Carrier. 2014. "Overcoming skepticism with education: Interacting influences of worldview and climate change knowledge on perceived climate change risk among adolescents." *Climatic Change* 126 (3–4):293–304.

Stiglitz, E. Joseph. 2001. "Introduction to: The great transformation: The political and economic origins of our time." Boston: Beacon Press. https://inctpped.ie.ufrj.br/spiderweb/pdf_4/Great_Transformation .pdf

Stirling, Andy. 2015. "Emancipating transformations – from controlling the transition to culturing plural radical progress." In *The politics of green transformations*, edited by Ian Scoones, Melissa Leach, and Peter Newell, 54–67. New York: Routledge, Earthscan.

Stone, Diane. 2008. "Global public policy, transnational policy communities, and their networks." *The Policy Studies Journal* 36 (1):19–38.

Stripple, Johannes, and Harriet Bulkeley, eds. 2013. *Governing the climate, new approaches to rationality, power and politics.* New York: Cambridge University Press.

Sullivan, Rory, and Craig Mackenzie. 2017. "Shareholder activism on social, ethical and environmental issues: An introduction." In *Responsible investment,* edited by Rory Sullivan, and Craig Mackenzie, 150–157. New York: Routledge.

Summerville, A. Jennifer, A. Barbara Adkins, and Gavin Kendall. 2008. "Community participation, rights, and responsibilities: The governmentality of sustainable development policy in Australia." *Environment and Planning C: Government and Policy* 26 (4):696–711.

Suter,Imogen.2018."NERCTrans.MISSION:Communicatingclimatechange with art." www.goodenergy.co.uk/blog/2018/06/25/communicating-climate-change-with-art/

Sutherland, Neil, Christopher Land, and Steffen Böhm. 2014. "Anti-leaders(hip) in social movement organizations: The case of autonomous grassroots groups." *Organization* 21 (6):759–781.

Sveriges Radio. 2010. "Vattenfall tog grönmålarpriset Climate Greenwash Award 2009." https://sverigesradio.se/sida/artikel.aspx?programid=3345&artikel=3385314

Swyngedouw, Erik. 2010. "Apocalypse forever?: Post-political populism and the spectre of climate change." *Theory, Culture & Society* 27 (2):213–232.

Swyngedouw, Erik. 2009. "Civil society, governmentality and the contradictions of Governance-beyond-the-State: The Janus-face of social innovation." In *Social innovation and territorial development,* edited by Diana MacCallum, Frank Moulaert, Jean Hillier, and Serena Vicari Haddock, 63–80. Farnhamn: Ashgate.

Sühlsen, Kathrin, and Matthijs Hisschemöller. 2014. "Lobbying the 'Energiewende'. Assessing the effectiveness of strategies to promote the renewable energy business in Germany." *Energy Policy* 69:316–325.

Szulecki, Kacper. 2018. "Conceptualizing energy democracy." *Environmental Politics* 27 (1):21–41.

Talisse, B. Robert. 2005. "Deliberativist responses to activist challenges: A continuation of Young's dialectic." *Philosophy & Social Criticism* 31 (4):423–444.

Taro Lennerfors, Thomas. 2013. "Beneath good and evil?" *Business Ethics: A European Review* 22 (4):380–392.

Taylor, Phil, and Peter Bain. 2003. "'Subterranean worksick blues': Humour as subversion in two call centres." *Organization Studies* 24 (9):1487–1509.

The Body Shop. 2020. "Activist – As a top reviewed range, this collection is a must have for men. With a lasting warm and spicy scent, it's just right for guys on the go." www.thebodyshop.com/range/activist/c/c00072?clear=true

The British Academy. Principles for Purposeful Business. https://www.thebritishacademy.ac.uk/publications/future-of-the-corporation-principles-for-purposeful-business/

The Economist. 2015. "Meet Shinzo Abe, shareholder activist." *The Economist*, 4 June. https://www.economist.com/leaders/2015/06/04/meet-shinzo-abe-shareholder-activist

The New European. 2022. "'I don't know if being an MP is the best route for me…': eco entrepreneur Dale Vince makes his move into politics." www.theneweuropean.co.uk/dale-vince-ecotricity-interview/

The Sunday Times. 2015. "Dale Vince V Elon Musk: Electric car tsars at war over motorway charging stations." www.driving.co.uk/news/dale-vince-vs-elon-musk/

Thunberg, Greta. 2019. "Greta Thunberg: 'Sweden is not a Role Model'." We don't have time. https://medium.com/@wedonthavetime/greta-thunberg-sweden-is-not-a-role-model-6ce96d6b5f8b

Toffler, Alvin. 1980. *The third wave*. New York: Bantam Books.

Toke, David. 2011a. *Ecological modernisation and renewable energy*. Basingstoke: Palgrave Macmillan.

Toke, David. 2011b. "Ecological modernisation, social movements and renewable energy." *Environmental Politics* 20 (1):60–77.

Tönnies, Ferdinand. 1887. *Gemeinschaft und gesellschaft – Abhandlung des Communismus und des Socialismus als empirischer Culturformen*. Leipzig: Fues's Verlag.

Tönnies, Ferdinand. 1957/2002. *Community and society*. Mineola: Dover.

Townley, Barbara. 1998. "Beyond good and evil: Depth and division in the management of human resources." In *Foucaut, management and organization theory*, edited by Alan McKinlay, and Ken Starkey, 191–210. London: Sage Publications.

Tsing, Anna Lowenhaupt. 2015. *The mushroom at the end of the world: On the possibility of life in capitalist ruins*. Princeton: Princeton University Press.

Tushman, L. Michael, and J. Thomas Scanlan. 1981. "Boundary spanning individuals: Their role in information transfer and their antecedents." *Academy of Management Journal* 24 (2):289–305.

Uetake, Tomo. 2018. "Activist investors say their voices are being heard by Japan Inc." *Reuters*. www.reuters.com/article/us-japan-stocks-activist/activist-investors-say-their-voices-are-being-heard-by-japan-inc-idUSKBN1H51AT

United Nations. 2006. *Ending violence against women: From words to action*. New York: Study of the secretary-general, United Nations Publication.

United Nations. 2018. Sustainable, resilient and inclusive societies – the path towards transformation. https://sustainabledevelopment.un.org/content/documents/18829Together2030_Sectoral_Paper_HLPF2018.pdf

United Nations. 2020. "Making Global Goals Local Business – Indonesia." www.unglobalcompact.org/take-action/events

Uusi-Rauva, Christa, and Pasi Heikkurinen. 2013. "Overcoming barriers to successful environmental advocacy campaigns in the organizational context". *Environmental Communication* 7 (4):475–492.

Valentine, Scott, K. Benjamin Sovacool, and Marilyn Brown. 2019. *Empowering the great energy transition: Policy for a low-carbon future*. New York: Columbia University Press.

Vallely, Lois. 2016. "Interview: Dale Vince, founder and chief executive, Ecotricity." Utility Week. https://utilityweek.co.uk/interview-dale-vince-founder-and-chief-executive-ecotricity/

Van Der Schoor, Tineke, and Bert Scholtens. 2015. "Power to the people: Local community initiatives and the transition to sustainable energy." *Renewable and Sustainable Energy Reviews* 43:666–675.

Van Maanen, John. 2010. *Identity work and control in occupational communities*. London: Cambridge University Press.

Vasi Bogdan, Ion. 2011. *Winds of change: The environmental movement and the global development of the wind energy industry*. New York: Oxford University Press.

Vattenfall. 2006. "Curbing Climate Change." https://corporate.vattenfall.com/globalassets/corporate/sustainability/reports/curbing_climate_change.pdf

Vattenfall. 2007a. "The Vattenfall song." www.youtube.com/watch?v=mi4gL9HnokA

Vattenfall. 2007b. "Young people invited to Combat Climate Change." http://news.cision.com/vattenfall/r/young-people-invited-to-combat-climate-change,c263216

Vattenfall. 2009a. "Press release. Response to accusations about Greenwashing" www.vattenfall.se/www/vf_se/vf_se/518304omxva/525534media/525654arkiv/1685974news-/index.jsp?pmid=78557

Vattenfall. 2009b. "Sign up for the climate. Vattenfall Climate Manifesto." www.youtube.com/watch?time_continue=2&v=0Ubhr4MWbyo

Vattenfall. 2015. "Vattenfall AB: Sale of Vattenfall's German lignite and hydro activities." https://corporate.vattenfall.se/globalassets/corporate/startpage/lignite_sale-process_2015-09-22.pdf

Vattenfall. 2017. "Press release, 2007-04-26, Vattenfall will half its CO2-emissions by 2030." www.vattenfall.se/www/vf_se/vf_se/518304omxva/525534media/525654arkiv/1685974news-/index.jsp?pmid=107091

Vattenfall. 2019a. "Wind power at Vattenfall."

Vattenfall. 2019b. Year-end Report 2018. https://corporate.vattenfall.com/globalassets/corporate/investors/interim_reports/2018/q4_report_2018_.pdf

Vattenfall. 2020. "What's Happening – A story of progress." www.youtube.com/watch?v=0sK7xuHJybk&t=13s

Vattenfall. 2021a. "Roadmap to fossil freedom." https://group.vattenfall.com/what-we-do/roadmap-to-fossil-freedom

Vattenfall. 2021b. Års-och hållbarhetsredovisning 2020, framsteg för klimatet – det händer nu. https://group.vattenfall.com/se/siteassets/sverige/om-oss/finans/arsrapporter/2020/ars-och-hallbarhetsredovisning_2020.pdf

Vaughan, Adam. 2018. "Global energy giants forced to adapt to rise of renewables." The Guardian, 17 March. www.theguardian.com/global/2018/mar/16/eon-rwe-asset-swap-shakeup-german-energy-renewables

Veenhoven, Ruut. 1999. "Quality-of-life in individualistic society." Social Indicators Research 48 (2):159–188.

Vered, Amit, ed. 2002. Realizing community: Concepts, social relationships and sentiments. London and New York: Routledge.

Vlavo, A. Fidèle. 2018. Performing digital activism: New aesthetics and discourses of resistance. New York: Routledge.

Walker, Gordon, Noel Cass, Kate Burningham, and Julie Barnett. 2010. "Renewable energy and sociotechnical change: Imagined subjectivities of 'the public' and their implications." Environment and Planning A: Economy and Space 42 (4):931–947.

Walker, Gordon, Patrick Devine-Wright, Sue Hunter, Helen High, and Bob Evans. 2010. "Trust and community: Exploring the meanings, contexts and dynamics of community renewable energy." Energy Policy 38 (6):2655–2663.

Walker, Gordon, Sue Hunter, Patrick Devine-Wright, Bob Evans, and Helen Fay. 2007. "Harnessing community energies: Explaining and evaluating community-based localism in renewable energy policy in the UK." Global Environmental Politics 7 (2):64–82.

Wapner, Paul Kevin. 1996. Environmental activism and world civic politics. Albany: SUNY Press.

Warland, Geneviève. 2012. Public sphere and Gelehrtenpolitik in Wilhelminian Germany: Friedrich Paulsen (1846–1908) and Ferdinand Tönnies (1855–1936). 36th Annual Conference of the German Studies Association, 1–15.

Weber, Klaus, and Brayden King. 2014. "Social movement theory and organization studies." In The Oxford handbook of sociology, social theory, and organization studies – contemporary currents, edited by S. Paul Adler, Paul Du Gay, Glenn Morgan, and I. Michael Reed, 487–509. Oxford: Oxford University Press.

Weber, Shandwick. 2016. "Employee Activism: The Next Frontier of Employee Engagement." www.webershandwick.com/news/article/employee-activism-the-next-frontier-of-employee-engagement

Weintrobe, Sally. 2012. "The difficult problem of anxiety in thinking about climate change." In *Engaging with climate change*, edited by Sally Weintrobe, 55–77. London and New York: Routledge.

Weiskopf, Richard, and Yvonne Tobias-Miersch. 2016. "Whistleblowing, parrhesia and the contestation of truth in the workplace." *Organization Studies* 37 (11):1621–1640.

Wenger, Etienne. 1998. *Communities of practice: Learning, meaning, and identity*. Cambridge: Cambridge University Press.

Wenger, Etienne. 2010. "Communities of practice and social learning systems: The career of a concept." *Social Learning Systems and Communities of Practice* 3:179–198.

Werther Jr, B. William, and David Chandler. 2010. *Strategic corporate social responsibility: Stakeholders in a global environment*. London: Sage Publications.

West, Joel, and Karim Lakhani. 2008. "Getting clear about communities in open innovation." *Industry and Innovation* 15 (2):223–231.

Wickert, Christopher, and M. Stephan Schaefer. 2015. "Towards a progressive understanding of performativity in critical management studies." *Human Relations* 68 (1):107–130.

Willmott, Peter. 1989. *Community initiatives: Patterns and prospects*. London: Policy Studies Institute.

Wilson, Charlie. 2012. "Up-scaling, formative phases, and learning in the historical diffusion of energy technologies." *Energy Policy* 50:81–94.

Wilson, John Campbell. 2012. *A history of the UK renewable energy programme, 1974–88: some social, political, and economic aspects*. PhD thesis.

Wilson, Japhy, and Erik Swyngedouw. 2014. *Post-political and its discontents: Spaces of depoliticisation, spectres of radical politics*. Edinburgh: Edinburgh University Press.

Wittneben, B. F. Bettina, Chukwumerije Okereke, Bobby Subhabrata Banerjee, and L. David Levy. 2012. "Climate change and the emergence of new organizational landscapes." *Organization Studies* 33 (11):1431–1450.

Wolf, Cam. 2017. "Patagonia Is Suing the Trump Administration." *GQ*, 5 December. www.gq.com/story/patagonia-trump-lawsuit

Wood, Davida. 2016. Electric activism: Analysis, alliances, and interventions. *Economic Anthropology* 3 (1):174–185.

Wright, Christopher, and Michael Mann. 2013. "Future imaginings and the battle over climate science: An interview with Michael Mann." *Organization* 20 (5):748–756.

Yates, Luke. 2015. "Rethinking prefiguration: Alternatives, micropolitics and goals in social movements." *Social Movement Studies* 14 (1):1–21.

Yaziji, Michale, and Jonathan Doh. 2010. *NGOs and corporations: Conflict and collboration, business, value creation, and society.* New York: Cambridge University Press.

Yusoff, Kathryn. 2010. "Biopolitical economies and the political aesthetics of climate change." *Theory, Culture & Society* 27 (2–3):73–99.

Zachrisson Winberg, Johan. 2016. "EU-granskning försenar Vattenfalls brunkol-affär." Sveriges Television Nyheter. www.svt.se/nyheter/ekonomi/eu-granskning-forsenar-vattenfalls-brunkol-affar

Zald, N. Mayer, and A. Michael Berger. 1978. "Social movements in organizations: Coup d'Etat, insurgency, and mass movements." *American Journal of Sociology* 83 (4):823–861.

Zebrowski, Chris, and Daniel Sage. 2017. "Organising community resilience: An examination of the forms of sociality promoted in community resilience programmes." *Resilience* 5 (1):44–60.

Zietsma, Charlene, and I. Monika Winn. 2008. "Building chains and directing flows: Strategies and tactics of mutual influence in stakeholder conflicts." *Business & Society* 47 (1):68–101.

Zito, R. Anthony. 2001. "Epistemic communities, collective entrepreneurship and European integration." *Journal of European Public Policy* 8 (4):585–603.

Zito, R. Anthony. 2018. "Instrument constituencies and epistemic community theory." *Policy and Society* 37 (1):36–58.

Index